THE METAPHYSICAL NOVEL IN ENGLAND
AND AMERICA

· EDWIN M. EIGNER ·

The Metaphysical Novel in England and America

Dickens, Bulwer, Melville, and Hawthorne

UNIVERSITY OF CALIFORNIA PRESS

Berkeley · Los Angeles · London

University of California Press
Berkeley and Los Angeles, California
University of California Press, Ltd.
London, England
Copyright © 1978 by
The Regents of the University of California
ISBN 0–520–03382–5
Library of Congress Catalog Card Number: 76–50246
Printed in the United States of America

1 2 3 4 5 6 7 8 9

For Ruth

Contents

Acknowledgements

This book, although it contains nearly everything I know, is very much a joint effort, and I am grateful for the generous assistance I have been given over the past ten years. It is indeed staggering to tally up the debt. The work has been supported by grants from the University of Kansas, the University of California, the Fulbright-Hays Commission, and the National Endowment for the Humanities. The University of Kansas has my special gratitude for the confidence it encouraged and the healthy climate for research it created. Two of my Kansas colleagues, Professors George J. Worth and Max Keith Sutton, helped me to formulate many of the ideas. The following have read the entire manuscript and have offered both encouragement and correction: Professors Ruth ap Roberts, Allan Christensen, Linda Jones, U. C. Knoepflmacher, and Marshall Van Deusen, all of the University of California, Prof. Dr. Hans-Joachim Lang of the Universität Erlangen-Nürnberg, and Professor Marshall Waingrow of the Claremont Graduate School. Professor Ralph Hanna, Professor Stanley Stewart, and the late Professor Kathleen Williams, Riverside colleagues, helped with portions of an early draft. I wish also to thank the scores of librarians across Germany, England, and the United States who were patient and helpful, and Mrs. Marlene Bosanko, Mrs. Clara Dean, Mrs. Dale Flynn, and Mrs. Nora McGuinness, who assisted with the manuscript. Mr. Richard Evidon is the best and most literate of copy editors. My wife, Ruth Eigner, has been a constant proofreader and a full partner in matters of prose style. If anything in this book is clearly expressed, the reader has her to thank for it. My most recent debt is to Professor Eliott Leader of Westfield College (University of London), who provided a suitable remoteness, a room next to those of his colleagues in elementary particle physics, for the subversive contemplation of novels metaphysical.

London, 1977

Note on Sources

Unless otherwise indicated, citations will be to the following collections of works:

For Bulwer —*The Knebworth Edition*, London, 1873–77.

For Dickens —*The Nonesuch Dickens*, edited by Arthur Waugh, Hugh Walpole, Walter Dexter, and Thomas Hatton, London, 1937.

For Hawthorne—*Centenary Edition of the Works of Nathaniel Hawthorne*, edited by William Charvat et al., Columbus, Ohio, 1962–.

For Melville —*The Writings of Herman Melville: The Northwestern–Newberry Edition*, edited by Harrison Hayford et al., Evanston and Chicago, 1968–.

Introduction: The Different Kinds of Prose Fiction

If he were writing today, Richard Chase, who argued that the great works of American fiction were not novels but romances, would not have been forced to the anomaly of calling his book *The American Novel and Its Tradition.* After a long period of disuse, and thanks in large part to Chase's own brilliant efforts, the term "romance" has regained a wide currency among critics. It remains, however, a troublesome designation, hinting connections with ancient Greek and medieval genres, connections which are suggestive but do not always hold. The term seems also to claim a special relationship with principles of Romanticism which influenced all forms of literature in the nineteenth century. Moreover, Leslie Fiedler is certainly right when he objects that "to speak of a counter-tradition to the novel, of the tradition of 'the romance,' as a force in our literature . . . is certainly to fail to be specific enough for real understanding."[1]

On the other hand, Fiedler is overly reductive when he calls the American romance "a gothic fiction, naturalistic and negative, sadist and melodramatic—a literature of darkness and the grotesque."[2] Gothic is only one form of the romance, either the American or the British. Walter Scott's "white Gothic" (Fiedler's term) has also its legitimate place in the tradition, and so have the sentimental "novels" of Mrs. Southworth's school and even the naturalistic romances of Frank Norris. This is to say that there are a number of sub-subgenres even of the romance. It is beneficial, therefore, to point out the general characteristics which bind together the entire tradition, but necessary also to understand the specific features of the individual movements within it.

The chapters which follow will deal frequently with the larger romance tradition and even at times with the much larger tradition of narrative. I shall concentrate, however, on the works of Dickens, Bulwer-Lytton, Melville, and Hawthorne, and I shall pay some special attention to a fifth romancer, Emily Brontë. I have chosen to call their subgenre "the meta-

1. *Love and Death in the American Novel* (New York, 1960), p. xxiv.
2. *Ibid.*

physical novel," after a term which Bulwer used to distinguish his own fiction and that of his school both from works of mimetic realism, on the one hand, and from prose satires, on the other. Thus Bulwer wrote:

> Besides the multiform representation of real life, the narrative fiction takes two other shapes. . . . And these two shapes are of one species—both may be called the philosophical. The first appertains to the philosophy of wit—the second to that of poetry. I will call the first the satirical, the second the metaphysical, novel.[3]

The satirical novel for Bulwer included *Gulliver's Travels, Candide,* and *Jonathan Wild.* An Aristotelian critic would call it rhetorical fiction as opposed to mimetic. The metaphysical novel, by contrast, is best exemplified by *Wilhelm Meister* and, while Bulwer felt in the 1830s that the genre was as yet undeveloped in the English-speaking world, he saw the beginnings of a viable tradition in the "dark tales of Godwin and the far inferior compositions of [Charles Brockden] Brown."[4] As opposed to the realistic novel, and like satire, metaphysical fiction is "not to be regarded as the mere portraiture of outward society," and it "wanders from the exact probability of effects, in order to bring more strikingly before us the truth of causes."[5] It differs from satire in that it "often invests itself in a dim and shadowy allegory."[6]

To this point the distinctions seem rudimentary, and it must appear that we shall gain little by replacing even such vague terms as poetic fiction or symbolic romance with the even slipperier designation of metaphysical novel, especially when in the nineteenth century metaphysical could mean psychological, philosophical, or even mystical. Moreover, there threatens an inevitable confusion with the seventeenth-century metaphysical poets, who influenced our writers very little. Nevertheless, I find the term necessary, although for reasons which sometimes go beyond Bulwer's explicit arguments.

In the first place, as no one needs to be told any more, the partisan Bulwer was wrong to characterize mimetic realism condescendingly as "the mere portraiture of outward society." On the other hand, he was perceptive when he implied that the realists were more concerned with effects than with causes. Realism is profoundly psychological precisely in the sense that it is interested in the effects of experience on individuals. Metaphysical romance is more seriously concerned with the nature of experience

---

3. "On the Different Kinds of Prose Fiction with Some Apology for the Fiction of the Author," in *The Disowned* (London, 1835), I, vii–viii.
    4. *Ibid.,* I, ix.
    5. *Ibid.*
    6. *Ibid.*

itself. Thus when we understand *The Scarlet Letter* as a story about the influence of sin on several clearly defined characters, we are reading it, often quite fruitfully, as realism. If, however, we interpret the characters as the faculties of the mind or as the elements of an archetypal society, then the sin itself, as the title might suggest, becomes the subject matter rather than merely the impetus to psychological action. Moreover, the book's inquiry, given such an interpretation, is of a radically different sort, one which may justly be called metaphysical, for it is primarily concerned with explaining the *why* rather than the *how* of reality, its philosophical or metaphysical meanings rather than its psychological effects.

Such a definition of the metaphysical novel, however, might qualify it to substitute as a term for romance of almost any sort in the nineteenth century. The romancers of all schools never tired of saying that they were concerned with man rather than with men. But there is still another sense in which "metaphysical" applies to the specific writers on whom we shall concentrate. And here again Bulwer can be helpful, for when he writes about the "dim and shadowy allegory" which, he believes, distinguishes the metaphysical novel from satire, he goes on to emphasize the peculiarly mixed nature of this form. The metaphysical novel, he writes, "deserts or resumes" its allegory "at will," and Goethe's fiction, he believes, is neither "wholly allegory, or wholly matter-of-fact—but both at times."[7]

Of course, prose narrative had almost always been an impure business. The Greek sophistic romance came properly into being when Achilles Tatius thought to combine an intellectual burlesque form with a serious, naïve, ideal type of fiction.[8] Moreover, mixed genres and multiple modes of storytelling continued to characterize the wider narrative tradition in Europe and Asia, in poetry and prose, right up until the late nineteenth century. The Gothic romance itself began when Horace Walpole decided, as he said, "to blend the two kinds of romance, the ancient and the modern."[9]

In Bulwer's time, however, most fiction was struggling to refine away such impurities. The realistic novel was set on a course leading to the pristine unity of *The Ambassadors*, where the narrative mode is so single that the author refuses to render even the letters his hero reads. In the name of form, the realists of the nineteenth century did away with nearly

---

7. *Ibid.*

8. Ben Edwin Perry, *The Ancient Romances: A Literary-Historical Account of Their Origins* (Berkeley and Los Angeles, 1967), pp. 114–115. Perry argues further that the English novel came into being when Fielding repeated this precise combination.

9. "Preface to the Second Edition," *The Castle of Otranto* (ed.) W. S. Lewis (London, 1969), p. 7.

all the "nonessential" elements which had characterized the earlier fiction: dramatically gratuitous characters, authorial intrusions, episodes, inset stories, digressions, multiple narrators, subplots, and generic contrasts.

Romantic fiction also, in many of its subgenres, participated with realism in this trend towards greater narrative simplicity. Poe, Wilde, and, to a lesser extent, R. L. Stevenson, were among the most outspoken of the structural purists. Most romances tended to be single-minded in other ways, as well. In the fantastic-Gothic of M. G. Lewis, Hoffmann, and Maturin, our feet are seldom permitted to touch the ground of common reality. In the terms of Henry James' famous metaphor, the cable connecting the balloon of experience to the realities of earth is "insidiously . . . cut,"[10] permitting the imagination to float absolutely and dizzingly free. Moreover, the nineteenth century was an age in which ideologies were often carried to extremes. Thus, sentimentalism left little place for skeptical reservation—Mercutio was not a possible character in the Victorian love story—and idealistic or transcendental romancers seldom paid any attention to positivist philosophy except to scorn it. Speaking generally of the second and lower levels of American romantic fiction, H. R. Brown characterizes its writers as

> gentle dreamers like Donald Grant Mitchell and George William Curtis; moralists and teachers like Mrs. Hale and Mrs. Child; sensationalists like Mrs. Stephen and Mrs. Southworth. In general, they were either too much above or too far below life to find the truth. The mirror they held up to nature was either concave or convex; the reflection was not that of life itself, but a distortion of it.[11]

"The darker aspects of the new industrialism," Brown goes on to say, "were either blithely ignored or bathed in the warm glow of optimism."[12] On the other hand, the naturalist-romancers of the end of the century gave only these darker aspects of the new industrialism and therefore expressed a pessimism which most "nonbelievers" had to regard as simply another one-sided distortion of reality.

The group of romancers whom we shall call the metaphysical novelists differed from other writers of their age in that their works usually retained and built upon the structural impurities of the earlier fiction and, which is perhaps more significant, featured rather than avoided the clash

---

10. "Preface" to *The American*, Volume II in *The Novels and Tales of Henry James* (Cambridge, Mass., 1907–09). Reprinted in *The Art of Fiction: Critical Prefaces by Henry James* (ed.) R. P. Blackmur (London, 1934), p. 34.

11. *The Sentimental Novel in America* (Durham, N.C., 1940), p. 332.

12. *Ibid.*, p. 363.

of world views. Richard Chase has noted these characteristics in some of
the greatest works of American fiction. He explains the juxtapositions and
the absence of conventional unity by arguing that the American imagination is stirred "by the aesthetic possibilities of radical forms of alienation,
contradiction, and disorder." [13] I believe it is possible to conclude differently,
both as to the exclusively American nature of this sort of fiction (even
Chase permits Emily Brontë into his tradition) and regarding its alleged
penchant for contradiction and disorder.

We shall find that the nature of metaphysical fiction, American *and*
English, is divided in virtually every aspect. Its works are, as we have heard
Bulwer testify, a mixture of allegory and the matter-of-fact. Correspondingly, its characters are sometimes presented on one page as ideal types
and on another as realistic portraits. In the matter of setting, the metaphysical novelists did not use either the never-land of their Gothic prede-
cessors or the everyday, Dutch-genre-painting world of the realists. Rather
they tried for what Hawthorne called "a theatre, a little removed from
the highway of ordinary travel," not an absolute, but only "a suitable remoteness." [14] And most dramatically, their structures, in defiance of all
the rules of unity, are usually divided, quite consciously, into two distinct
parts. In all these respects, not only *Wuthering Heights*, but also *Bleak
House* and most of the works of Bulwer, are as radically double as is *Moby-
Dick*, with its transcendental blubber, its down-to-earth Hamlets, its commercial ship of fools, and its dual heroes.

Half the world of the metaphysical novel appears legitimately to warrant the designation of novel as opposed to romance. This half is firmly
based in what the nineteenth century commonly regarded as reality. Its
philosophy is positivist and/or utilitarian, its psychology and aesthetics
are associational, its materialistic world view derives from John Locke
and his empirical followers. This is the aspect which may have accounted
for the popularity of both Dickens and Melville in their own times, and
it continues to find them some champions today. Barbara Hardy, for instance, who has serious and intelligent reservations about Dickens on his
ideal side, believes he was nevertheless a major novelist because he presented "a new kind of truthfulness about social conditioning." [15] She
finds Dickens' mystical conversions baffling, but she is fully convinced by
the painstakingly presented, cause-and-effect degenerations which often
precede them.

Realism, as the metaphysical novelists well knew, was the only genre

13. *The American Novel and Its Tradition* (Garden City, N.Y., 1957), p. 2.
14. "Preface" to *The Blithedale Romance*.
15. *The Moral Art of Charles Dickens* (London, 1970), p. 14.

of fiction which both readers and critics would surely accept. William Charvat states that when Melville informed his publisher that he intended to write *Mardi* as a romance,

> he announced his departure from those current traditions of fiction which few but Poe and Hawthorne and Brown had thus far managed to escape from, and they only at the cost of popularity. At a time when all vendible American fiction was based on either history or "real" contemporary life, Melville conceived an imagined narrative which, though it derived from Rabelais and Swift (and the tradition of allegory), was not classifiable with anything that readers were currently consuming.[16]

This desired realism was, admittedly, of a soft variety according to modern standards. American critics insisted, as Charvat has also pointed out, "on a selectivity which eliminated certain objectionable elements," such as "pessimism, radicalism, 'low' details, and 'immorality' of any kind."[17] But saturated as they were with the principles of the Scottish realistic philosophers, the critics insisted also on a strict adherence to the empirical method and on a classicism in fiction "which dealt with the society as most of them knew it."[18]

> Critics showed a tendency to keep a hold on reality and to insist on probability and credibility. They disliked "Gothic" wonders and miracles, and supernaturalism. They liked always to find the glow of humanity and the solidity of real people.[19]

Even the sentimental fiction of the American lady novelists dealt essentially, as James Hart confirms, with "the life of the home, and the way of the household" and was valued because "it did not fly off into the misty idealized world of poetry."[20] And in England, where John Locke was an even more powerful influence, the critical taste was identical. Thus Carolyn Washburn writes that "the criteria which dominated the consideration of narrative prose fiction" in England were that "a novel be true to life, probable, based on experience; and that it be moral. Both requisites characterized the opinions of . . . the whole period, 1832–1860."[21] Myron F. Brightfield, who

16. *The Profession of Authorship in America* (Columbus, Ohio, 1968), pp. 218–219.
17. *The Origins of American Critical Thought, 1810–1835* (New York, 1968), p. 153.
18. *Ibid.*, p. 150.
19. *Ibid.*, p. 60.
20. *The Popular Book: A History of America's Literary Taste* (Berkeley, 1963), pp. 90–91.
21. "The History, from 1832 to 1860, of British Criticism of Narrative Prose Fiction," diss. Univ. of Illinois, 1937, p. 20.

has looked into all the corners of mid-century English fiction, writes of "the complete dominance of realism between 1840 and 1870."[22]

It might be argued that the realistic portions of metaphysical novels were included to placate the sensibilities of this down-to-earth reading public or to throw sand in the critics' eyes. But the strategy, if these were, as I doubt, the intentions, did not usually succeed. The presence of realistic elements in such works tended not to hide, but rather to accentuate the mysticism and to render it more objectionable. The "narrative of facts" beginnings of *Mardi* and *Moby-Dick* make the allegories of the middle chapters much more conspicuous, and reviewers were quick to point this out. Similarly, the dissolutions into mystical romance which occur in the final chapters of *The House of the Seven Gables* and *The Marble Faun* have seemed less satisfactory to readers precisely because of the contemporary realism and guidebook factuality which come before. In the late Dickens, down-to-earth comic passages reminded the audience that the author could have been giving them more *Pickwick Papers*, if only he would, and the tough-minded narrator of one-half of *Bleak House* has helped to make Esther Summerson, the narrator of the other half, distasteful to a critic like Barbara Hardy, who has no difficulty at all with Cinderella or the purely fantastic characters of Beckett and Kafka.[23] This was also the reaction of W. D. Howells, who therefore characterized Dickens negatively as "romantistic" rather than legitimately "romantic."[24]

The combination of positivist and visionary strains is, as many readers have perceived, a central problem of Dickens studies, as it is also in critiques concerning Hawthorne and Melville. I shall maintain, however, that the two resulting genres do not exist together in the metaphysical novel either to please the critics or, as Richard Chase has suggested, to express a sense of alienation and disorder by mutual undercutting. Barbara Hardy and Howells argue that the realism in Dickens discredits the mysticism. The intention of the authors, however, appears to have been precisely the opposite: to negate the realism with the romance. And they did not wish for us simply to welter in a resulting confusion of world views. The metaphysical novelists tried to defeat the one philosophy in order to set up the other, to expose materialism and its consequences, so that metaphysics, which the positivists had banned from philosophy, might be restored as a legitimate province for human inquiry.

The metaphysical novelists believed that such a shift in thought was requisite to the spiritual salvation of their contemporaries. Bulwer, in his *England and the English*, lamented that painting, literature, and the whole

22. *Victorian England in Its Novels*, 4 vols. (Los Angeles, 1968), I, 68.
23. *Dickens: The Later Novels* (London, 1968), p. 10.
24. *Heroines of Fiction* (New York, 1901), pp. 118–119.

fabric of life in his country was entirely governed by a materialistic frame of mind which had developed from Locke, Condillac, Adam Smith, Helvétius, and Bentham.

> We as yet live under the philosophy of Adam Smith. The minds that formerly would have devoted themselves to metaphysical and moral research, are given up to inquiries into a more material study. Political economy replaces ethics; and we have treatises on the theory of rents, instead of essays on the theory of motives. It is the age of political economists; and while we see with regret the lamp of a purer naphtha almost entirely extinct in England. . . . the spirit of the age demands political economy now, as it demanded moral theories before.[25]

Elsewhere in the same book, he wrote:

> The philosophy of Locke is still the *system* of the English. . . . Few . . . know or conjecture the influence which one mighty mind insensibly wields over those masses of men. . . . I think it is to our exclusive attention to Locke that I can trace much of the unspiritual and material form which our philosophy has since rigidly preserved.[26]

The great spiritual necessity of his age, as Bulwer understood it, was to free itself from this intellectual bondage, and the tools which he recommended to work this jailbreak were visionary literature and German idealism. Like Carlyle, he believed that English life and English aesthetics had grown impotent because they proceeded from a false epistemology. Carlyle rejected English poetic theory because, from Hume to Alison, it was wholly derived from association. Its "external" or "merely intellectual" origins had led to a poetics incapable of ethical revitalization because it made its appeal to the understanding rather than to the reason, to *Verstand*, not *Vernunft*. German Romantic aesthetic theory, on the other hand, was "underived,"[27] according to Carlyle, and was "born in the inmost spirit of man." Thus he continues:

> The Kantist, in direct contradiction to Locke and all his followers, both of the French and English or Scotch school, commences from within, and proceeds outwards; instead of commencing from without, and, with various precautions and hesitations, endeavouring to proceed inwards. The ultimate aim of all Philosophy must be to interpret appearances,—from the given symbol to ascertain the thing. Now the first step towards this, the aim of what may be called Primary or Critical Philosophy, must be to find some indubitable principle; to fix ourselves on some unchangeable basis; to discover

25. *England and the English* (New York, 1833), II, 104–05.
26. *Ibid.*, I, 228.
27. "State of German Literature" [1827], *The Works of Thomas Carlyle*, 30 vols. (London, 1899), XXVI, 55–56.

what the Germans call the *Urwahr*, the Primitive Truth, the necessarily, absolutely and eternally *True*. This . . . absolute basis of Truth, Locke silently, and Reid and his followers with more tumult, find in a certain modified Experience, and evidence of Sense, in the universal and natural persuasion of all men. Not so the Germans: they deny that there is here any absolute Truth. . . . They deny . . . that Sense is the only inlet of knowledge, that Experience is the primary ground of Belief. Their Primitive Truth, however, they seek, not historically and by experiment in the universal persuasions of men, but by intuition, in the deepest and purest nature of Man.[28]

Both Carlyle and Bulwer championed Goethe as the writer most capable of bringing about the great personal and public conversions they insistently called for, although in *England and the English*, to which J. S. Mill contributed an appendix, Bulwer spoke also for Wordsworth in this regard. Wordsworth's genius, he felt, was "particularly German," and his poetry was

of all existing in the world the most calculated to refine—to etherialize—to exalt;—to offer the most correspondent counterpoise to the scale that inclines to earth. It is for this that I consider his influence mainly beneficial. His poetry has repaired to us the want of an immaterial philosophy—it *is* philosophy, and it is of the immaterial school. No writer more unvulgarizes the mind.[29]

Bulwer and Carlyle tried to save their own contemporaries by substituting the visionary and intuitive for the material and experiential. But, like Goethe and Wordsworth, neither of them attempted to effect this conversion by ignoring the material world and its philosophy, as the sentimental idealists did, or, like Novalis and other transcendentalists, by somehow finding their ways to the infinite through the finite. There is plenty of the material world in *Sartor Resartus* and in the romances of Bulwer, but it remains devil's-dung until it is metamorphized by such visionary truths as cannot be derived by merely scrutinizing or contemplating it, either as fact or as symbol. The result is the metaphysical novel, an oxymoron, in which experience is presented first in purely materialistic or associational or positivistic terms, which are then contradicted from the idealist point of view so that experience is mystically transformed and a new reality is established.

Such a pattern of conversion by contradiction is evident in a number of Dickens' novels, most clearly, perhaps, in *Hard Times*. Transfiguration is a key term with Hawthorne. *The House of the Seven Gables* shows the dead-end nature of a collective psyche derived only from a materialism which

28. *Ibid.*, 79–81.
29. II, 69.

had rigidly shut out the imagination; then it demonstrates how that psyche can be made productive when a single door is left prayerfully unbarred to the mystical or imaginative element. And Melville's Ishmael cannot be saved, either literally or spiritually, until he has fully pursued and absolutely abandoned both his transcendental and his scientific quests into the nature of reality.

This dual aspect of the metaphysical novel, which I take to be its essential feature, renders it more seriously a romance than any of the other subgenres of nineteenth-century fiction which have been called romances. Frye notes that basic philosophical and psychological contradictions are a significant characteristic of the genre. "However conservative . . . [the romancer] may be," Frye observes, "something nihilistic and untamable is likely to keep breaking out of his pages."[30] And of Shakespeare's "late, fifth-phase 'romances'," he writes:

> they do not avoid tragedies but contain them. The action seems to be not only a movement from a "winter's tale" to spring, but from a lower world of confusion to an upper world of order. The closing scene of *The Winter's Tale* makes us think, not simply of a cyclical movement from tragedy and absence to happiness and return, but of bodily metamorphosis and a transformation from one kind of life to another.[31]

In the Greek romances, serious violence in the forms of rape and murder coexist with true love and happy endings.[32] The form, throughout its long history, combines tragic premises with comic conclusions, and always for positive purposes, never for the sake merely of expressing what we have heard Chase call "radical forms of alienation, contradiction, and disorder."

Such a genre was obviously in deep trouble during the nineteenth century, not only because of its ultimate allegiance to a forbidden mysticism, but precisely because of its essentially mixed nature. As the critics began to perceive that most fiction was refining itself in single directions, they came more and more frequently to conclude that one or the other aspect of a metaphysical novel must constitute a misdirection, a changed intention, a dishonestly imposed happy ending, or an impurity.

Bulwer had therefore to argue that the best fiction of his century (not only his own fiction) was being systematically misunderstood because reviewers could not or would not fathom the basic intentions of the genre to which the works belonged. Instead, the critics judged the metaphysical

30. *Anatomy of Criticism* (Princeton, 1957), p. 305.
31. *Ibid.*, p. 184.
32. Reynolds Price, one of the few serious writers of our own times who calls his works romances, speaks of the necessary balance in his fiction of wish fulfillment and "the arousal and examination of a number of our oldest fears." "News from the Mineshaft," *Virginia Quarterly Review*, XLIV (1968), 652.

novel according to the practices of writers who derived their notions of form from the rules of the drama rather than of the epic and who consequently valued unity of effect over comprehensiveness of statement. These writers, as we have already seen, produced not only the realistic novel, but also several varieties of unmixed romance. Since the latter were generally minor subgenres, however, we shall find it most profitable in the following chapters to derive our understanding of the metaphysical novel by contrasting its principles and practices with those of realistic fiction, which was, after all, the chief rival, both as to form and philosophy.

Before we proceed, some disclaimers are perhaps necessary. In the first place, genres, even those which strive for purity, are seldom absolute, and we critics are anyway much more interested in them than imaginative writers are. Perhaps no work is entirely of a single genre, and certainly no important author wrote always in one form. I shall, for instance, regard *Huckleberry Finn, Sister Carrie,* and *The Ambassadors* as works of realism, but I do not mean to deny, indeed I suppose, that they contain many romance characteristics, and I certainly do not wish even to imply that the authors of these novels were always realists in works of theirs which I do not undertake to discuss.

In this regard, Walter Scott is perhaps the most significant case. As the only British novelist of his generation whom the Victorians considered both major and durably popular, he had, of course, a profound effect on all the fiction which came after him. Moreover, there are a sufficient number of the elements of romantic fiction in his works to justify the usual critical practice of calling him a romancer. But the metaphysical novelists largely rejected him, at least consciously; and, regarded as an influence, Scott is most valuably seen as a figure, perhaps, indeed, the most important figure, in the development of the nineteenth-century realistic or dramatic novel. He gave the genre its first great popularity, its principal theme of disillusionment, and its serious and overriding interest in characters presented apparently for their own sakes. His attitude towards his craft, his habits of composition, and his instincts for structure gave a tone and a direction for the realists of Europe and America, who excused Scott's romantic proclivities as nonessential to his art or, at least, dismissed them as irrelevant to their own. For these reasons, I shall speak of Scott as a realist, without prejudice, I hope, to those interpreters who place him in some romance category other than the metaphysical.[33]

33. While I am in the mood to apologize, let me also beg pardon for using such terms as realist, realism, realistic novel, and realistic fiction so unhistorically. I should have preferred to use the words novelist and novel as opposed to romancer and romance, but I am presenting the metaphysical *novel* as a subgenre of romance, containing elements of the novel.

Secondly, I do not intend, by including a consideration of both American and English fiction in a single book, to show any disrespect for the developing disciplines of American and Victorian Studies. No doubt, the American experience formed Hawthorne and Melville in ways that made them significantly different from Dickens and Bulwer, and I do not question that these differences are reflected in their fiction. The present study, however, is a description of an international genre, and, like most criticism, it probably distorts some aspects in its attempt to clarify others. If the similarities I argue are valid and suggestive, the essential national distinctions will be made by scholars with different orientations from my own, for all literary study is a continuing discussion.

A final disclaimer relates to Bulwer-Lytton, whom we shall continue to use as a spokesman for the principles of the metaphysical novel. He has been recognized by most commentators[34] as the most voluble, the most conscientious, the most eloquent champion of his school. Moreover, his important theories are admirably illustrated in much of his fiction, which is coming into its own with a rapidity I did not conceive possible when I began writing.[35] Nevertheless, there will be no attempt here to present Bulwer as a major novelist who deserves equal place with Dickens, Hawthorne, and Melville on aesthetic grounds. Nor will this study discover any long neglected masterpieces by other hands. I hope, however, that our consideration of the metaphysical novel will provide a context in which such generally acknowledged yet still troublesome works as *Bleak House*, *The House of the Seven Gables*, and *Moby-Dick* may be even better appreciated, and their intentions, perhaps, more clearly understood.

34. David Masson, Bulwer's contemporary and a relatively stern critic of his work, wrote that "of all British novelists, he seems to have worked most consciously on a theory of the Novel as a form of literature (*British Novelists and Their Styles*, Cambridge and London, 1859, pp. 228–29). A hundred years later, Richard Stang called him "the most articulate advocate" of the idealistic school of fiction (*The Theory of the Novel in England, 1850–1870* [New York, 1959], p. 153). And Carolyn Washburn names Bulwer's "On Art in Fiction" as "the most intensive . . . analysis of technique in prose fiction" during the entire period she covers in her excellent, unpublished dissertation ("The History, from 1832 to 1860, of British Criticism of Narrative Prose Fiction," p. 53).

35. The reader is referred especially to Robert Lee Wolff, *Strange Stories: Explorations in Victorian Fiction—the Occult and the Neurotic* (Boston, 1973) and Allan Christensen, *Edward Bulwer-Lytton: The Fiction of New Regions* (Athens, Ga., 1976). A major biography by Sibylla Jane Flower is very nearly completed.

·I·

A Charted Voyage: Visions and Revisions

If the novelist be contented with the secondary order of Art
in fiction, and satisfied if his incidents be varied, animating,
and striking, he may write from chapter to chapter, and grope
his way to a catastrophe in the dark. But if he aim at loftier
and more permanent effects, he will remember that to execute
grandly, he must conceive nobly. He will suffer the subject he
selects to lie long in his mind, to be resolved, meditated,
brooded over until from the chaos breaks the light, and he sees
distinctly the highest end for which his material can be used,
and the best process by which they can be reduced to harmony
and order.

—EDWARD BULWER-LYTTON, *"On Art and Fiction"*

There are a number of highly charged issues in the criticism of nineteenth-century fiction which this study cannot well avoid. They indicate, on the healthy side, that readers take the genre with deep seriousness; but the emotionalism sometimes interferes with clear judgment, and it is therefore unfortunate that logic requires us to begin with a topic which seems always to provoke hostility—the matter of preconception.

A certain class of readers becomes annoyed at "ingenious" critics who are always trying to prove, compulsively in the view of these readers, that the works of Dickens, Melville, Emily Brontë and others are always perfect. In many cases the impatience is amply justified, but often the unlucky critic is only attempting to show that some eccentric masterpiece was planned, that it did not simply grow by accident or inattention into its fantastic shape. Plans, of course, need not be perfect. But such an admission or distinction would do little to calm the outrage. Nor is the bad temper all on one side of the argument. According to a sarcastic Perry Miller, some highly influential American reviewers, who disliked Melville, were also critical of Bulwer-Lytton because of what they regarded as his "shameless admission that he composed romances according to an a priori scheme, that he wrote not at all as an excited child."[1] We are concerned, therefore,

1. *The Raven and the Whale: The War of the Wits in the Era of Poe and Melville* (New York, 1956), p. 33.

with basic and deep-rooted attitudes towards fiction, but since they are central to the distinction between the realistic and metaphysical novel, we must try our best to regard them dispassionately.

Bulwer's American critics were right in their facts, at least. The most outspoken of the metaphysical novelists had indeed made such an admission without a trace of shame and on many occasions. Bulwer had even gone so far as to criticize other writers, Byron and especially Scott, for writing *without* a preconceived plan:

> It is common to many novelists to commence a work without any distinct chart of the country which they intend to traverse—to suffer one chapter to grow out of another, and invention to warm as the creation grows. Scott has confessed to this mode of novel writing; but Scott, with all his genius, was rather a great mechanist than a great artist. His execution was infinitely superior to his conception. . . . He conceives a story with the design of telling it as well as he can, but is wholly insensible to the high and true aim of art, which is rather to consider for what objects the story should be told. Scott never appears to say to himself, "Such a tale will throw a new light upon human passions, or add fresh stores to human wisdom: for that reason I select it." He seems rather to consider what picturesque effects it will produce, what striking scenes, what illustrations of mere manners. He regards the story with the eye of the *property man*, though he tells it with the fervour of the poet. It is not thus that the great authorities in fiction have composed. . . . With Shakespeare the conception itself is visible and gigantic from the first line to the last.[2]

On the other hand, Perry Miller's loaded characterization of Bulwer's enemies, who wanted their novelists to write like excited children, is not completely fair. The attitude the critics represented, even if it was so naïvely expressed as Miller implies, had wide and deep philosophical roots in both American and English thought.[3] It was not only a matter of modish literary criticism. The empirical position, as it applied in criticism of fiction, legislated that meaning be derived from a close observation of the imitated experience, and the realistic or dramatic novel was thoroughly law-abiding in this respect, a compliance which goes a long way towards explaining the ultimate acceptance of the genre. The metaphysical novel, on the other hand, which set about to contradict the experiential world view, was

2. "On Art in Fiction" (1838), in *Pamphlets and Sketches* (London, 1887), pp. 333–34.

3. G. N. G. Orsini has written, "The very notion of pure a priori thinking arouses hostility in people brought up in the deeply-rooted Anglo-Saxon empirical tradition. Nothing is so suspect, indeed nothing seems to be so . . . feared as the a priori ratiocinative approach: the "high Priory Road," as Pope ridiculed it in the *Dunciad*." *Coleridge and German Idealism* (Carbondale, Ill., 1969), pp. 76–77.

bound to offend. It was uncomfortable in the prevailing philosophical current and at odds, therefore, with the resulting literary criticism.

Bulwer, who kept insisting on the necessity of preconception, had to be rejected by intellectually respectable critics who shared the national distaste for a priori thought. The other metaphysical novelists were somewhat better at disguising their methods, and they were therefore treated differently. It is no longer fashionable to argue that Dickens and Emily Brontë were wild, unregulated improvisers. But until scholars adduced an overwhelming amount of intrinsic and extrinsic evidence to the contrary—schema, plot outlines, number plans, etc.—these writers were almost universally so regarded. In a sense, the critics, by celebrating Dickens and Brontë as untutored geniuses, were unconsciously saving two obviously appealing writers for the Anglo-Saxon tradition. Versions of Hawthorne's notebooks have been public for a much longer time, and the task for his apologists has been to argue that his romances are not *merely* "thoughts fictionalized."[4] The critics have been able to make a respectable, though a difficult case, which I shall later attempt to modify somewhat. As for Melville, there has been no use denying that he was a visionary thinker of the metaphysical school, but his saving graces, in the eyes of some conventional readers, have been his apparent lack of skill as a narrative craftsman and the generally accepted notion, which has never been properly documented, that he found his truths in the course of composition and therefore kept changing his plans.

The realistic or dramatic novelists have not presented critics with such difficulties, for a calculated lack of premeditation was both a valuable technique and a legitimate principle with them. Bulwer was right, of course, in ascribing the practice to Scott, who had written in his journal, "I never could lay down a plan—or, having laid it down, I never could adhere to it; the action of composition always dilated some passages, and abridged or omitted others; and personages were rendered important or insignificant, not according to their agency in the original conception of the plan, but according to the success or otherwise with which I was able to bring them out."[5] Scott even went to some pains proudly to document this "failure" in the introduction to *Guy Mannering*. "The manner in which the novels were composed cannot be better illustrated," he wrote, "than by reciting the simple narrative on which *Guy Mannering* was originally founded, but to which, in the progress of the work, the production ceased to bear out even the most distant resemblance."

4. Hyatt Waggoner, *Hawthorne: A Critical Study* (Cambridge, Mass., 1963), p. 74.
5. *The Journal of Sir Walter Scott* (ed.) J. G. Tait, 2 vols. (Edinburgh, 1939), I, 100.

It may be worth acknowledging that the practice of the novelist who simply lets his story happen did not begin with Scott. Auerbach, the great critic of realism, believed that in *Don Quixote* "Cervantes allowed himself to be guided by the momentary situation, by the demands of the adventure in hand. . . . Gradually and without any preconceived plan, the two personages evolve, each in himself and also in their relation to each other."[6] This is, of course, debatable speculation,[7] but Rousseau gives personal testimony that he wrote two parts of *La Nouvelle Héloïse* without "having any plan formed, and not foreseeing . . . [he] should one day be tempted to make it a regular work."[8]

Scott is no innovator, therefore, in this department; still the improvised novel occurs more often or is at least admitted more frequently and more complacently after him and among those writers whom he influenced. Balzac and Stendhal are immediate followers in this respect as in many others. Trollope, one of whose favorite novels was *Ivanhoe*, speaks in much the same accents as Scott: "I have never found myself thinking much about the work that I had to do till I was doing it. I have indeed for many years almost abandoned the effort to think, trusting myself, with the narrowest thread of a plot, to work the matter out when the pen is in my hand."[9] And he goes on to say, "When I sit down to write a novel I do not at all know, and I do not very much care, how it is to end."[10]

To a certain extent, Scott and Trollope are striking here the novelist's characteristic pose of modesty, which we shall discuss in the next chapter, but they are also giving an accurate description of one part of the realist's essential mode of composition. A recent critic of Thackeray writes that those who would "vindicate *Vanity Fair* as a carefully prestructured whole are really working against the grain of Thackeray's genius. The novel does indeed have its structural strength. . . . [but] the predominant feel of the book is one of brilliantly resourceful improvisation."[11] Even when a realist begins with a definite aim—for instance, Flaubert in *Madame*

6. *Mimesis* (Princeton, 1953), p. 354.

7. In Chapter 71 of Part II, Don Quixote expresses his highest contempt for writers who work without a conscious plan and accept "whatever it turns out to be," but Cervantes' characters, of course, do not always speak his thoughts. *The Ingenious Gentleman Don Quixote de La Mancha*, 2 vols. (trans.) Samuel Putnam (London, 1953).

8. *Confessions of Jean Jacques Rousseau* (London, 1923), p. 349.

9. *An Autobiography*, 2 vols. (Edinburgh and London, 1888), I, 207–08.

10. *Ibid.*, II, 81.

11. J. I. M. Stewart, "Introduction," to *Vanity Fair* (London, 1968), p. 8. J. A. Sutherland, the author of *Thackeray at Work* (London, 1974), shares this view. He writes, "I have been unable to locate a complete set of plans for any Thackeray novel, and I doubt whether any were ever made" (p. 133).

Bovary—it comes out seriously modified after the writing. As Henry James wrote in the preface to *The Wings of the Dove*, "One's plan, alas, is one thing and one's result another." But sometimes the novelist begins with no conscious aim at all. Dreiser claimed to have started writing *Sister Carrie* with literally nothing in his mind except the title. The only part of Mark Twain's very brief outline for *Tom Sawyer* which was realized in the novel were the words "boyhood and youth," and *Huckleberry Finn* appears to have been started with even less planning. Twain's "characteristic method," according to a recent biographer, was "improvising from chapter to chapter . . . letting the story shape itself."[12]

In many ways, realism is as romantic as romance. The practitioners of both forms were mystics to the extent that they believed in inspiration; the difference between them in this respect was that one group thought vision came during the act of writing and the other believed it should come beforehand. Twain believed that a presence like that of the Holy Ghost sat beside him as he wrote. His own function in regard to his story was merely one of "listening as it goes along telling itself,"[13] of not interfering with the mystic process. "Since there is no plot to the thing," he wrote to Howells concerning *The Adventures of Tom Sawyer*, "it is likely to follow its own drift. . . . I won't interpose."[14]

Some novelists have felt that well-conceived characters tend to achieve a life of their own to the extent that they independently refuse to perform some of the actions which their creators had intended for them. In *Aspects of the Novel* E. M. Forster complains of this sort of character rebellion and advises writers to treat it with a firm, repressive hand. Better realists than Forster, however, have preferred to abandon intentions rather than stifle a character who may be leading the author empirically to the real truth behind the experience which the novel is imitating. In *The Portrait of a Lady*, James set his well-defined and significantly idealized heroine free in a situation and asked himself only the "primary question: 'Well, what will she *do*?' " The answer of the other characters, who "had simply, by an impulse of their own, floated into my ken," seemed to be "that if I would trust them, they would show me; on which, with an urgent appeal to them to make it at least as interesting as they could, I trusted them."[15]

12. Justin Kaplan, *Mr. Clemens and Mark Twain* (New York, 1966), p. 179.

13. Quoted in Warner Berthoff, *The Ferment of Realism* (New York, 1965), p. 72.

14. Letter to Howells, 21 June [1875]. *Mark Twain-Howells Letters* (eds.) Henry Nash Smith and William Gibson (Cambridge, Mass., 1960), I, 87–88.

15. "Preface" to *The Portrait of a Lady*, Volume III in *The Novels and Tales of Henry James* (Cambridge, Mass., 1907–1909), reprinted in *The Art of Fiction, Critical Prefaces by Henry James* (ed.) R. P. Blackmur (London, 1934), p. 53.

He was following, he writes, Turgenev's basic plan of imagining a character and providing a context for her. Elsewhere, as with *The Princess Casamassima*, James did not know the ending of his story until he had written a considerable portion of it.[16] Trollope was always in this position and therefore refused to publish serial parts of works-in-progress. "And it had already been a principle with me in my art, that no part of a novel should be published till the entire story was completed. . . . An artist should keep in his hand the power of fitting the beginning of his work to the end. . . . When some young lady at the end of a story cannot be made quite perfect in her conduct, that vivid description of angelic purity with which you laid the first lines of her portrait should be slightly toned down."[17]

We have traveled a considerable distance among realists from Twain to Trollope, who would have scouted any suggestion that the Holy Ghost was mixed up in his solid employment. Nevertheless, the process of composition was remarkably similar with both men. Their technique was to invest themselves entirely in the lives of their characters to the abandonment of all other preconceptions, either thematic or narrative. Where Twain refuses to interpose himself against the natural drift of his work, Trollope sees himself as an enthusiastic coachman, whose job it is, not to control, but rather to encourage the horses of his story, which are its characters. "I have been impregnated with my own creations," he writes, "till it has been my only excitement to sit with the pen in my hand, and drive my team before me at as quick a pace as I could make them travel."[18] Similarly, Thackeray, when Sarah Hennell asked him about the coming number of *The Newcomes*, answered, "The characters once created *lead me*, and I follow where they direct. I cannot tell the events that wait on Ethel and Clive."[19] And Miss Hennell's friend, George Eliot, at the beginning of her career, when she was in her realist phase, wrote to her publisher, "My stories always grow out of my psychological conception of the dramatis personae."[20]

16. In contrast to this picture of Henry James as improviser, it might be argued that he wrote prospectuses for two of his works, *The Wings of the Dove* and *The Ambassadors*. The sketch for the first of these is lost, and no case can be made from it. The prospectus for *The Ambassadors*, since it runs about twenty thousand words and contains a number of short scenes of dialogue, might better be regarded as a shorter first draft than a preconception of the Bulwer, Dickens, or Hawthorne variety. Moreover, the "germ" for the story, the anecdote concerning Howells in Paris, is, like most of James' starting points, an experience rather than an idea.

17. *An Autobiography*, I, 185–86.

18. *Ibid.*, I, 234.

19. Quoted in Lady Ritchie's "Introduction to *The Newcomes*, 1853–1855," *The Works of William Makepeace Thackeray*, 26 vols. (London, 1911), XII, xlvii–xlviii.

20. Letter to John Blackwood, 18 Feb. 1857. *The George Eliot Letters*, 7 vols.

If the realist's commitment to his characters was intense enough, then he could do very nicely without prearranged plots; for, as Howells wrote, "The true plot comes out of the character; that is, the man does not result from the things he does, but the things he does result from the man, and so plot comes out of character: plot aforethought does not characterize."[21] And the realist could do also without preconceived meanings because for him a meaning is something which comes empirically out of a story, not something that goes a priori into it. The ideal realist, if one can imagine such a contradiction, chooses characters and an experience only because they move him emotionally and because he has confidence that there must be discoverable significance behind his visceral reaction. Then he submerges himself so completely in his creations that he drowns out all the irrelevant parts of himself—his politics, his religion, even his aesthetics. Thus the writer achieves a discipline; and the hoped-for result of his unconcern with form and message is that he produce a work which is both shapely and meaningful.

This aesthetic of the realist may sound somewhat swashbuckling, but the resulting method is also in keeping with his down-to-earth, empirical approach. It is based on the belief that form and meaning, psychological meaning, not metaphysical, exist in the experience to be imitated and on the further belief that truth can be discovered by close observation during tedious hours of execution. Like laboratory experiments, the process can be wasteful of the writer's time, for experiences and characters do not always keep their bright promises. Think of all Mark Twain's fragments and of the many times even *Huckleberry Finn* came to a dead stop because the writing seemed to be leading nowhere. But when the method works, when Huck, the author, and the reader discover simultaneously that you cannot pray a lie, there is nothing quite like it in the experience of literature, and such a success is worth, perhaps, any number of failures.[22]

Huck Finn's apotheosis presents the realistic novelist not only in his most glamorous aspect, but in his most humdrum, as well. The chapter

(ed.) Gordon S. Haight (New Haven, 1954), II, 299. As she became less of a realist (see U.C. Knoepflmacher, *George Eliot's Early Novels: The Limits of Realism*, Berkeley and Los Angeles, 1968), her works were carefully laid out before she began writing.

21. "My Favorite Novelist and His Best Book," *Munsey's Magazine*, April 1897. Reprinted in *Criticism and Fiction and Other Essays* (eds.) Clara Marburg Kirk and Rudolf Kirk (New York, 1965), p. 99.

22. I have heard a modern-day romancer, James B. Hall, who is an advocate of "pre-writing," caution the students of a creative writing class that if they wished to indulge so "romantic" a method as improvisation, they had better own good sized wastepaper baskets; and I have heard a realist, Mitchell Goodman, respond to this remark by thanking God for receptacles.

in which it appears was completely rewritten, and Twain devoted eight months to the revision of the entire manuscript.[23] It is in this department that Scott was least adequate as a model for the realists, whose aesthetics virtually demanded revision. For if you do not know what you intend to say until your characters have said it, you must not only go back to make the first chapter fit the last, as we have heard Trollope say was his practice, you must sometimes recast the entire work in accordance with the late achieved vision. Joyce's rewriting of *Stephen Hero* into *A Portrait of the Artist as a Young Man* is a case in point. Scott had neither the patience nor the time for revision. Balzac, on the other hand, who averaged two thousand pages a year over a period of about twenty years, spent more of his working hours revising than writing. Stendhal improvised the first writing of *The Charterhouse of Parma*, but at Balzac's suggestion he revised it laboriously.[24] We need not rehearse at length, I presume, the story of Henry James' elaborate labors on the New York Edition of his works or Thackeray's practice of adding the morals, or of Joyce's and F. Scott Fitzgerald's technique of putting in the symbols. All these writers were operating under the assumption that the more and closer they worked with the real or imagined experience they were imitating, the more completely they were likely to understand it; and this remains a valid position if we grant the premises (1) that there is, indeed, some meaning behind experience and (2) that man can comprehend it. Study the object long and well and piously enough, both the transcendentalists and the positivists had been preaching, and it will reveal itself at last. And these premises are not difficult to grant when the sought-after meaning behind experience is only a psychological truth.

The metaphysical novelists, with the probable exception of Melville, were poor hands at revision. "Bulwer-Lytton," as a recent commentator testifies, "was known to rewrite hardly at all,"[25] and Dickens had what he called "an insuperable aversion . . . to trying back."[26] "I never copy," he wrote to his protégé, John Overs, "[I] correct but very little, and that invariably as I write."[27] And yet a comparison of their practices in this

23. See Walter Blair, *Mark Twain and Huck Finn* (Berkeley and Los Angeles, 1960), p. 353.

24. Harry Levin writes that while composing the first draft, Stendhal was "never quite certain what would happen in the next chapter." *The Gates of Horn: A Study of Five French Realists* (New York, 1963), p. 93.

25. Richard Eugene Lautz, "Bulwer-Lytton as a Novelist" (diss. Univ. of Pennsylvania, 1967), p. 9.

26. Letter to Bulwer. Aug. 4, 1848. *The Letters of Charles Dickens*, 3 vols. (ed.) Walter Dexter (London, 1938), II, 113.

27. 7 [?] February 1840. *The Pilgrim Edition of the Letters of Charles Dickens* (eds.) Madeline House and Graham Storey (Oxford, 1965), II, 19.

branch of composition with the writing habits of Scott would be misleading. For the aesthetics of the metaphysical novel do not require revision;
indeed, when carried to logical conclusions, the romance aesthetics actually
oppose rewriting. Allen Ginsberg does not rewrite because to do so would
be to falsify what he had originally said. Another modern poet, Robert
Duncan, fears that if he permitted himself to revise he would be tempted
not to get his poems right the first time.[28] Such writers are disciples of the
Shelleyan tradition, which holds that time and thought and contemplation bring the artist farther away from the quick-fading vision, not closer
to the meaning of it. Victor Hugo believed that romances "should spring
forth at one bound, and then stay as they are for good and all. Once it is
made, the thing admits of no revising, no retouching," he warned. "The
book once published, the sex, virile or not, once recognized and proclaimed,
the babe's cry once heard, it is born—there it is—such as it is—father or
mother can no longer better it—it is in the world—in the sun and air—let
it take its chances to live or die![29]

A result of this policy against revision is that some metaphysical novelists are not such fine craftsmen as most realists, who naturally straighten
up sloppy scenes and sentences as they recast for clearer meaning. But the
metaphysical novelist did not need to rewrite in order to find a deeper
truth in his material; he already had more truth before he began to write
than he was likely ever to be able to express. Disraeli's Contarini Fleming
despaired of becoming a poet because he could find no adequate words to
recreate visions which were absolutely clear to him. And the metaphysical
novelist did not share Trollope's need to make his beginning consistent
with his ending. With the romancer, the beginning, since it was usually
closer in time of composition to the informing vision than was the ending,
stood therefore as the least distorted part of his work. Dickens did not
hesitate to publish fiction serially while it was in-progress, and as Trollope himself had to recognize, albeit somewhat snidely, "His first numbers always are well done."[30] Indeed, modern critics have recognized that
the opening chapters of Dickens, which were written before anything else
and hardly ever revised, provide the thematic and symbolic keynotes for
what is to follow.

And, of course, visionary novelists who did not publish works while

28. I do not know whether either Ginsberg or Duncan has ever published the
portion of his poetics here ascribed to him, but I have heard each of them make the
statements I have paraphrased.

29. "Note Added to the Edition of 1832," *Notre-Dame of Paris* (trans.) J.
Carroll Beckwith, 4 vols. (London, 1895), I, x.

30. *The Warden, The Writings of Anthony Trollope* (Philadelphia, 1900),
I, 182.

they were in-progress were not bound by Dickens' necessity of beginning
with the first chapter and then writing seriatim. The realistic novelist, we
should note, ought to proceed in this fashion since it is his technique to
follow the development of his central character sequentially. But the idealist is usually free to begin with the scene that most clearly embodies his
vision or illustrates his idea, no matter where in the story the scene may
occur. Thus Godwin began his work on *Caleb Williams* by constructing
the third volume,[31] and his daughter started writing *Frankenstein* with
what was later to become the fifth chapter, making, as she says in the
introduction of 1831, "a transcript of the grim terrors of my waking
dream."[32] Starting thus with the philosophic kernel, the a priori truth, a
philosophical romancer has little difficulty giving the rest of his story a
thematic unity, if not a dramatic consistency.

Up to this point we have been using the words "idea" and "vision" inter-
changeably, but now that Godwin and Mary Shelley have been mentioned,
it is possible, perhaps, to make a distinction. Godwin had already developed
the ideas he wished to express in *Caleb Williams* when he wrote *Political
Justice.* The vision of Caleb's flight then gave him an opportunity to attempt to embody his ideas in a romance.[33] *Frankenstein*, like Stevenson's
Strange Case of Dr. Jekyll and Mr. Hyde, is supposed to have begun in the
author's mind with what in earlier times would have been called a dream
vision. But neither story literally began with the dream. Stevenson had long
been searching for a vehicle to express his conception of man's duality, and
his daytime reading of the French psychologists had as much to do with
Jekyll and Hyde as did the nightmare murder of Sir Danvers Carew. Similarly, Mary Shelley's dream was preceded by a series of scientific and
"philosophical" discussions between Byron and her husband. "Invention,"
she writes in the 1831 introduction, "does not consist in creating out of
void, but out of chaos; the materials must, in the first place, be afforded: it
can give form to dark, shapeless substances, but cannot bring into being the
substance itself."[34]

Thus the vision comes after the idea and is perhaps the symbol or symbolic experience which not only embodies it, but raises the story from the
level of allegory to that of myth. Students of Hawthorne's notebooks are

31. "Preface" to the 1832 edition of *Fleetwood.* Reprinted as "Appendix II"
of *Caleb Williams* (ed.) David McCracken (London, 1970).

32. *Frankenstein; or, The Modern Prometheus* (London, 1831), p. xi.

33. Many readers have felt that Godwin did not succeed in this attempt to
embody his philosophy. Robert Kiely believes that he failed because his "imagination showed itself to be superior to his power of abstract conceptualization. (*The
Romantic Novel in England*, Cambridge, Mass., 1972, p. 95).

34. *Frankenstein*, p. ix.

well familiar with the process, although Hawthorne did not literally dream his symbols. Without adequate embodiments, however, his ideas were useless to him, as the anguished asides in the manuscripts of the late, unfinished romances fully indicate. "I have not yet struck the true keynote of this Romance," Hawthorne interrupted his narration of *The Ancestral Footstep* to remind himself, "and unless I do, I shall write nothing but tediousness and nonsense."[35] Yet he was never at a loss as to the idea he wished to express. He wrote several preliminary sketches for *Dr. Grimshawe's Secret*, all of them failures, and ultimately, in desperation, he plunged into the narrative itself, still without having made any proper connection between his idea of the proudly independent though root-hungry American—the theme of *Our Old Home*—and the emblem or vision of the bloody, ancestral footstep. Consequently, he complained in his manuscript, "I don't see the modus operandi. . . . Oh, Heavens! I have not the least notion how to get on. I never was in such a sad predicament before."[36] Improvisation, in the manner of Scott and Trollope, was both foreign to his technique and beyond his capability.

A younger, more fruitfully visionary, and far more self-confident Hawthorne is described by his wife:

> When he is evolving a work of art, he waits upon the light in such a purely simple way that I do not wonder at the perfection of each of his stories. Of several sketches, first one and then another come up to be clothed upon with language, after their own will and pleasure. It is real inspiration, and few are reverent enough and patient enough to wait for it as he does. . . . He does not meddle with the clean true picture that is painted on his mind. He lifts the curtain, and we see a microcosm of nature, so cunningly portrayed that truth itself seems to have been the agent of its appearance.[37]

Hawthorne occupied himself with the idea of *The Scarlet Letter* for more than five years. The actual composition was a matter of less than six months.[38] *The House of the Seven Gables* and *The Blithedale Romance*, both subjects of long preconception, took even less time in the writing.

Yet one must be careful not to overstate the case with Hawthorne. Bulwer, who always represents the extreme or purist position of the romancer, once wrote that "an author is generally pleased with his work"

35. *The Complete Works of Nathaniel Hawthorne* (Cambridge, Mass., 1883), XI, 491.

36. *Hawthorne's Doctor Grimshaw's Secret* (ed.) Edward H. Davidson (Cambridge, Mass., 1954), p. 164.

37. Quoted in "Introductory Note," *Mosses From an Old Manse* (Boston, 1900), p. xv.

38. See Randall Stewart, *Nathaniel Hawthorne: A Biography* (New Haven, 1948), pp. 93–94.

less in "proportion as it is good, than in proportion as it fulfils the idea with which he commenced it."[39] Hawthorne may have come around to something like this position, for late in his career he made a similar statement to explain his preference for drawings over finished paintings. He felt that "the first idea of a picture is real inspiration, and all the subsequent elaboration of the master serves but to cover up the celestial germ with something that belongs to himself."[40] Nevertheless, Hawthorne, at least as a very young writer, felt otherwise. In "Passages from a Relinquished Work" (1835), which used sometimes to be read as a fragment of a spiritual autobiography, he notes, "I cannot remember ever to have told a tale which did not vary considerably from my preconceived idea, and acquire a novelty of aspect as often as I repeated it. Oddly enough, my success was generally in proportion to the difference between conception and accomplishment."[41] And his wife confirms also this image of a Hawthorne who sometimes reconceived as he wrote: "I have known him to be in inextricable doubt, in the midst of a book or a sketch, as to the probable issue, waiting upon the muse for the rounding in of the sphere which every true work of art is."[42]

Thus Hyatt Waggoner is essentially correct when he concludes that none of Hawthorne's notebook jottings "can serve as even an approximately adequate statement of the meaning of the story to which it finally led, or in which it got embodied."[43] He is correct, but he goes too far in his attempt to recreate Hawthorne as a fashionable symbolist when he insists that the stories represent fictional thinking rather than thoughts fictionalized. Hawthorne's stories are both of these things, as, by necessity, are the stories of all romancers, indeed of all writers of fiction. Thoughts fictionalized or embodied in vision may be the ideal of romance, as Bulwer says it is, but it is an ideal as unlikely of complete fulfillment as the opposing ideal of the realist who sits down to his writing without a single preconception or moral attitude. No realist can come to his work newborn, and no romancer can entirely turn off his thought processes after he has dreamed his vision. Nor would it be a good thing for fiction if either could. Despite the transcendental mystique, the truth which the writer of the realistic novel discovers while imitating the experience is surely one which he already knew, although perhaps unconsciously. And since, as Shelley says, the glowing

39. "Dedicatory Epistle to John Auldjo," *Deveroux: A Tale* (London, 1852), I, iv.

40. "The French and Italian Notebooks of Nathaniel Hawthorne" (ed.) Norman Holmes Pearson (diss. Yale Univ., 1941), III, 499–500.

41. *Complete Works of Hawthorne*, II, 470.

42. Letter to Henry Chorley concerning *The Marble Faun*. Quoted in Julian Hawthorne, *Hawthorne and His Wife* (Boston and New York, 1884), I, 361.

43. *Hawthorne: A Critical Study*, p. 74.

coal of the romancer's vision fades even as he writes[44] and thus seems less and less adequate to him as an expression of the truth, he must substitute fresher thoughts for the quickly disappearing features of his original design. Therefore, a certain amount of reconception is both inevitable and desirable. But it is still possible to make a distinction between the young Hawthorne, who welcomed the enrichment and complexity which his preconceived visions achieved as he rendered them, and a Mark Twain who, in *Huckleberry Finn*, first discovered his thoughts in the unfolding of a story.

The American reviewers who criticized Bulwer most severely for his technique of preconception, the writers for the *Knickerbocker*, were also the most hostile critics of Herman Melville and his school. Melville, it has always been felt, both preconceived and reconceived, so that his most ambitious books—*Mardi, Moby-Dick, Pierre*—have frequently been read as welters of changed intentions. On the other hand, the best scholars of Melville's works—Willard Thorp, Harrison Hayford, Hershel Parker— have pointed out that despite its wide currency, the two-*Moby-Dicks* hypothesis remains unproven.[45] I disagree with the theory entirely, but it is only necessary to state at this point that whether or not Melville "found" or changed his ideas in the course of composition, he certainly did not do so

44. In "Defence of Poetry" (1821).

45. The best historical discussion of the hypothesis is a dissertation by James Barbour, "The Writing of Moby Dick" (UCLA, 1970). Barbour, who argues for three Moby Dicks, is nevertheless painstakingly honest in separating the theories on which he and others have built their cases from the meager "undisputed facts of composition": "And the facts are these: Melville began writting *Moby Dick* after his return from England early in 1850, probably during the first week in February. He wrote to his English publisher that summer that he expected to have it ready for publication in the fall. The book was not published, however, until the fall of the following year, more than one year after a friend had reported that the book was "mostly done." Around these facts the theories of revision have been constructed, [to the result]. . . . that there is a tradition of opinion that *Moby Dick* was written twice. There is, however, no consensus of opinion as to the nature of the two versions, nor the manner in which the revised novel was conceived and written." (pp. 1–2 and 24–25)

The two- or three-Moby-Dicks theory, then, must be understood as the product of a tradition of opinion, one which began with the first English reviewer, who, puzzled by the book's difficulties, concluded, on the basis of even fewer facts, that "Mr. Melville's purpose must have changed." (*The Athenaeum*, Oct. 25, 1851. Reprinted in *The Melville Log; A Documentary Life of Herman Melville, 1819–1891*, 2 vols. ((ed.)) Jay Leyda ([New York, 1969], I, 430). A similar "tradition of opinion" has it that the political allegory in *Mardi* was added after the rest of the work was complete. It is true that Melville makes references to some events which took place after a draft of *Mardi* had been copied for the publisher, but it is possible that these references took the places of others, which the fast-moving politics of the late 1840s had made stale.

in the empirical way of the realists; that is to say, he did not discover his meanings by imitating and closely observing the experience at hand.

The best clues to Melville's mode of composition occur in *Pierre* and *Mardi*, where the practices of two writers, Pierre Glendinning and Lombardo, who have both been taken to represent Melville himself, are described in some detail. Pierre alters the style, the meaning, the very nature of his book while he is writing it, but there is never any suggestion that the changes are inspired by anything that happens within his manuscript. Rather Pierre's novel changes because Pierre changes. The alterations in his book are brought about by his own development, of which the developing manuscript is an effect and an index, never a cause. The novel he is writing, so far as we know, never teaches him anything.

The case in *Mardi* is more difficult because we are not provided with much information about Lombardo's nonliterary life and because part of what information we do have seems to confirm, or at least has commonly been taken to confirm, the view that Melville was himself an undisciplined improviser. Babbalanja states in Chapter 180 that "when Lombardo set about his work, he knew not what it would become. He did not build himself in with plans; he wrote right on; and so doing, got deeper and deeper into himself; and like a resolute traveler, plunging through baffling woods, at last was rewarded for his toils." This, indeed, sounds something like the practices of the realists, described earlier, but, once again, Babbalanja does not say that the writer learns anything about his *subject* by all this directionless writing. Lombardo does not get deeper and deeper into his material, but "deeper and deeper into himself." His reward is not an insight into the nature of some experience he is trying to come to grips with; it is a state of mind which permits of inspired writing. "I have created the creative," he says. Moreover, he describes the "full fifty folios" of improvisation as "trash" which must be destroyed, not revised, after the true conception has been achieved.

> He read them over attentively; made a neat package of the whole: and put it into the fire. . . . And now the whole boundless landscape stretched away. Lombardo panted; the sweat was on his brow; he off mantle; braced himself . . . and gave himself plenty of room. On one side was his ream of vellum—

In other words, having written his way into the vision, he is now first ready to embody it, which is a far different thing from the empirical realist who discovers his meaning through execution.

Outside of the fiction itself, Melville has left us remarkably little evidence to throw light on this matter of preconception versus improvisation. His correspondence with Hawthorne seems to indicate that he approached the Agatha material as a realist rather than a metaphysical novelist—he seems to have been struck by the experience itself, not immediately by any idea it symbolized—but, of course, Melville never published the Agatha story, and he may not even have got round to writing it. On the side of preconception, there are marks, which probably indicate approval, in the margins of Melville's copy of *The Literary Works of Joshua Reynolds*, emphasizing two separate passages which argue that greatness in art is largely a matter of total conception and general effect.[46] There are also a pair of letters, one to his publisher and the other to his friend, Evert Duyckinck: in the first he speaks, concerning *Mardi*, of "the plan I have pursued,"[47] and in the letter to Duyckinck, written while he was composing *Moby-Dick*, Melville comments that "taking a book off the brain, is akin to the ticklish and dangerous business of taking an old painting off a panel."[48] This remark parallels Babbalanja's description in *Mardi* of Lombardo's Shelleyan attitude towards his great poem, that it "ever seemed to him but a poor scrawled copy of something within, which, do what he would, he could not completely transfer" (Chap. 180).

Manuscripts, if we had them in quantity, might settle the question, but very few have survived. The drafts of *The Confidence-Man* at Harvard show heavy revisions and at least one fresh start, but the material is too fragmentary to generalize from. The *Billy Budd* manuscripts, though they do not represent Melville in his prime, offer, perhaps, more light. Before the appearance of the Hayford and Sealts edition, it had been argued and, I believe, generally accepted, that *Billy Budd* was begun novelistically as an attempt by Melville to understand and exorcise his cousin Guert Gansevoert's guilty part in the *Somers* mutiny incident. Analogies were in order here to Scott's effort in *The Fair Maid of Perth* to accept the cowardice of his own cousin or to Henry James' repeated attempts to come to terms with Minny Temple's early death. But the recent editors show that the *Somers* material did not enter the manuscripts until the story was quite matured, and they suggest that we must hunt for sources, if we feel so inclined, not in the author's experiences but in other fiction or in Melville's thought. "*Billy Budd* developed," Hayford and Sealts conclude, "from exposition into dramatization";[49] that is to say, in the a priori manner, from abstract thought to particularizing experience, not vice versa, as it had been commonly supposed.

46. However, Melville did not read this book until 1870. It is now in the Houghton Library.

47. To John Murray, Jan. 1, 1848. *The Letters of Herman Melville* (eds.) Merrell R. Davis and William H. Gilman (New Haven, 1960), p. 68.

48. Dec. 13, 1850. *Ibid.*, p. 117.

49. *Billy Budd Sailor* (*An Inside Narrative*) (Chicago, 1963), p. 36.

The *Billy Budd* manuscripts also show that, unlike the other metaphysical novelists, Melville was painstaking at revision. The nature of the revisions, however, as the judgment of Hayford and Sealts suggests, implies that Melville rewrote in order to make his meanings more dramatic rather than to gain a closer understanding of his material. Lombardo of *Mardi* also included revision as an indispensable part of his aesthetics, but not revision in the manner of Thackeray, who pointed up the morals behind his story, or of Balzac, who greatly augmented his novels, rendering them at once more dramatic *and* more meaningful. Lombardo's reworking was a process of excision, designed to eliminate all reminders of the fact that his book was put together in a highly self-conscious, "unnatural" manner, reminders that Lombardo did not write his masterpiece like an excited child, as the *Knickerbocker* people would have preferred, or in the sequential mode, which the aesthetics of the dramatic novel required.

> Ere Mardi sees aught of mine, I scrutinize it myself, remorseless as a surgeon. I cut right and left; I probe, tear and wrench; kill, burn, and destroy. . . . stab false thoughts, ere hatched. . . . pull down wall and tower, rejecting materials which would make palaces for others. Oh! could Mardi but see how we work, it would marvel more at our primal chaos, than at the round world thence emerging. It would marvel at our scaffoldings, scaling heaven; marvel at the hills of earth, banked all round our fabrics ere completed.—How plain the pyramid! In this grand silence, so intense, pierced by that pointed mass,—could ten thousand slaves have ever toiled? ten thousand hammers rung?—There it stands,—part of Mardi: claiming kin with mountains;—was this thing piecemeal built?—It was. Piecemeal?—atom by atom it was laid. (Chap. 180)

Thus Melville seems to have been more concerned with execution than were the others in his school. Perhaps the need to write his way into the visionary state of mind made him value composition as a creative experience, while the others, who conceived their stories in dreams, in brief notebook entries, or on mechanical number plans, may have regarded execution as a lesser, performing art. Or it may be that he needed to revise because his own life, like Pierre's, was changing so rapidly that, while a book was on the stocks, new visions and conceptions kept crowding in and had to be reconciled with one another. But in any event, vision in Melville appears to have preceded composition, whether of whole books or of parts of them, and he seems certainly to have written always in the a priori mode, never in the empirical.

Dickens used to be thought of as the most spontaneous and as one of the least consciously artistic of writers. It was known that he did not much revise, and it was supposed that he did not plan. Howells once explained this view of Dickens in reference to the serial mode of publication, which, he felt, "was always against form, against balance."

> Dickens issued his novels, until he started *Household Words*, in numbers; George Eliot published hers in the same way, and I believe wrote them from month to month as they appeared, as Mr. Hardy still writes his. A novel was not completed when its publication began. In fact, from number to number, the author hardly knew what was going to happen.[50]

And Poe, who admired both Dickens and Bulwer, contrasted the spontaneity of *The Old Curiosity Shop* with the carefully preconceived effects of Bulwer's *Night and Morning*.[51] He assumed that Dickens gained his triumph through sheer force of genius and in despite of all rules, according to the manner in which, as Poe was later stridently to insist, he had not written "The Raven."

More recently, since scholarly attention has been focused on Dickens' number plans, his detailed plot outlines, Poe's notion of Dickens as an unselfconscious improviser has been largely abandoned, at least as regards the middle and late works. We know him now as a careful planner who made himself into a highly conscious craftsman until he could school Bulwer himself in the demanding art of serial publication.[52] We know, moreover, that it was his practice from fairly early in his career to plan a novel by first selecting a theme, and envisioning it as a fable, then inventing relevant characters and incidents, and finally constructing a plot to connect all the meaningful elements.[53]

But even the very early works were much less haphazardly written than had previously been supposed. Dickens may have started his first novel, as he tells us, by simply thinking of Mr. Pickwick, but recent scholarship has made it apparent that he very shortly thereafter began thinking of other, more thematic matters.[54] *Oliver Twist* is another early work which

50. "My Favorite Novelist and His Best Book," in *Criticism and Fiction and Other Essays*, pp. 98–99. Except in respect to *Romola*, Howells is completely mistaken about George Eliot, and he very much simplifies Dickens' mode of composition.

51. "The Old Curiosity Shop and Other Tales," *Graham's Lady's and Gentleman's Magazine* (May 1841), pp. 248–251.

52. See the letters in *Letters of Dickens*, Volume III, surrounding the publication of *A Strange Story*.

53. See John Butt and Kathleen Tillotson, *Dickens at Work* (London, 1957).

54. Particularly significant in this regard is the work of Robert L. Patten with the so-called interpolated tales in *Pickwick Papers*, which had always been regarded as mere fillers, junk left over from *Sketches by Boz*, and interesting only as they cast light on Dickens' own psychological problems. Patten has shown that the tales are important elements of the novel's total scheme: that they were taken seriously by Dickens, that at least two of them were not interpolated but composed

did not simply find its own development in the fashion of a realistic novel. Dickens conceived his characters long before he introduced them, and he thought them out intellectually before he imagined them dramatically. Thus he writes to Forster on November 3, 1837, "I am glad you like Oliver this month—especially glad that you particularise the first chapter [Chap. 16]. I hope to do great things with Nancy. If I can only work out the idea I have formed with her, and of the female who is to contrast with her [Rose Maylie, who does not appear in the narrative until the following May] I think I may defy Mr. Hayward and all his works." [55]

Dickens' letters also provide evidence that *The Chimes*[56] and *Dombey and Son*[57] were preconceived in great detail. The surviving number plans for the later novels, as we have said, show even more conclusively that Dickens worked out his stories in advance of composition. And the difficulties expressed in the *David Copperfield* plans for reintroducing and exculpating Miss Mowcher, show how seriously Dickens took his blueprints; it was no easy thing for him to change a formulated intention.[58]

Of course, Dickens, like the others in his school, could make some alterations as he wrote, and he often did. The second version of Miss Mowcher, just referred to, and the revised ending of *Great Expectations* are perhaps the best-known examples of such changes. The most serious reconceptions occur in *Dombey and Son*, where Edith is allowed to keep her virtue because Lord Jeffrey "positively" refused to believe she would become Carker's mistress,[59] and where Walter Gay, who was originally ticketed for degeneration, comes back to the Dombey world reborn by virtue of a shipwreck.

These changes, however, are in character and plot, never in theme or fable. Theme, once again, was Dickens' starting point. Characters and incidents were invented only in the second place to help embody the vision. If it seemed to Dickens as he wrote that the originally conceived character

---

seriatim, and that they are fully relevant to a theme which governs the entire work. In short, Dickens used the tales in *Pickwick* in the same way that he used characters and incidents in his later works, as parts of an overall thematic plan, which, after the false start, must have been fully preconceived. "The Art of *Pickwick's* Interpolated Tales," *ELH*, XXXIV (1967), 349–367. See also his unpublished dissertation, "Plot in Charles Dickens' Early Novels" (Princeton, 1965).

55. *Pilgrim Letters*, I, 328.

56. Letter to Forster, 18 Oct. 1844. *Letters of Dickens*, I, 630. After giving a summary of his plan for *The Chimes* Dickens laments, "Ah, how I hate myself, my dear fellow, for this lame and halting outline of the vision I have in my mind."

57. Letter to Forster, 25 July 1846, *Ibid.*, I, 770–772, provides a remarkably full plan for *Dombey and Son* written one month after the beginning of that work.

58. See Butt and Tillotson, *Dickens at Work*, Chap. VI.

59. Letter to Forster, 21 Dec. 1847. *Letters of Dickens*, II, 63.

illustrated his giant metaphor poorly, he was free to make changes. When he did so for extraliterary reasons, as in the case of Miss Mowcher, he needed only be careful that the theme would not suffer too seriously. He was free to invent new characters and incidents as he composed, he could even add whole sections, as with the American chapters of *Martin Chuzzlewit*, so long as the new inventions were thematically relevant. Afterthoughts of this type were, indeed, proper to his procedure, since characters, incidents, and plots were really afterthoughts to begin with. The two-part format of his number plans seems, in fact, designed to accommodate just such changes and additions—one column was for the number as originally planned, while the other left room for improvements —and the preconceived summary of *Dombey and Son* which Dickens sent to Forster is similarly careful to allow for branches and meanderings which might come up. But such changes in Dickens are never of the type which Scott encouraged, the sort which lead the author to a different truth than he had originally intended to express. Moreover, they are the exception rather than the rule. As Butt and Tillotson write, "From 1846 on. . . . improvisation . . . was within the limits of a foreseen plan, which might be modified in detail, but not radically."[60]

The way in which Dickens kept control of his stories, the way he refused to learn from them, is evident in even so early a work as *The Old Curiosity Shop*, a reconceived, but by no means an improvised novel. Dickens planned and actually published the first chapters as a short story, which he then expanded, without revision, into a full-length romance. At first glance this process appears to be the sort of thing that happens frequently in dramatic or realistic fiction when an author discovers that his heroine is more complex than he had thought, that she has possibilities which the necessarily limited experience of a short story cannot exhaust. The story then becomes a first chapter, and the realist puts his heroine through more extended paces to see what she *can* do and to discover what she *does* mean. But something quite different happened in the case of *The Old Curiosity Shop*.

In the first place, the decision to expand was at least partially dictated, not by aesthetic considerations, but by the commercial motive of saving *Master Humphrey's Clock* from failure. Dickens' cherished plan for editing a magazine of short fiction had to be abandoned when the readers, who had bought up the first number eagerly expecting a new novel by Boz in deliriously exciting weekly instead of monthly parts, were disappointed to find they were being offered a sort of miscellany of German-style tales. Dickens had to satisfy the desire for a long story or risk losing his audience, and in "The Old Curiosity Shop" he perceived an opportunity

60. *Dickens at Work*, p. 66.

for expansion. But it was not a realist's possibility which Dickens saw. Nell changes by becoming physically weaker and weaker as the book goes on until she dies at last, but her complexities are all exhausted during the short story portion. Those critics who are disappointed with Dickens because he did not allow his heroine to grow up into the sexual stage are reading in the wrong genre, for there is nothing of the progressive in Dickens' conception of Nell or of her book. She is an icon, like Browning's Pippa, who was perhaps modelled after her, and it is unreasonable for us to expect her to develop.

In the 1848 preface to *The Old Curiosity Shop*, Dickens explained that "in writing the book I had it always in my fancy to surround the lonely figure of the child with grotesque and wild, but not impossible companions, and to gather about her innocent face and pure intentions, associates as strange and uncongenial as the grim objects that are about her bed when her history is first foreshadowed." Of course, as they were originally intended, the innocent face and the grim objects were not the foreshadowing, but the accomplishment of Nell's history. But after we have read all the subsequent chapters, it is still impossible for us to go beyond Master Humphrey's statement of the case, delivered after his first visit to the curiosity shop:

> all that night, waking or in my sleep, the same thoughts recurred, and the same images retained possession of my brain. I had, ever before me, the old dark murky rooms—the gaunt suits of mail with their ghostly silent air— the faces all awry, grinning from wood and stone—the dust, and rust, and worm that lives in wood—and alone in the midst of all this lumber and decay and ugly age, the beautiful child in her gentle slumber, smiling through her light and sunny dreams.[61]

The intention of the expanded story is not dramatically to bring Nell into meaningful collision with this fallen world but lyrically to repeat the initial vision with variations, to manufacture more grotesques with which to surround the ever-beautiful child. Properly speaking, there is no action in her story,[62] for *The Old Curiosity Shop* exists outside the phenomenal world of progressive cause and effect. In the ordinary sense, at least, Nell and the world of grotesques which Dickens multiplies to juxtapose against her have no influence on one another. We do not have a character *in* a situation but a character *and* a situation. Nell takes to the road, but in the

---

61. *The Old Curiosity Shop*, Chap. I.

62. Edgar Johnson, Dickens' best modern biographer, writes that *The Old Curiosity Shop* "is composed simply of . . . contrasting pictures, the rough men and the bad places, and the child passing through them all, untouched and unstained." *Charles Dickens: His Tragedy and His Triumph* (New York, 1952), I, 324.

old rather than the new-fashioned picaresque tradition; like Gil Blas and unlike Huck Finn and Augie March, she is not changed by what she sees. Instead she guides us on a walk through a microcosmic wax museum with reduplicating episodes of horror, demonstrating that not only London but all of England and, since the journey also goes backward in time, all of history, is an old curiosity shop whose hideousness cannot touch her purity. As Steven Marcus observes, "the decaying Arcadia in which she dies resembles nothing so much as that other pile of rubble, the Shop itself."[63] And Nell's gentle death or ascension is a more dramatic replaying of the quiet sleep which ended the first section of her story.

These repetitions make up the main part of Dickens' expansion of *The Old Curiosity Shop*. They show how it was possible for him to lengthen a story without radical reconception. The rest of Dickens' additions consist of two subplots in which Kit Nubbles and Dick Swiveller find their salvations with substitute Nells. We shall discuss the meaning behind this general structure in a subsequent chapter, but the essential point to make now is that either one of these subplots might easily have run away with the book, the Dick Swiveller plot especially, since Dick is the only character in the story with real possibilities for development and change. And Dick does run away with the books of most novel-oriented critics, just as Quilp fascinates the psychoanalysts of the literary profession. Dickens, in contrast, keeps all his characters firmly in their places as subordinates to Nell, whom they try, with equal ineffectiveness, either to help or to hurt. The subplots are also carefully controlled; they flank Nell's story, never preempting it, never even becoming parts of it in any cause-and-effect way.

These two heroes, Kit and Dick, represent the redeemable part of the fallen world. It is Nell who saves them, not directly, as we shall see, but only as a vague religious influence which always keeps Kit up to the mark and leads Swiveller to recognize her type in the miserable small servant, the prisoner of a grotesque, underground curiosity shop of her own. Thus even the developed subplots of the expanded story repeat a principal motif of the original version, in which the vision of Nell's innocence among all the ugliness redeems the uninvolved narrator, the nightwalking and melancholic Master Humphrey.

Against readers who pleaded for Little Nell's life and critics who thought she was butchered for market, Dickens always maintained that the death was a necessary and long preconceived part of his design. And it is interesting that Bulwer, whose *Night and Morning* Poe singled out as a contrast to the untutored spontaneity he thought he perceived in Nell's adventures, should have backed Dickens in his claims. Thus Dickens wrote to Thomas Latimer:

63. *Dickens from Pickwick to Dombey* (New York, 1965), p. 147.

I have always fancied the Old Curiosity Shop to be my XXX [best], and . . . I never had the design and purpose of a story so distinctly marked in my mind, from its commencement. All its quietness arose out of a deliberate purpose; the notion being to stamp upon it from the first, the shadow of that early death. I think I shall always like it better than anything I have done or may do. So much for authorship. Bulwer who read it through t'other day holds exactly my opinion.[64]

In contrast to *The Old Curiosity Shop*, *Martin Chuzzlewit* is famous as the first of the novels which Dickens consciously tried to control in order to express a theme. Thus he wrote in the preface to the first edition (1844) that he had "endeavoured in the progress of this tale, to resist the temptation of the current Monthly Number, and to keep a steadier eye upon the general purpose and design." Forster confirms another point of the preface when he writes that "the notion of taking Pecksniff for a type of character was really the origin of the book; the design being to show, more or less by every person introduced, the number and variety of humours and vices that have their root in selfishness."[65] The structure of the comic plot, also according to Forster, was devised in the first stages of composition: "as early as the third number he drew up the plan of 'old Martin's plot to degrade and punish Pecksniff.' "[66]

Using intrinsic evidence, moreover, it is possible to see how carefully Dickens articulated the thematically relevant pattern of the melodramatic counterplot in *Martin Chuzzlewit*. This intricate structure is based upon a series of partnerships, which amount really to *Doppelgänger* relationships. Thus, in the early chapters, Anthony and Jonas Chuzzlewit are virtually indistinguishable partners, and so are Chevy Slyme and Montague Tigg. A partnership can be a means to defeat selfishness, as Anthony first points out in conversation with Pecksniff and later indicates to the reader by the selfless manner of his own dying, and as Mark Tapley ultimately

64. March 13, 1841, *Pilgrim Letters*, II, 233. Forster, of course, contradicts Dickens' claim that Nell's death was planned. *The Old Curiosity Shop*, he writes, "grew into a full proportioned story under the warmth of the feeling it had inspired its writer with; its very incidents created a necessity at first not seen; and it was carried to a close only contemplated after a full half of it had been written." *The Life of Charles Dickens*, (ed.) A. J. Hoppé, 2 vols. (London, 1966), I, 124. On the other hand, a more recent scholar, Stanley Tick, has argued in a paper delivered at the 1973 meetings of the Philological Association of the Pacific Coast that the "manuscript itself strongly suggests that Dickens knew exactly what task he was upon quite early in his composition—at the same moment, I would say now, when he realized, that there would be no finishing of this 'little child-story' in a handful of short chapters."

65. *Life of Dickens*, I, 274.

66. *Ibid*.

proves to *his* partner, young Martin. But such a relationship cannot work when one of the principals is himself double, as, for instance, Sairey Gamp, who has invented an alternate identity to support her hypocritical self-image, and Pecksniff, who philanthropically warms his own hands. Jonas Chuzzlewit and Montague Tigg, who later appears as Tigg Montague, are also such doubles-by-division,[67] and it is not surprising, therefore, that they rather quickly dissolve their original partnerships and band together for the purpose of defrauding the world. Their actions provide a more startling, if not a more sophisticated, demonstration of the chemical concept of elective affinities than Goethe was able to mount in his novel.

The new compound, however, proves even less stable than the old ones, as each of the elements strives continually towards its true affinity, to combine with itself. At length the nightside of Jonas' psyche cancels the bond entirely by murdering his shape-shifting confederate. The structure to this point, if one may be allowed to change the metaphor, resembles the precision of the elimination chart in some athletic tournament:

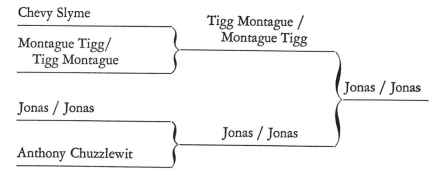

Chevy Slyme

Montague Tigg/
Tigg Montague

Tigg Montague /
Montague Tigg

Jonas / Jonas

Jonas / Jonas

Anthony Chuzzlewit

Jonas / Jonas

Jonas / Jonas

This careful structuring, especially when we mark its thematic relevance, argues a considerable amount of preconception. The case becomes stronger when we note that Dickens insisted in bringing both of the originally rejected partners—Anthony Chuzzlewit and Chevy Slyme—back into the plot to assist in destroying the champion monster of selfishness, Jonas Chuzzlewit, the ultimate self-partner. Through the agency of Chuffey, who is described as a breathing corpse, dead Anthony testifies from the grave, exposing his son and erstwhile partner. And in a still more surprising turn, Chevy Slyme, long, long absent from the novel, is reintroduced (as a policeman!) to facilitate Jonas' suicide, which is the final dissolution of the man's partnership even with himself. Reduced thus to diagram, the

67. See Ralph Tymms, *Doubles in Literary Psychology* (Cambridge, England, 1949).

melodramatic plot of this novel, it appears, was as carefully blueprinted as that of *Wuthering Heights* has been shown to have been.[68]

On the other hand, there is a great deal of improvisation in the comic plot of *Martin Chuzzlewit*. Much of it is of the afterthought variety we discussed earlier. Mrs. Gamp is an inspired addition to the gallery of selfishness, and, whether Dickens included the American chapters for commercial or artistic reasons, they provide a powerful reinforcement to the original theme. At least one reader argues, however, that as *Martin Chuzzlewit* was being written, its thematically inspired characters, especially the improvised Mrs. Gamp, developed in ways which contradict Dickens' intended vision and render the preconceived plot faulty. Thus James Kincaid has written:

> In the process a whole new morality grows up which makes the original view of selfishness seem hopelessly puerile and which makes old Martin Chuzzlewit, as the chief instrument in the development of the original design, the most unsatisfactory character in all of Dickens. There is, as a result, a split between the simple, didactic surface and the more complex sub-surface of the novel, keeping the comedy from being fully realized or satisfactorily completed. This split is most clearly apparent at the end of the novel where both Pecksniff and Mrs. Gamp are denounced by old Martin and sent packing. . . . By this point the novel belongs not to old Martin but to Sairey and Seth, not because they are more 'real' but because the morality they live by is much more humane and more adequate to the demands of the bleak world realized here than is Martin's simplistic copy-book code. As in *Oliver Twist*, then, the plot gets in the way of the pattern.[69]

This interesting analysis, with which I shall have ultimately to disagree, assumes a major point I have been trying to make: that Dickens did indeed preconceive both the plot and meaning of his book. As to the conflict between Dickens and Mrs. Gamp, the metaphysical novelists knew all about character rebellions, for they were always struggling to put them down. Without laws—preconceived plots—there can, of course, be no rebels. In 1835 the young Hawthorne wrote the following story idea in his notebook:

> A person to be writing a tale, and to find that it shapes itself against his intentions; that the characters act otherwise than he thought; that unforseen events occur; and a catastrophe comes which he strives in vain to avert.[70]

---

68. My reference is to C. P. Sanger's study of the family relationship: *The Structure of Wuthering Heights* (London, 1926), and to the many articles which have followed from this seminal work.

69. *Dickens and the Rhetoric of Laughter* (Oxford, 1971), pp. 133–34.

70. *Passages from the American Note-Books of Nathaniel Hawthorne*, 2 vols. [(ed.) Sophia Hawthorne] (Boston, 1868), I, 16–17. Oct. 25, 1835.

And the neophyte author in Bulwer's *My Novel* protests that "the author may beget a character, but the moment that character comes into action, it escapes from his hands—plays its own part, and fulfils its own inevitable doom" (Bk. XII, Chap. 1). Dickens was always busy disparaging such acts of independence, and even if the characters of *Martin Chuzzlewit* did out-grow their original designs, a point which I do not concede, Dickens' strong commitment to his preconception is clear from the fact that he insisted on imposing it right up to the end. And twenty years later, when he employed the same pattern again in *Our Mutual Friend*, he was still more rigorous in its execution.

After *Martin Chuzzlewit*, if we can judge from the plot summaries and elaborate number plans, Dickens took pains to preconceive his novels even more carefully, and he never again indulged a character as he had Mrs. Gamp. Many readers have regretted this change after *Martin Chuzzlewit*, feeling that the real fun is thenceforth out of Dickens, that the inimitable freedom is gone. Dickens himself must have regarded the matter differently, concluding that by limiting his characters' exuberances, he was liberating his own visions from their tyranny. Thus he wrote to an aspiring writer:

> I have no means of knowing whether you are patient in the pursuit of this art; but I am inclined to think that you are not, and that you do not disci-pline yourself enough. When one is impelled to write this or that, one has still to consider: "How much of this will tell for what I mean? How much of it is my own wild emotion and superfluous energy—how much remains that is truly belonging to this ideal character and these ideal circumstances?" It is in the laborious struggle to make this distinction, and in the determi-nation to try for it, that the road to the correction of faults lies. (Perhaps I may remark, in support of the sincerity with which I write this, that I am an impatient and impulsive person myself, but that it has been for many years the constant effort of my life to practise at my desk what I preach to you.) [71]

Thus, after *Martin Chuzzlewit*, Dickens seldom allowed his characters to develop so much life that they could refuse to follow his thematically oriented directions and thereby threaten to contradict the original vision.[72] Put another way, he did not permit himself to be instructed by the ex-

71. Letter to Miss Emily Jolly, 13 May 1857. *Letters of Dickens*, II, 850.
72. I think that Edith Dombey is the single great exception to this statement, and I suspect that when Jeffrey refused to believe she would go to bed with Carker, he was expressing not so much Victorian prudery, but rather a sensitive response to a well-developed character, who could not be forced to work out the author's theme at the expense of her own integrity. It is interesting that after this rebellion, Dickens banished Edith from the novel.

periences of his characters, especially of those characters like Mrs. Gamp, whom he had preconceived as negative examples of the virtues he had determined to inculcate, and who, if left to their own devices, would naturally develop a plausible world view at odds with his own.

This restraint, once again, is a matter of deep regret for many readers who feel that the late Dickens is not only less enjoyable than the early, but also less honest. They criticize him, as they deprecate Hawthorne of *The House of the Seven Gables*, for his unwillingness to be convinced by the "logic" of his story, for following what Barbara Hardy calls "dogmatic" rather than "organic" form.[73] But surely such disappointment is an example of the Anglo-Saxon prejudice in favor of a posteriori reasoning we noted at the beginning of this chapter, and we must try to forgive the metaphysical novelists for not sharing it. Believing that their century had been crippled or driven mad by its general adherence to the experiential world view, they were adamant in rejecting such a logic. They wrote frequently about characters who, trapped in the malignant times spirit, wasted aimless, ad hoc lives or, like Melville's Taji, pursued wild quests, chartless voyages. Nevertheless, the metaphysical novelists insisted, against the "evidence," that visions, preconceptions, had the power to liberate them and their contemporaries from what Bulwer called the "tyranny of every-day life."[74]

73. See her chapter, "Dogmatic Form: Defoe, Charlotte Brontë, and E. M. Forster," in *The Appropriate Form: An Essay on the Novel* (London, 1964), pp. 51–82.

74. *A Strange Story, The Knebworth Edition*, p. 267.

·II·

The Writer and His Audience

Frankly, it is not my words that I mistrust but your minds. I
could be eloquent were I not afraid you fellows have starved
your imaginations to feed your bodies. I do not mean to be
offensive; it is respectable to have no illusions—and safe—
and profitable—and dull. Yet you, too, in your time must
have known the intensity of life, that light of glamour
created in the shock of trifles, as amazing as the glow of
sparks struck from a cold stone—and as short-lived, alas!
                                    —JOSEPH CONRAD, *Lord Jim*

It is frequently assumed that the a priori optimism of the metaphysical
novelists and other romancers put them in a cozy relationship with their
readers and gave them an advantage over the realists, who told honest,
painful truths, derived from hard experience. Most critics believe, for instance, that Dickens let himself be talked into changing the pessimistic
ending of *Great Expectations* because he wanted to maintain such a relationship and to keep such an advantage. Even those critics who prefer the
changed ending on artistic grounds seem, nevertheless, to distrust Dickens'
motives.[1] The general picture of accommodation is perhaps accurate if we
compare our writers with the late-century naturalists, who regarded themselves not as realists, but as romancers of a different school, or even if we
compare them with their contemporaries in France, where different philosophical attitudes and prejudices prevailed and where realism was far less
compromising. But the assumption is invalid when we regard the metaphysical novelists along with the early- and mid-century realists of England and America.

A happy ending is a generic necessity for most forms of romance, but
this does not always mean, as R. L. Stevenson once suggested, that the
author has decided to lie like a gentleman out of deference to the sensibilities

---

1. J. Hillis Miller, who makes the best case for the changed ending, says that
the advice came from "Mrs. Grundy in the mask of Bulwer Lytton" (*Charles
Dickens: The World of His Novels*, Cambridge, Mass., 1958, p. 278), and Sylvère
Monod urges, without irony, that in justice to Dickens we try to forget that Bulwer
originated the change (*Dickens the Novelist*, Norman, Okla., 1967, pp. 476–77).

of his reader.[2] A more valid index of a writer's relationship or, better, of his desired relationship with his readers can be found in the tone of his private and public comments on his work, especially in his prefaces and authorial intrusions. An examination of the tone of these comments will show that while the romancers may have been happier with the world than were the realists, they were, once again, less comfortable with the prevalent world view; that while they sound surer about the truth of their visions, they were not nearly so certain of the efficacy of fiction as a means of communicating truth; and that while they may have been ultimately at peace with the universe, they seem, in the meantime, to have been seriously at war with their readers. Such an examination will also reveal that for both realistic and metaphysical novelists the relationship between author and reader is often a consciously manipulated tool of strategy, for an author's comments on his work not only tell the reader what he is desired to look for, in the direct manner of a Wordsworthian or Zolaesque manifesto, they also indicate, and are sometimes intended to indicate, whether the narrator regards the reader as his friend, his protégé, his audience, his recalcitrant student, or his congregation. And when properly established, each of these relationships facilitates a different kind of book, usually with a different intention and sometimes with a different world view.

Walter Scott, who was one of the great masters of this subtle strategy, created the characteristic stance or pose which many English realists took throughout most of his century. It is an attitude of modesty, simplicity, and good sense. Thus he wrote in the general preface to the Waverley Novels:

> The habits of self-importance which are . . . acquired by authors are highly injurious to a well-regulated mind; for the cup of flattery, if it does not, like that of Circe, reduce men to the level of beasts, is sure, if eagerly drained, to bring the best and the ablest down to that of fools.[3]

And he claimed, consequently, that he regarded his own works "without any feeling of exultation, because, whatever may have been their temporary success, I am well aware how much their reputation depends upon the caprice of fashion."[4] *The Monastery*, he admitted, was "a sort of light literature."[5]

Scott's works, therefore, would not, in his estimation, be read forever.

2. Letter to J. M. Barrie, Nov. 1, 1892, *The Works of Robert Louis Stevenson*, 26 vols. (London, 1922–1923), XXIII, 170.

3. Reprinted in *Sir Walter Scott on Novelists and Fiction* (ed.) Ione Williams (London, 1968), pp. 417–418.

4. *Ibid.*, p. 427. "Introduction" to *Chronicles of Canongate*.

5. "Introduction" to *The Monastery* (London, New York, and Melbourne, 1888–98), p. xii.

Nor, although he was a serious antiquarian, did he affect to pretend that they derived from a long and noble lineage, for the novel, according to his view of literary history, was a new genre. *Pamela*, Scott felt, represented a fresh start in narrative, an "unexpected return to truth and nature,"[6] and as "the discoverer of a new style of writing," its author could be mentioned along with "Cooke or Parry."[7] Richardson himself had thought that his works were more traditional, that with *Clarissa* he had written a legitimate tragedy;[8] but Scott valued the natural and unsophisticated in art, and he presented himself as a modest man, who commonsensibly suspected the self-puffery inherent in such grandiose claims. He admits that

> Fielding had high notions of the dignity of an art which he may be considered as having founded. He challenges a comparison between the Novel and the Epic. Smollett, Le Sage, and others, emancipating themselves from the strictness of the rules he has laid down. . . . have been satisfied if they amused the reader upon the road, though the conclusion only arrived because the tale must have an end, just as the traveller alights at the inn because it is evening.[9]

Thus the novel, as Scott saw it, was a significant discovery, but hardly earth-shaking, because, "after all, the immediate object of the novelist, as of the poet [is] to please,"[10] and he did not consider the novelist as standing high even in the ranks of imaginative literature.[11]

Generally, the nineteenth-century English realists accepted this modest self-estimate. "The Victorian novelist," as Bradford Booth has pointed out, "did not take himself very seriously. Since he wrote for a disparate, heterogenous group and aimed primarily at amusement, he did not often assume the mantle of the poet or the prophet."[12] Thus Thackeray wrote, "I often say I am like the pastry-cook, and don't care for tarts, but prefer bread and cheese; but the public love the tarts (luckily for us), and we must bake and sell them."[13] And Trollope, to whom this humble observation of

6. "Samuel Richardson," in *Lives of the Novelists* (1825). Reprinted in *Sir Walter Scott on Novelists and Fiction* (ed.) Ione Williams (London, 1968), p. 22.

7. *Ibid.*, p. 40.

8. *Clarissa: or, The History of a Young Lady* (Oxford, 1930), VII, 132–135.

9. "Introductory Epistle" [1822], *The Fortunes of Nigel* (Edinburgh, 1822), pp. xiv–xv.

10. "Jane Austen's Novels," *Quarterly Review* (Jan. 1821). Reprinted in *The Miscellaneous Prose Works of Sir Walter Scott, Bart* (Edinburgh, 1835), XVIII, 221.

11. "Preface," *The Abbot, Waverley Novels* (Boston, 1893), XX, xxii.

12. *Anthony Trollope: Aspects of His Life and Art* (Bloomington, Ind., 1958), p. 23.

13. Letter to Anthony Trollope, 28 Oct. 1859, *The Letters and Private Papers*

Thackeray's was addressed, explained his choice of a profession in terms even more self-effacing:

> I had often told myself since I left school that the only career in life within my reach was that of an author, and the only mode of authorship open to me that of a writer of novels. . . . Parliament was out of the question. I had not means to go to the Bar. . . . Poetry I did not believe to be within my grasp. The drama, too, which I would fain have chosen, I believed to be above me. For history, biography, or essay writing I had not sufficient erudition. But I thought it possible that I might write a novel.[14]

Scott, of course, would have preferred to have been a soldier, and he turned to fiction only after Byron's popularity forced him to abandon verse.

To a certain extent, this modesty on the part of the novelists may have been a conscious pose. Cooper believed that in Scott it was simply an instance of snobbery.[15] Mark Twain may have used it defensively, for certainly he did not always feel modest about his writing. Thus he said somewhat loftily in his *Autobiography* that "Humorists of the 'mere' sort cannot survive," and that humor must both teach and preach "if it would live forever." Then the characteristic self-effacement reasserted itself like a shield. "By forever, I mean thirty years. I have always preached. That is the reason that I have lasted thirty years." But as an artist Twain was clear on at least one point: "Humor must not professedly teach and it must not professedly preach."[16] Similarly Scott advised that "any *direct* attempt at moral teaching" must be "managed with the utmost discretion."[17]

Trollope genuinely admired and perhaps even envied Bulwer-Lytton's erudition, but he criticized Bulwer for the too obvious use of it. "I cannot say . . . that he lived with his characters," Trollope criticized; "he lived with his work, with the doctrines which at the time he wished to preach."[18] Bulwer had philosophical pretensions, which, to a realist like Trollope, meant acting uppity. W. D. Howells expresses much the same attitude towards Bulwer:

> He meant extremely well by literature; he had ideals so tall that he enjoyed something like a moral elevation from them; he respected the novelist so highly that he wished to call him the Poet, and did call him so in his prefaces; he was a man of polite learning, or at least, of scholarly reading;

of William Makepeace Thackeray (ed.) Gordon N. Ray (Cambridge, Mass., 1946), IV, 158–159.

14. *An Autobiography*, 2 vols. (Edinburgh and London, 1888), I, 70–71.

15. "Lockhart's Life of Scott." *The Knickerbocker* (Oct. 1838).

16. *The Autobiography of Mark Twain* (ed.) Charles Neider (New York, 1959), pp. 272–273.

17. "Jane Austen's Novels," p. 221.

18. *An Autobiography*, II, 72.

he wished always to do better than he did; in the lack of artistic instincts he had artistic principles, which if mistaken were sincere; and with all he was thoroughly mediocre.[19]

I do not mean to imply that the realists were not moralists or even that they did not take their didactic responsibilities so seriously as did the metaphysical novelists. The quotations from both Twain and Scott would anyway contradict such an inference. I suggest only that their particular art benefitted from an unphilosophical pose, and that they were somewhat suspicious of patent intellectuality which smacked, once again, of a priori thought. In this light, Howells' preference for artistic instincts over artistic principles is instructive. The nineteenth-century public demanded an improving as well as an amusing meal, and Scott, Thackeray, Trollope, Twain, and certainly Howells were not reluctant to provide it. They were all sages by Falstaffian instinct, if not on principle. There were limits, however. A novelist might dispense home truths born of commonsense wisdom, or he might even present philosophy, so long as it was modern, hard-nosed, and thoroughly empirical, and so long as it did not call itself philosophy. But the realist-author could not appear excessively learned in comparison with his readers. Thus George Eliot, when she was a doctrinaire realist, hid her own education in a digressive aside from "The Sad Fortunes of the Reverend Amos Barton":

> And, now, here is an opportunity for an accomplished writer to apostrophise calumny, to quote Virgil, and to show that he is acquainted with the most ingenious things which have been said on that subject in polite literature. But what is opportunity to the man who can't use it? An unfecundated egg, which the waves of time wash away into nonentity. So, as my memory is ill-furnished, and my notebook still worse, I am unable to show myself either erudite or eloquent apropos of the calumny whereof the Rev. Amos Barton was the victim.

Instead, she showed herself wise by describing the situation with a homely analogy out of the reader's own experience.

> I can only ask my reader,—did you ever upset your ink-bottle, and watch, in helpless agony, the rapid spread of Stygian blackness over your fair manuscript or fairer table-cover? With a like inky swiftness did gossip now blacken the reputation of the Rev. Amos Barton, causing the unfriendly to scorn and even the friendly to stand aloof.[20]

And with even more grace, Mark Twain struck a similar pose in his tongue-in-cheek "preparatory" to *Roughing It*:

19. *Heroines of Fiction* (New York, 1901), pp. 118–119.
20. *Scenes of Clerical Life, The Works of George Eliot* (Edinburgh, 1878), I, 78.

This book is merely a personal narrative, and not a pretentious history or a philosophical dissertation. It is a record of several years of variegated vagabondizing, and its object is rather to help the resting reader while away an idle hour than afflict him with metaphysics, or goad him with science. Still there is information in this volume. . . . I regret this very much, but really it could not be helped: information appears to stew out of me naturally, like the precious attar of roses out of the otter. Sometimes it has seemed to me that I would give worlds if I could retain my facts; but it cannot be. The more I caulk up the sources, and the tighter I get, the more I leak wisdom. Therefore, I can only claim indulgence at the hands of the reader, not justification.[21]

As the century progressed, the intellectualizing author, even of the sage or cracker-barrel variety, became less and less tolerable in the realistic novel. Howells banished him because he believed that the writer's general ideas would necessarily interfere with the inductive experiment he was conducting in his work. Preconceived morality, Howells felt, could be as crippling and as distracting to a novelist as to a laboratory scientist. Henry James believed that George Eliot's fiction was too thought-oriented. And in our own century, James himself, the hero of an aesthetic he helped create, has been valued as one who had "a mind so fine that no idea could violate it."[22] Thoughts were frequently perceived as having penetrated the coarser brains of Hardy and Dreiser, and so they have been held up sometimes as disreputable examples of writers who could not find complete satisfaction within the bounds of their marriages to the muse.

I have gone over this familiar material in order to establish a contrast for the ideals and practices of the metaphysical novelists. To put the matter as simply as possible, the writers of philosophical romance do not usually appear modest. It is true that Hawthorne made humble noises, especially in public, about his preferences for realistic fiction. He even caused Trollope to believe that he wanted to write books like the Barchester novels, "solid and substantial, written on the strength of beef and through the inspiration of ale."[23] But the extent even of Hawthorne's arrogance is evident in his reaction to the English reviewers of *The Marble Faun*: "These beer-sodden beefeaters," he said, "do not know how to read a Romance."[24]

21. (Hartford, 1873), p. iii.

22. T. S. Eliot, "On Henry James," *The Egoist* (1918). Reprinted in *The Question of Henry James* (ed.) F. W. Dupee (New York, 1945), p. 110.

23. Trollope quotes this from a late letter of Hawthorne's (*An Autobiography*, 192–93), and modestly comments by calling Hawthorne "a brother novelist very much greater than myself."

24. Quoted in Randall Stewart, *Nathaniel Hawthorne: A Biography* (New Haven, 1948), p. 211.

The philosophical romancers were generally unhappy with Scott's estimate of the writer as mere entertainer. Taking their cues perhaps from Carlyle, they complained of Scott's lack of seriousness, and they refused to be defined by it. According to Bulwer, Sir Walter needed "a little more thought and purpose,"[25] and Hawthorne wrote that he "could not have been really a wise man, nor an earnest one, nor one that grasped the truth of life;—he did but play."[26] Even Dickens, who was inordinately proud of his father-in-law's friendship with Scott, was upset by the "clumsy shifts and inartistic treatment of machinery" in the Waverley Novels.[27] And Dickens could never forgive the novelist's pose in Thackeray, whose parodies of contemporary novelists he sternly regarded as examples of unprofessional conduct. "We had our differences of opinion," Dickens felt constrained to say even in his obituary tribute to Thackeray. "I thought that he too much feigned a want of earnestness, and that he made a pretence of undervaluing his art, which was not good for the art that he held in trust."[28]

The romancers attempted to establish their own high estimate of their calling by reminding the reader, time and time again, of the long heritage of narrative tradition in which they partook. William Gilmore Simms, for instance, insisted that "the romance is of loftier origin than the novel."[29] Unassuming realists needed no tradition, felt, in fact, freer to imitate nature directly without one. Thus we have seen Scott's refusal to look behind Richardson or Fielding for a predecessor. On the other hand, almost at the very beginning of English Gothic fiction, Clara Reeve wrote *The Progress of Romance* (1785), which tried to argue the great antiquity of her genre as compared to the upstart novel. Her aim in *The Old English Baron*, as she explains in the preface to that work, was to write a somewhat less violent *Castle of Otranto*. William Harrison Ainsworth was later to attempt an English *Mysteries of Udolpho*.[30] The larger fry of romantic fiction, as we shall see, sought more prestigious ancestors.

Some romancers did better than others in presenting themselves as the heirs of a long intellectual and artistic dynasty. Hawthorne, for instance,

25. Letter to Owen Meredith, Oct. 28, 1861, quoted in *The Life of Edward Bulwer, First Lord Lytton* by The Earl of Lytton (London, 1913), II, 396–97.
26. *The English Notebooks*, Randall Stewart (ed.) (New York, 1941), p. 344. A similar attitude towards Scott is expressed in Hawthorne's story, "P's Correspondence."
27. See Percy Fitzgerald, *Recreations of a Literary Man* (London, 1882), I, 142.
28. "In Memoriam: W. M. Thackeray," *Cornhill Magazine*, Feb., 1864. Reprinted in *Collected Papers* (London, 1938), I, 98.
29. "Preface" [1853] to *The Yemassee* (New York, 1856), p. vi.
30. "Preface" [1849] to *Rookwood* (London, 1898), p. xxxiv.

seems to have succeeded almost without trying, but the appearance of ease may be deceiving. To be sure, his prefaces do not flaunt the facts of his wide reading and his deep study of the narrative tradition. Instead, a Hawthorne preface, especially during the years when he was creating his public image, takes the form of what he called "a little preliminary talk about his external habits, his abode, his casual associates, and other matters entirely upon the surface."[31] But these little talks are, and have always been recognized as, considerable artistic achievements. They blend magnificently into the works which follow them; they are highly wrought; and, as witness "The Old Manse" and "The Custom House," they are sometimes quite extensive. Certainly the *Il Penseroso* tone Hawthorne painstakingly evokes in them must have done much to establish him as a sort of American Milton, a man so deeply familiar with the literature of the past that his own works fall naturally and without conceit into the tradition.

Melville, in strong contrast, tried desperately and obviously to demonstrate his intellectual and artistic roots, and *he* managed to convince hardly anybody. He was prevented from writing the kinds of introductions Hawthorne used because his publishers had an interest in presenting him as a rough-and-ready sailor, not much given to reading and reflection, a true speaker, but absolutely careless as to matters of art. Such an image of himself rankled, however, and the effort to contradict it is clearly discernible in what critics frequently regard as the erudite excesses of *Mardi*. Melville's attempt in this direction is even more obvious in *Moby-Dick*, where he prefaces the narrative with an "etymology" on the word "whale" and with no less than seventy-nine "extracts" on whaling, beginning with *Genesis* and ending with a modern song. Nevertheless, the extent and depth of Melville's reading escaped his contemporaries and came rather as a surprise to the early workers in the author's revival. Moreover, although nearly every doctoral dissertation on Melville for the last forty years has discovered another profound influence, the conception of Melville as a great natural genius still somehow prevails. Curiously, Evert Duyckinck's amused and snobbish condescension towards the enthusiastic sailor who devoured his library holds current in many academic circles. Our distaste for the a priori remains so strong that we want, it appears, to believe it is Melville and not Ishmael who says that a whaling ship was his Harvard and Yale. The literary references in "Fragments from a Writing Desk," published in May 1839 when Melville was still technically a teen-ager, and before he saw a whale ship, are admittedly sophomoric, but few sophomores in creative writing classes today could produce such hothouse flowers as this

31. "Dedicatory Letter" to *The Snow Image and Other Twice-Told Tales* (Boston, 1879), p. vi.

young schoolteacher did. Thus Melville failed to establish an intellectual image for himself, but not from lack of trying.

Melville said about the prefatory beginning of Hawthorne's *Mosses from an Old Manse* that it shows an author who "takes great delight in hoodwinking the world—at least with respect to himself. Personally, I doubt not that he rather prefers to be generally esteemed but a so-so sort of author."[32] And Hawthorne wrote of his own prefaces that they "hide the man, instead of displaying him."[33] We shall suggest, however, that the hiding and the hoodwinking may have had a motive beyond simple modesty.

On the other hand, Bulwer-Lytton, as the reactions from Trollope and Howells have already indicated, was the least subtle, the most immodest of the romancers at the business of displaying his erudition. Bulwer's prefaces render him the most exposed of all the writers in his genre. This is what makes him so very useful to our study. Moreover, he experimented with and theorized about virtually every form of narrative and most other genres of literature: plays, poems, essays, biographies, and translations. As David Masson wrote of him in 1859, "of all British novelists, he seems to have worked most consciously on a theory of the Novel. . . . This, indeed, may be the very cause of his versatility."[34] If he had only possessed the talent to go with his remarkable ambition, inventiveness, versatility, persistence, and energy, he might have been another Dryden, whose qualities of mind he sometimes shows. As it is, he remains the chief apologist for romantic fiction, the best contemporary spokesman for the others in his school.

Bulwer, who could never resist the urge to preface, explained and defended himself at every stage of his long career. His need to explain, we shall deal with later; his need to defend himself stemmed in part from charges made against the immorality of his fiction. Very early in his career he had reestablished the genre of the criminal novel, which, both in his hands and as exploited by Ainsworth, was considered a highly dangerous influence on public morality. It invited the reader to identify and perhaps to sympathize with a criminal hero. *Paul Clifford* (1830) was additionally dangerous as a political document because Bulwer seemed to preach in it that society and society's laws are responsible for the creation of criminals. Psychologically and morally, *Eugene Aram*, which shows that a good and respectable man may also be a criminal, was an even more disturbing book. An article, almost certainly by Lockhart, a political enemy, condemned it

32. "Hawthorne and His Mosses," *The Literary World* (Aug. 17 & 24, 1850). Reprinted in *The Portable Melville* (ed.) Jay Leyda (London, 1952), p. 417.
33. "Dedicatory Letter" to *The Snow Image and Other Twice-Told Tales*, p. **vi**.
34. *British Novelists and Their Styles*, p. 228–29.

as a work "of evil and pernicious example." [35] Bulwer, the article goes on to say, encourages "a modern, a depraved, a corrupting taste." [36]

Bulwer, of course, believed that his taste was neither depraved nor corrupting. As a philosophical romancer, he believed equally that it was not modern, and when *Lucretia* (1846) was treated even more harshly than his early Newgate novels had been, Bulwer responded automatically by defending his art on the very basis of its antiquity. To justify the criminal hero, he cited Oedipus, Medea, Clytemnestra, Orestes, Phaedra, Richard III, Macbeth, and Othello.

> Crime, in fact, is the essential material of Tragic Drama. . . . Whatever aims at the tragic effect, whether on the stage or in the more sober narrative, cannot dispense with the evil which works to mischief—excites to terror—involves the innocent in its own ruin, and conduces to the tragic passions of our pity and awe. . . . *The very Statue of the Tragic Muse is represented with the dagger in one hand, and the poison bowl in the other.*[37]

But what Bulwer seemingly could not learn, or perhaps what he stubbornly refused to acknowledge, was that he was living in a defensively self-confident age when tradition, and especially literary tradition, was not highly valued. To show that men in barbarous times had chosen to indulge their savage tastes with the depiction of crime would not serve to justify tragedy to the more enlightened 1840s. Thus, *The Westminster and Foreign Quarterly Review*:

> "Crime," says Sir Edward, "is the essential material of *tragic* drama." If so, we should be disposed to assert that the decline of the drama, as far as tragedy is concerned, is not a subject for lamentation; and the fact that many tragedies formerly popular, and still considered classic, have been driven from the stage, we trace to the tendencies of a growing civilisation. . . . A distaste for symbolic terrors is a natural consequence of this improvement. Sophocles, were he among us, would find the parricide of Oedipus a subject only for minor theatres. 'Titus Andronicus' could not now be written; and how much would have been softened by Shakespeare, even in the best of his tragedies, had they been addressed to an educated audience of the nineteenth-century.[38]

This response and others like it finally frightened Bulwer away from "immoral" literature, but it did not cure him of the habit of justifying his

35. "A Good Tale Badly Told by Mr. Edward Lytton Bulwer," *Fraser's Magazine*, V (Feb. 1832), 107.

36. *Ibid.*, 112.

37. *A Word to the Public* [Printed here with *Lucretia; or The Children of Night* (London, 1853), but originally published as a pamphlet in 1847], pp. 305–08.

38. XLVII (Apr. 1847), 2.

works by references to the traditions out of which they came. He described his next novel, *The Caxtons*, as "in style aiming at something between Sterne and Goldsmith,"[39] and he wrote that *My Novel* (1853) was modeled after "Miss Austen; Mrs. Gore in her masterpiece of 'Mrs. Army- tage'; Mrs. Marsh, too; and then (for Scottish manners) Miss Ferrier!"[40] In the preface to *King Arthur* (1849) Bulwer announced that "the Ro- mance from which I borrow is the Romance of the North" (Vol. I, p. ix).

Nor is this ancestor-identifying tendency in Bulwer confined to his mid- dle period and associated only with his defensive stance. In the 1830s he was particularly interested in German literature. Thus *The Pilgrims of the Rhine* (1834), which consists of a series of imitations from German ro- mantic fiction, contains a fairly extensive and a rather good critique of that genre. The 1840 preface to *Ernest Maltravers* acknowledges *Wilhelm Meister* as its model. At this point in his career he was also anxious to find roots for his school in the works of Godwin, Smollett, Fielding, and Le Sage.[41] Much later, when he was no longer under attack, he connected it with Apuleius, Fénelon, La Motte Fouqué, Swift, Walpole, and Reeve.[42] And he found his ultimate source in the Greek romances.[43]

What all this amounts to is a good deal more than the wild farrago of names and titles which my quick catalog necessarily makes it appear. Bulwer was attempting, conscientiously and throughout his career, to establish a narrative tradition to serve as a barricade against the attacks of the realists, who insisted upon the value of originality. There is nothing of modesty in Bulwer's frequent acknowledgements. He is proudly proclaim- ing himself (at one point he takes Dickens under his wing;[44] at another, Hawthorne[45]) as a participant in a literary heritage which has reigned as the chief glory of the past two thousand years and is likely to survive any aberrations in taste caused by Scott's temporary and unmerited popularity.[46]

39. Letter to Richard Bentley, Dec. 11, 1847, in the Bodleian Library, Shelf- mark MS Eng. Lett. d. 90.

40. *My Novel; or, Varieties in English Life* (Edinburgh, 1853), Book I, Chap. I.

41. "Preface to the Edition of 1835," *Pelham* (London, 1835), p. 5.

42. "Preface" to *A Strange Story* (London, 1861).

43. "Preface" to *The Lost Tales of Miletus* (London, 1866).

44. "1845 Preface" to *Night and Morning, The Knebworth Edition.*

45. "On Certain Principles of Art in Works of the Imagination," *Caxtoniana* (Edinburgh and London, 1863), II, 151–152. Originally published in *Black- wood's,* 1862.

46. It is interesting that while Bulwer doesn't mind equating his own aims with those of Shakespeare, he scouts any comparison of Scott and Shakespeare, for Scott represented the opposite school. Thus in "On Art in Fiction" (1838): "It is a sign of the low state of criticism in this country, that Scott has been compared to Shakspeare. No two writers can be more entirely opposed to each other in

He is proclaiming himself as Melville did when he equated Hawthorne (and by extension compared himself) with Shakespeare.[47] Hawthorne's mother-in-law was quite right in commenting dryly that it never does a writer any good to be so compared, but Melville and Bulwer were ambitious men, seemingly insensible to the requirement of humility which their century and their profession imposed. In times of the unheroic common man and the tradesman author, they were anxious to enroll themselves in the cult of genius.

The romancers kept insisting on their places in the long tradition of narrative primarily because they wished to gain a serious, intellectual reading for their works. The technique, especially as practiced by Melville and Bulwer, was not subtle, but some romancers disliked taking chances. They were in fact willing, as we shall see, to use even more blatant means for shocking the reader into an understanding of their intentions. Realists derive a benefit from an opposite kind of reading since the philosophy of their novels is more readily forthcoming when, as Conrad said in the preface to *The Nigger of The Narcissus*, we forget to ask for it, when we simply allow it to develop out of the narrated experience. To secure such a reading, realists needed to reinforce rather than discourage an easygoing instinct in their audience, and this could sometimes be done with the utmost in charm and subtlety. Mark Twain's famous preface to *Huckleberry Finn* provides a succinct example of the novelist's *professed* attitude towards a serious reading of his work:

Notice

> Persons attempting to find a motive in this narrative will be prosecuted; persons attempting to find a moral in it will be banished; persons attempting to find a plot in it will be shot.

A romancer usually speaks in less humorous and in much more offensive tones. Thus, Victor Hugo:

> It is not to be doubted that these recovered chapters will find little value in the eyes of such readers as—with no imputation on their taste or judg-

---

the qualities of their genius, or the sources to which they were applied. Shakspeare, ever aiming at the development of the secret man, and half disdaining the mechanism of external incident. Scott, painting the ruffles and the dress and the features and the gestures—avoiding the movements of the heart—elaborate in the progress of the incident. Scott never caught the middle of Shakspeare, but he improved on the dresses of his wardrobe, and threw artificial effects into the scenes of his theatres. . . . Shakspeare could have composed the most wonderful plays from the stories of Scott; Scott could have written the most excellent stage directions to the plays of Shakspeare." (*Pamphlets and Sketches* [London, 1887], pp. 333–338.)

47. "Hawthorne and His Mosses," *The Literary World* (Aug. 17 and 24, 1850).

ment—will never look for more in *Notre-Dame* than the run of the action and the development of the plot. But there are possibly other readers who will not deem it useless to study the hidden aestheticism and philosophy of the book, who, while reading *Notre-Dame* will take pleasure in detecting under the guise of the romance something very different from romance, and will be delighted to pursue through the fanciful vision of the poet—pardon such conceited expressions—the ever present system of the historian and the constant aim of the artist.[48]

This practice of blatantly calling the reader's attention to the truths he might otherwise miss is itself a very old tradition. It appears in *Guzmán de Alfarache*, which Alemán begins with a very arrogant preface "To the Vulgar," followed by a humble explanation of his book's serious purpose addressed "To the Discreet Reader." The narrator of *Gil Blas* also cautions us not to read too casually:

> If you cast your eye over my adventures without fixing it on the moral concealed under them, you will derive very little benefit from the perusal; but if you read with attention you will find that mixture of the useful with the agreeable, so successfully prescribed by Horace.[49]

In *Don Quixote* two voices occur. First Cervantes presents himself as very ignorant about philosophers and critical authorities. He claims to be only a casual writer, with no great aim in his book besides the destruction of the chivalric romance, a dead horse which could be beaten without much effort or offense. Later, however, and speaking through an erudite character, he defends the loose method of his work as suitable for the presentation of all branches of knowledge.[50] Which voice we listen to, depends, of course, on how we read the book, and this choice depends in turn on whether our disposition is for realism or romance.

But the romancers of the period we are most concerned with were often unwilling to allow the reader such a choice. Thus Godwin, whom Bulwer claimed as one of his nearest literary ancestors, alerts us in his preface to *Caleb Williams* that it was his intention to form an epoch in the reader's mind.[51] Percy Shelley's preface to *Frankenstein* explains that Mary was not "merely weaving a series of supernatural terrors."[52] Charles Brockden

---

48. "Note Added to the Edition of 1832," *Notre-Dame of Paris* (trans.) J. Carroll Beckwith, 4 vols. (London, 1895), I, xi–xii.

49. Alain René Le Sage, *The Adventures of Gil Blas of Santillane*, trans. Tobias Smollett (New York, n.d.), I, vi.

50. *The Ingenious Gentleman Don Quixote de La Mancha*, 2 vols. (trans.) Samuel Putnam (London, 1953), Part I, Chap. 47.

51. "Preface" to the 1832 edition of *Fleetwood*. Reprinted in *Caleb Williams* (ed.) David McCracken (London, 1970), p. 338.

52. [1817] (Garden City, N.Y., n.d.), p. 5.

Brown claimed in the "advertisement" to *Wieland* that he "aimed at the illustration of some important branches of the moral constitution of man."[53] His purpose, he insisted, was "neither selfish nor temporary." These are philosophic romances, and the writers, unlike Scott, are desperately concerned lest we mistake their works for simple entertainments.

Hawthorne's prefaces are masterpieces for making the same point, but, once again, without giving offense. Usually he pretends that he would prefer to have written a realistic and unphilosophical novel. Thus he points out the true nature of the work to follow without the arrogance which usually attends such statements by other writers. Trollope, as we have noted, believed in Hawthorne's humility, and so have some other non-Yankees.[54] The beginning of "Rappaccini's Daughter," in which the "translator" takes the "author" to task for his "inveterate love of allegory,"[55] most successfully does the job of alerting the reader to allegoric significances, and at the same time keeping his hackles down. Still, the technique could be annoying to readers who did not wish to take fiction very seriously. Thus Emerson, for whom Scott was one of the very few novelists worth mentioning, objected that "Hawthorne invites his readers too much into his study, opens the process before them. As if the confectioner should say to his customers, 'Now, let us make the cake.' "[56]

Emily Brontë is the least obtrusive of the metaphysical novelists and therefore the least offensive. *Wuthering Heights* does without an authorial preface of any sort, and it stands almost alone among Gothic novels in its freedom from erudite references.[57] Indeed, the elaborate structure of its narration appears to have entirely removed the shy author's personality from the story she is telling. Yet this same technique is the subtle device by which the writer indirectly controls the reader's reactions, alerting him to meanings he would otherwise miss, forcing him into a psychology he would otherwise reject, and involving him directly in the act of creation.

Almost all the characters of *Wuthering Heights* help to tell the story, but it may be significant that the three most active narrators, Isabella Linton, Lockwood, and Nelly Dean, are the most ordinary, least demon-ridden of the actors. What does the author mean by forcing us to view her melodramatic, passionate, mystical action through such commonplace

53. *Wieland; or, The Transformation* (Port Washington, N.Y., 1963), p. 23.

54. The present writer, who arrogantly affects to see through Hawthorne's devices, is also a native of Essex County, Massachusetts.

55. *Mosses from an Old Manse* (Boston, 1879), I, 100.

56. May 1846. *Journals of Ralph Waldo Emerson*, 10 vols. (London, 1909–14), VII, 188.

57. See Robert Kiely, *The Romantic Novel in England* (Cambridge, Mass., 1972), pp. 233–34.

lenses? One critic has suggested an answer as regards the use of Nelly as narrator:

> Nelly is an admirable woman whose point of view, I believe, the reader must reject. She is good-natured, warmhearted, wholesome, practical, and physically healthy. Her interpretation of her reading and her experiences, her feelings on various occasions, are, to a large extent, the consequence of her physical health. When the reader refuses to accept her view of things, which he continually does and must do, he is forced to feel the inadequacy of the normal, healthy, hearty, good-natured person's understanding of life and human nature. He is consequently forced into an active participation in the book. He cannot sit back and accept what is given him as the explanation of the actions of the characters. He must continually provide his own version.[58]

And if Nelly Dean's practical and thus wrong-headed analyses of Heathcliff and Cathy are intended to put us on our guard, to warn us that we must drop our own everyday view of things if we are to fathom the story, so, to an even greater extent, are the clearly superficial reactions of Lockwood and Isabella. Thus Emily Brontë gentles us out of our normal mode of perception by encouraging us to rise above it.

Her sister Charlotte, on the other hand, operates much more directly, much more offensively, but perhaps to the same effect. In *Jane Eyre*, as Sylvère Monod has pointed out, the narrator constantly bullies her reader "because she distrusts him," because she thinks his views are "lazily traditional," because she finds him a "contemptible being, conventional, silly, cowardly, ignorant, and vain."[59] Monod believes that *Jane Eyre* succeeds despite the superior attitude which the author or narrator takes toward us, but it is indeed possible we might have read her book in the imbecile way she feared if she had not so shamed us.

Melville was another distrusting author, who appears never to have anticipated that he might be on good terms with his audience. Thus William Charvat points out that his "conflict with his readers, which lasted the whole ten years of his professional life and ended in a defeat . . . began in the first paragraph of his first book, *Typee*, [where] the conventional, cozy, reader-writer relationship of the second sentence is promptly undermined by the apostrophe to "state-room sailors," his contemptuous term for his public.[60] From this bad start, the situation worsened considerably

58. John K. Mathison, "Nelly Dean and the Power of *Wuthering Heights*," *Nineteenth-Century Fiction*, XI (1956), 106.

59. "Charlotte Brontë and the Thirty 'Readers' of Jane Eyre," in *Jane Eyre: A Norton Critical Edition* (ed.) Richard J. Dunn (New York, 1971), pp. 500, 502, and 504.

60. *The Profession of Authorship in America* (Columbus, Ohio, 1968), p. 204.

as Melville's readers gave him little reason to believe in their power to understand subtlety, and as he showed even less disposition to afford them fresh chances to redeem themselves. The author's preface to *Mardi* indicates the tone of the relationship:

> Not long ago, having published two narratives of voyages in the Pacific, which, in many quarters, were received with incredulity, the thought occurred to me, of indeed writing a romance of Polynesian adventures, and publishing it; to see whether the fiction might not possibly be received for a verity: in some degree the reverse of the previous experience.

"What they call the public," he has the poet Lemsford say in *White-Jacket*, "is a monster, like the idol we saw in Owhyhee, with the head of a jackass, the body of a baboon, and the tail of a scorpion!" (Chap. 45). And the picture which Melville himself painted of Pierre Glendinning's stupid public is even less flattering. As Charvat writes:

> Melville here seems to take perverse satisfaction in abusing, satirizing, and insulting the reading public and its representatives—editors and publishers. He excoriates the kind of novels that they make popular. He accuses them of "unforgivable affronts and insults" to great authors like Dante in the past; of missing the "deeper meanings" of Shakespeare; of judging literature as they do morals; of praising an author's worst books, or liking his best ones for the wrong reasons.[61]

Melville's one attempt at the sort of introduction Hawthorne could write so skillfully is a demonstration of how unsuited he was to use his countryman's subtle preface strategy. "The Piazza," unlike "The Old Manse" and "The Custom House," turns into a story in its own right, and its narrator, since he becomes a fictional character, loses his ability to form an authorial relationship with the reader. Melville, therefore, found more obvious ways within the texts themselves of announcing that he was a deep thinker. Very few readers of *Mardi* or *Moby-Dick* have missed this intention, at least. I believe that the books which immediately preceded these works, *Typee* and *Omoo*, *Redburn* and *White-Jacket*, are also philosophical romances, at least, if not metaphysical novels, and it is possible that the too obvious, perhaps blatant intellectualism of Melville's more ambitious works is, in part, a product of his impatience at the perfectly literal readings his other romances had been accorded. *Omoo*, for instance, is a complex work, containing many of the elements of the metaphysical novel which we shall be discussing in the later chapters of this book. It was understood, however, either as a factual account of Melville's own wanderings, or it was disbelieved as a tissue of mindless, though

61. *Ibid.*, p. 252.

amusing, tall tales, with some vitriol for the missionaries thrown in for spite or good measure. In *Mardi*, Melville made such a reading impossible. *Omoo* was a book which one could read comfortably and condescendingly. *Mardi* contained depths which, as Hawthorne said, "compel a man to swim for his life,"[62] and so it has become common for surprised critics to gasp out the word "Sophomoric!" as they sink down in them for the third time.

Dickens is often taken as the model engineer of the undemanding author-reader association, and, indeed, he professed principles which should have led to such a pleasant relationship. "It is not for an author to describe his own books," he said in the preface to the 1847 edition of *Pickwick Papers.* "If they cannot speak for themselves, he is likely to do little service by speaking for them." Some time earlier, Dickens had written in a letter to G. H. Lewes, "The truth is, that I am a very modest man, and furthermore that if readers cannot detect the point of a passage without having their attention called to it by the writer, I would much rather they lost it and looked out for something else."[63] And years later, when he was publishing Bulwer's *A Strange Story* in his own magazine, he vigorously fought off the author's seemingly constitutional desire for an explanatory preface:

> I counsel you most strongly NOT . . . to enter upon any explanation beyond the title-page and the motto, unless it be in some very brief preface. Decidedly I would not help the reader, if it were only for the reason that that anticipates his being in need of help, and his feeling objections and difficulties that require solution. Let the book explain itself.[64]

"That the audience is good enough for anything that is well presented to it," he had written Bulwer a month earlier, "I am quite sure."[65]

But these expressions of confidence are somewhat belied by Forster, who reports that "Dickens felt criticism, of whatever kind, with too sharp a relish for the indifference he assumed to it . . . he believed himself to be entitled to higher tribute than he was always in the habit of receiving."[66] And they are contradicted by his own prefaces, which Dickens regularly used to justify some misunderstood or overlooked point of the narrative. The most famous of these justifications is the defense of the death by spontaneous combustion in *Bleak House,* but there are other prefaces authenti-

62. Letter to Evert Duyckinck, Aug. 29, 1850. *The Melville Log: A Documentary Life of Herman Melville, 1819–1891,* 2 vols. (ed.) Jay Leyda (New York, 1969), I, 391.

63. June 11, 1838. *The Pilgrim Edition of the Letters of Charles Dickens* (eds.) Madeline House and Graham Storey (Oxford, 1965), I, 404.

64. 18 Dec. 1861. *The Letters of Charles Dickens* (ed.) Walter Dexter (London, 1938), III, 268.

65. 20 Nov. 1861. *Ibid.,* III, 255.

66. *The Life of Charles Dickens,* 2 vols. (New York, 1900), II, 387.

cating the Yorkshire schools and the Cheeryble Brothers in *Nicholas Nickleby*, Betty Higden in *Our Mutual Friend*, Mr. Merdle and the Circumlocution Office in *Little Dorrit*, and the historical accuracy of *A Tale of Two Cities*. He also justifies the death of Little Nell, the narrative strategy of *Our Mutual Friend*, and the psychology of Mr. Dombey. Still other prefaces point up the lessons and the meanings in *Pickwick Papers*, *Barnaby Rudge*, *Martin Chuzzlewit*, and *A Christmas Carol*. Often, though not always, these explanations are made with a good deal of grace, but it should be noted that Forster had to talk Dickens out of his plan to begin *Martin Chuzzlewit*, his bitter exposé of selfishness and hypocrisy, with the motto: "Your homes the scenes, yourselves the actors, here." [67] And the preface to the third edition of *Oliver Twist* (1841) reads much like a passage out of Bulwer or Melville or even Hugo. Here Dickens justifies the criminal novel, as Bulwer was later to do, by pointing out precedents in Defoe, Goldsmith, Smollett, Richardson, and Mackenzie. Moreover, he goes on to vouch for the psychological reality of Nancy, and to express his strongest contempt for "people of so refined and delicate a nature, that they cannot bear the contemplation of these horrors." He has, as he says, "no respect for their opinion, good or bad."

If Dickens was himself incapable of following the advice he offered to Bulwer, it was perhaps unreasonable for him to expect compliance from his friend, who had never been able to pass up the opportunity to preface and who continued to proclaim his intellectualism up to and including his anonymously and posthumously published works. Once again, Bulwer is the philosophical romancer at his most exposed. As a result, critics have found him too radical for the 1830s, too immoral for the 1840s, too aesthetic for the 1850s, too mystic for the 1860s, too philosophic for the 1870s, too popular for the 1890s, and too vulgar for the 1920s. Since these times he has been very little read, but if he were, the claims shrilly voiced in his prefaces and in digressions throughout his works would be certain to gore whatever cattle we hold sacred today.

Unlike Hawthorne, Bulwer does not hint gently that his work ought to be read allegorically: taking no chances, he explains the allegory point by point:

> The more ingenious reader may, perhaps, already have perceived that . . . a metaphysical meaning runs throughout the characters and the story. In the narrator is embodied the SATIETY which is of the world; in Asmodeus is the principle of vague EXCITEMENT in which Satiety always seeks relief. The extravagant adventures—the rambling from the ideal to the common-

67. *Ibid.*, I, 296.

place—from the flights of the imagination to the trite affairs and petty pleasures of the day—are the natural results of Excitement without an object.[68]

And here is a passage from the preface to *A Strange Story*, which as we have seen, Dickens counseled Bulwer "most strongly NOT" to write:

Whatever may appear violent or melodramatic in the catastrophe, will perhaps be found, by the reader capable of perceiving the various symbolical meanings conveyed in the story, essential to the end in which the meanings converge and towards which the incidents that give them the character and interest of fiction have been planned and directed from the commencement.[69]

Zanoni, Bulwer wrote in his 1842 introduction, is "a romance and . . . not a romance. It is a truth for those who can comprehend it, and an extravagance for those who cannot." There is an insult to the reader in each one of these prefaces and a corresponding claim for the author's intellectuality. Moreover, such statements occur throughout Bulwer, who explained the serious purpose behind virtually everything he wrote.

All this arrogance, in Bulwer even more than in Melville, is extremely annoying, and one wonders that so practiced a craftsman did not realize after twenty or thirty years that his tone was more likely to infuriate the critics than to win them over. Probably he did realize and was simply unable to resist a good fight. It is also important to remember that he fully expected his work to outlive the fad of realism. The prefaces were addressed in part to a future generation which, Bulwer believed, would have returned to the main stream of intellectual literature and would therefore be less likely to resent a philosopher's just claims. Without denying these explanations, I should like to suggest still another possibility, in which I have somewhat less confidence, but which may help to show at least how both the humble nonintellectualism of the novelist and the philosophic arrogance of the romancer were strategic poses, equally important to the different effects each kind of writer attempted to achieve.

To explain the theory I wish tentatively to put forth, we must digress momentarily to the 1797 exchange of letters between Goethe and Schiller with which Auerbach begins *Mimesis*, his great book on realism, and which Lukács mentions in his important study of the historical novel. These letters are some of the most remarkable documents in the history of literary criticism, not only because of their influence, some of which we shall trace in this and succeeding chapters, but also because of the tre-

68. "Author's Note" to "Asmodeus at Large," [1832], *The Student and Asmodeus at Large*, p. 286.
69. "Preface," [1862], *A Strange Story*, p. viii.

mendous sense of discovery they contain. Here are two great writers formulating for their own sakes the laws of dramatic and epic poetry and then applying them to fiction. When they are finished, they open up their Aristotle—Schiller for the first time!—and are pleased to find where he agrees with them.

The exchange begins with a letter from Goethe, who assumes that the structural techniques of epic and drama are opposed to one another:

> One main characteristic of an epic poem is that it is ever going forwards and backwards; hence all retarding motives are epic. . . : Should this demand for retarding—which is fulfilled to excess in both of Homer's poems, and which also lay in the plot of mine [in *Hermann und Dorothea*]—be actually essential, and not to be dispensed with, then all such plots as proceed direct towards the end ought to be utterly rejected. . . . As regards the drama, it seems to me that the case is the reverse.[70]

Then, in three letters written during the next week, Schiller develops Goethe's statement into a full aesthetic, to the conclusion that on April 26 his friend "entirely agree[s]," commenting, "I have ever been accustomed to have my dreams read and explained to me by you."[71]

Schiller holds that the dramatist, whose only goal is mimesis, the representation of an action, seeks to make the viewer forget himself. The play is a vehicle in which the audience comfortably seats itself to be rushed unselfconsciously to a conclusion. "The tragic poet," writes this great dramatist, "robs us of our freedom of sentiment, and by leading and concentrating our powers in one special direction, he greatly simplifies his work, and places himself at an advantage while placing us at a disadvantage." He seeks, that is, to entrance the viewer. Any form of retardation breaks the charm and restores us to ourselves. On the other hand:

> Naked *truth*, drawn forth from the inmost sources, is the object which an epic poet has in view . . . his object is contained in every point of his movement; therefore we do not hurry on impatiently towards a goal, but linger lovingly at every step. He grants us the greatest freedom of sentiment, and by placing *us* at so great an advantage, he thereby makes his own aim the more arduous, for we now make of him all those demands which are founded upon the integrity and in the all-sided, unified activity of our powers.[72]

The epic poet, therefore, consciously works to retard the reader in order to keep him free and intellectually awake, for the epic is not a vehicle which hurries us spellbound through an action to a catastrophe, but rather, as

70. *Correspondence Between Schiller and Goethe from 1794 to 1805*, trans. L. Dora Schmitz (London, 1877), Apr. 19, 1797, I, 313.
71. *Ibid.*, I, 319–320.
72. Apr. 21, 1797, *Ibid.*, I, 314.

Schiller explains the following December, it is something like a garden, intended for alert, self-conscious contemplation.

> The dramatic action moves on before me, but I myself move round the epic action, which, so to say, is at a standstill. . . . If I move round the incident which cannot escape from me, I feel that I need not keep up a regular pace, I can stop for a longer or shorter time according to my subjective necessity, I can step backwards or forwards, etc.[73]

Only a few months after he formulated it, Schiller applied his own theory of epic and dramatic poetry to Goethe's prose fiction. The *Roman*, he felt, belonged clearly to the epic form, and *Wilhelm Meister*, as he wrote to Goethe on October 20, 1797, "evidently contains too much of tragedy. . . . In short, it seems to me that you have here made use of means which the spirit of the work did not authorise you to employ."[74] Even before the theory had been formulated, Schiller perceived that "a certain condescension towards the weak side of the public, has induced you to make more use of dramatic purposes and dramatic contrivances [in *Meister*] than is necessary or appropriate in a novel,"[75] although he was astonished "to find how much it is imbued both by an epic and a philosophical spirit."[76]

So far as I know, the letters in which Schiller and Goethe developed this theory never enjoyed much circulation among English and American romancers. The theory itself, however, gained wide currency in the mid-1830s through the agency of Bulwer-Lytton, who, in his search for a literary heritage, had openly imitated Goethe and was soon to write a life of Schiller as an introduction to his translation of Schiller's ballads. Carlyle is said to have credited Bulwer with being, after himself of course, the most influential of the British apostles of Germany.[77]

Bulwer presented Schiller's theory most fully in an essay entitled "On the Different Kinds of Prose Fiction, with Some Apology for the Fictions of the Author," which appeared as a preface to *The Disowned* in 1835. Here, unlike Schiller, he saw the possibility of a legitimate though definitely minor genre of fiction with rules derived from the drama. He allowed that even he had experimented with this form in *Eugene Aram* and *The Last Days of Pompeii*, although now he had indeed gone on to the greater and more traditional "Narrative (or Epic) Fiction,"[78] stemming from Apuleius, Sidney, Cervantes, Fénelon, Le Sage, Fielding, and

---

73. *Ibid.*, I, 454.
74. *Ibid.*, I, 421.
75. Letter to Goethe, July 8, 1796, *Ibid.*, I, 191.
76. Letter to Goethe, Oct. 19, 1796, *Ibid.*, I, 243.
77. See T. H. S. Escott, *Edward Bulwer: First Baron Lytton of Knebworth* (London, 1910), p. 5.
78. P. vii.

Smollett, more recently from Goethe, Godwin, Charles Brockden Brown, and Disraeli. The "Dramatic" novel, he believed, was much newer and of less noble parentage. "Horace Walpole's 'Castle of Otranto,' and Mrs. Radcliffe's Romances, were the first, as far as I am aware, which trespassed visibly upon the boundaries of the dramatic fiction." Then came Sir Walter, always the arch-villain for Bulwer.

> It was reserved for the glorious imagination of Scott to create and *perhaps* to perfect [the dramatic novel]—Not only in plot, in mystery, in incident, in catastrophe, are his fictions consumately dramatic, but his characters are essentially dramatic also. . . . Most of Scott's novels require little but the scissors to become plays. . . . The brilliant success of Scott has made, almost insensibly, the dramatic form of fiction not only the most popular, but also the sole criterion by which the critics are inclined to judge of fictitious compositions. They forget that there is another school of novel writing, equally excellent, to which all dramatic rules are inapplicable;—namely the *narrative*.[79]

Bulwer developed the Schilleresque rules relevant to the two forms of prose fiction nearly thirty years later in an essay which, by the way, welcomed Hawthorne into the fraternity of metaphysical novelists:

> The interest in a drama must be consecutive, sustained, progressive—it allows of no *longueurs*. But the interest of a novel may be very gentle, very irregular—may interpose long conversations in the very midst of action—always provided, however, . . . that they bear upon the ulterior idea for which the action is invented. Thus we have in 'Wilhelm Meister' long conversations on art or philosophy just where we want most to get on with the story—yet, without those conversations, the story would not have been worth the telling; and its object could not, indeed, be comprehended.[80]

It is worth noting that Anthony Trollope, who was perhaps of all novelists the most serious scholar of dramatic literature, strenuously objected to retarding elements, not only in Bulwer, but in Fielding and Cervantes, as well.[81] There is a certain amount of irony in this, for, getting back at last to our subject of the annoying author, Trollope has himself become a symbol for intrusive, nondramatic narration. He has Henry James to thank for this reputation,[82] which indicates, for one thing, that

79. *Ibid.*, pp. x–xiii.

80. "On Certain Principles of Art in Works of Imagination," *Caxtoniana* (Edinburgh and London, 1863), II, 163–164. Originally published in *Blackwood's*, 1862.

81. *An Autobiography*, 56–59.

82. "Anthony Trollope," *Century Magazine* (1883). Reprinted in *Anthony Trollope: The Critical Heritage* (ed.) Donald Smalley (London, 1969), pp. 535–36.

realists, careless of the need for a tradition, are unlikely to recognize their own. For the intrusions of Trollope and Thackeray have nothing in common with the episodes, digressive intrusions, and prefaces of Bulwer, and this essential difference illustrates well how the novelist's and the romancer's poses can each be of strategic importance.

Trollope's intrusions, his "little slaps at credulity," remind us, as Henry James objected, that what we are reading is, after all, only a story, "a make-believe." The prefaces of Scott perform much the same function, and so, with their emphasis on technique, do the prefaces of James himself. Bulwer, Hawthorne, and Melville, as we have seen, are anxious to tell us that we are reading something that is much more than a story. If Schiller and Bulwer are right, then the dramatic novelist gains his advantage over the reader by putting him off his guard, and one of the ways of doing this is to make guarantees that no strenuous intellectual and ethical demands will be required of him, that the only purpose of the work is to give him pleasure. Moreover, if the author is to appear in his story, he should not pose any threats to the reader's ego: he can be ironic, like Thackeray, but he must somehow get the feeling across that he would never regard the reader as an object of anything but the most loving, teasing satire; he can be wise, like the early George Eliot, but his learning must never appear to put his reader at a humiliating disadvantage; he can even assume omniscience, like Trollope, but, all the same, he'd better not be *too* clever. As James himself said of Trollope:

> he had an easy road to success; and his honest, familiar deliberate way of treating his readers as if he were one of them, and shared their indifference to a general view, their limitations of knowledge, their love of a comfortable ending, endeared him to many persons in England and America. . . . With Trollope we were always safe.[83]

Just so. The author of the dramatic novel, James as well as Trollope, must inspire confidence, so that we are not afraid to settle back in the carriage of his plot and leave the driving to him. When he intrudes, it is to reassure us that everything is going well up front, or perhaps it is to allow us to catch our breaths for a moment, but it is never an invitation, as in Goethe or Bulwer, for us to descend and have a personal look round. James discovered after much experiment, that he could keep us in the carriage most successfully by making himself both invisible and inaudible. But this practice, in contrast to Trollope's, is a difference of technique rather than of aim. "Dramatise, dramatise!" is the constant imperative of James' prefaces, and there is a natural progression in the dramatic novel from an inoffensive guide to no guide at all, as in an

83. *Ibid.*, p. 527.

actual drama on the stage. Even James, who regarded fiction with the utmost seriousness, and who makes us feel doubly alive as we read him, has an interest in tucking us in, so to speak, for he wants to turn off all our responses save the moral-aesthetic. Neither he, on dramatic grounds, nor Howells, for scientific reasons, wants to have us with what Schiller called "the all-sided, unified activity of our powers." Rather he wants to lead and concentrate our powers "in one special direction."

The metaphysical novelist, on the other hand, when he takes the aesthetics of his school most seriously, is at pains to keep us fully awake and fully ourselves. He realizes that his story, since it takes place in time, must resemble a journey more than the wished-for garden, and he knows that the very movement of his narration has a built-in hypnotic quality. But rather than capitalize on these features as the dramatic novelist can do, he must fight against them. Thus he puts obstacles in the roadway to retard our speed; as we shall see when we discuss structure, he sends us through a maddening series of digressive detours, he clutters the compartment with all sorts of Plinlimmon pamphlets on extraliterary subjects, he makes us change narrative horses and generic vehicles at every stopping place; he keeps us perennially off-balance and unsure of ourselves. The metaphysical novelist's use of characterization, as we shall also see, serves a similar purpose. And when *he* intrudes, it is not to reassure us or to help us gently over a difficult stretch in the roadway; it is to slap us rudely in the face, to tell us that because of our inattention, our sleepiness, or our downright stupidity, we have missed an important landmark and must go back.

The philosophical romancer doesn't make traveling very easy, and while we worry about all the luggage he has piled on us, we are justified in snapping at his pretentious arrogance, his sophomoric intellect, his Victorian Philistinism. After all, why shouldn't art give pleasure? And if we'd wanted this sort of thing, wouldn't we have booked with a legitimate philosopher? The romancer answers this last objection with his typically arrogant assertion that he is a legitimate philosopher, that simply because recent novelists have been content to play the ninny, we needn't question *his* brains. He philosophizes in fiction rather than in treatises because he stems, as he keeps on reminding us and reminding us, from a tradition much older than the modern separation of imagination from reason, of pleasure from thought, from a tradition older even than formal philosophy. He insists, though he lives in the nineteenth century and writes in prose, on being treated with the same rights as Virgil and Dante.

It is true that Virgil and Dante and indeed Goethe managed to secure these rights from their readers without resorting either to tricks or to insults, but, then, they didn't have Walter Scott and the modest realists to contend with. Nor, in their times, had the dramatic novel taken such a hold on the public as to establish an almost universal habit of reader expectation, inimicable to the purposes of romantic fiction. In light of this unfavorable situation, strong measures may have seemed justifiable.

The metaphysical novelists tended to believe, in their defensive arrogance, that they were the only legitimate philosophers in fiction. Of course, they were mistaken. For the realists' pose, which led the romancers into this error, had more than a dramatic function. The realists' pretense at ignorance was precisely what enabled them to use the novel as a legitimate philosophical instrument, as a method for discovering truth. There is no paradox here. The positivist philosophy, which most of the realists accepted, requires a starting point in ignorance. An erudite preface is like an a priori assumption. Mimetic realism was supposed to be an imitation and, at its best, an analysis of experience; therefore its wisdom had by necessity to be a truth derived from experience. The realist-sage could be wise only after the fact. When his hero had made a fool of himself, the writer could "philosophize" about it, preferably in a second draft, as Thackeray did in *Vanity Fair*. But he must not be suspected of writing preconceived exempla and, above all, he could not indulge himself with an idealism, which, by definition, had to be at odds with the phenomenal or experiential world he was reflecting. Positivism operates only in the absence of metaphysical speculation.

Moreover, the retarding principle, facilitated by the tone of the metaphysical novelists, works against the philosophic as well as the dramatic methods of realism. Like the scientists whom they paralleled, the realists were totally committed to a Lockean empiricism and to an unswerving faith in a cause-and-effect universe. The dramatic method, therefore, which transports the reader consecutively and uninterruptedly through a long series of causes and effects, is completely at one with the philosophical basis of the realistic novel. This is another reason why even the genially intrusive narrator was an embarrassment to the late realists and why the annoying author of romance was anathema to them.

On the other hand, the philosophical romancers, especially the writers of what Bulwer called the metaphysical novel, were, as the name suggests, opposed to British empiricism. We have seen that they regarded John Locke as the enemy and that they sought to overthrow the world view by which, they felt, he had bound the minds of their contemporaries, keeping them from their greater possibilities. To retard the progress of a narrative was to step in between two actions and therefore to weaken any supposed causal relationships between them, relationships which rest entirely upon the appearance of temporal proximity. In life there is no way for the idealist philosopher to control such proximities; actions seem to occur in quick succession, confirming and reconfirming our already strong belief in nonmetaphysical causality. But in fiction whole chapters, advancing alternative explanations, and short, jarring authorial intrusions can easily be interposed between actions in an otherwise seeming sequence. Not to retard, not to hold fast the reins of the story and frequently to brake it, would encourage the reader to form his own interpretation in the light of the Lockean world view by which he was already enslaved. Therefore the narrator or author of the metaphysical novel had to make himself conspicuous, perhaps even annoying and rude, in order to remain in control.

We have also seen that the metaphysical novelist does not proceed from ignorance, as the realist does, but from preconceived vision or truth. He does not discover his wisdom along with us in the progress of the narrative; rather he impresses his already established vision upon us. Thus he can gain an advantage from a preface and from digressive statements which foster the impression that, no matter how much we may resent it, he is wiser than we are.

The metaphysical novelist, therefore, may sometimes be annoying because he feels he has to be. The realist, even though the truths his novels discover are usually less palatable than the truths of the idealist, has an easier and more pleasant relationship with his readers. He can coast with them because, while he does not share their tendency to deceive themselves about particulars, he is not at odds with their general world view. He needs only encourage it; whereas the metaphysical novelist must violently or craftily reshape the readers' most basic habits of mind if he is to succeed in getting across his much more optimistic vision, his reviled and frequently rejected happy ending.

But this is only part of the battle which the metaphysical novelist had to wage with his reader and with his material. So far we have been speaking almost entirely in negative terms: of the habits of mind in the reader which had to be overcome and of the normal psychological effects of narrative which needed to be altered before the a priori vision could be communicated. But few advanced mystics believe that it is possible to make converts by simply narrating a vision, no matter what precautions have been taken to exclude the competing, nonvisionary world. It is not enough to build a solemn temple and speak piously there about miracles. No one is converted by someone else's mystery; the congregation itself must share the vision. And here again, the romancer's pose—his intrusive nature and his high visibility—offered an advantage to the metaphysical novelist, for if the reader could be forced to observe the creative process itself, not simply be permitted to watch the creation, he might become a participant in the vision rather than merely a spectator.

Hawthorne, as we have seen, preferred to keep a relatively low profile, but, as we have also seen, he employed subtle means in his prefaces and elsewhere to insure that his presence was felt in the narratives. Moreover, by writing stories in which artists—Hester, Miriam, Holgrave, and many others—appear as central characters, he encouraged the reader to identify with the creative process. *The Blithedale Romance*, of course, uses such an artist as its narrator.

Emerson, as we have noted, perceived this intention of Hawthorne's with cold disapproval, and it is perhaps one of the ironies of literary criticism that the first person of stature to recognize the greatness of Carlyle should have reacted so negatively to a technique which was, after all, that of *Sartor Resartus*. Probably, Emerson failed to make the connection because he did not read *Sartor* as a piece of fiction, but he should certainly have seen how laboriously Carlyle worked through his narrators to involve the readers in the process of the book, so that Teufelsdroeck's visions might become their own.

Dickens, Bulwer, and Melville also wrote novels about artists and novels narrated by artists. Moreover, they all took pains to keep the writer in evidence so that the creative process might be open to the reader. The technique of *Bleak House*, where a flashy omniscient author constantly juxtaposes himself against an easy, personal narrative, serves this function, among others. And in the same book, Dickens makes the invitation explicit when he invites the reader to join in the search for a principle which will unify all the diverse material he has presented:

> What connexion can there be, between the place in Lincolnshire, the house in town, the Mercury in powder, and the whereabouts of Jo the outlaw with the broom, who had that distant ray of light upon him when he swept the churchyard-step? What connexion can there have been between many people in the innumerable histories of this world, who, from opposite sides of great gulfs, have, nevertheless, been very curiously brought together! (Chap. 16)

Bulwer, as we have seen, always rendered himself conspicuous in his works, and his prefaces and digressions on literary subjects form a considerable, perhaps the most interesting, portion of his creative output. His most systematic attempt to draw the reader into the process of creation occurs in *My Novel*, where the central character is a poet, and the melodramatic action is frequently interrupted by playlets, in which the "author" and his friends, characters from a previous novel, interpret the story and discuss matters of technique. Thus the reader is by turns a spectator, a critic, and a collaborator, and the book might well have been entitled *Your Novel* or *Our Novel.*

But of all the metaphysical novelists, none worked more persistently at author-reader involvement than did Melville. His first five books are first-person narratives, and, as a recent critic points out, all of his "narrators are, in some way, portraits of the artist at work."[84] The third-person narrator of *The Confidence-Man*, which contains some of Melville's most important digressions on narrative art, is also such a portrait, and the discussions in *Pierre* on the status of the artist can be seen as attempts by Melville "to involve his readers in the creative process."[85]

The authors of two recent books on Melville come to the same interesting conclusion that his fiction is primarily concerned with the metaphysics of novel writing.[86] A third Melville scholar, William Charvat, puts forth a similar theory:

> To a generation of readers still predominantly governed by Scottish common sense with its official catalogues of approved responses to poetic stimuli, such a chapter [as "The Whiteness of the Whale"] offered training in a new kind of reading. But there is little evidence that the instruction was welcome, and we can assume that because it involved the reader in creative process, it was rejected.[87]

The relationship of the metaphysical novelist to his public, therefore, was a troublesome business. It was difficult because the author was forced by the conventions of fiction to use, as a part of his idealist visions, the world of experience, which had become the primary datum of the materialists. Moreover, he was in the position of having to teach his readers how to approach fiction before he could hope to reverse their most ingrained, scarcely conscious, philosophical habits of mind. He was not his readers' friend or guide or even their priest; he was his readers' missionary. If he sometimes lost patience with them, it may have been a sign of human weakness or it may have been a technique of instruction. If the readers more frequently lost patience with him, refusing to become his converts but throwing him instead into the cannibal stewpot, it may be an indication of the odds against which he was fighting.

84. Edgar Dryden, *Melville's Thematics of Form: The Great Art of Telling the Truth* (Baltimore, 1968), p. 29.
85. William Charvat, *Profession of Authorship in America*, p. 252.
86. They are Edgar Dryden and Joel Porte, the author of *The Romance in America: Studies in Cooper, Poe, Hawthorne, Melville, and James* (Wesleyan Univ., 1969).
87. *Profession of Authorship in America*, p. 247.

·III·

Character

The boy of act one is the mature man of act five. All in all.
In *Cymbeline*, in *Othello* he is bawd and cuckold. He acts and
is acted on. Lover of an ideal or a perversion, like José he
kills the real Carmen. His unremitting intellect is the horn-
mad Iago ceaselessly willing that the moor in him shall suffer.
... Every life is many days, day after day. We walk through
ourselves, meeting robbers, ghosts, giants, old men, young
men, wives, widows, brothers-in-love. But always meeting
ourselves.

—JAMES JOYCE, *Ulysses*

When we speak of the realistic novel of the nineteenth century, we think
immediately of characterization. As we have seen, the method of realism
was to place an interesting person in a taxing experience, and its technique
called for the author to identify fully with his protagonist and then allow
him free rein to develop meaningfully. What Bradford Booth says for
Trollope goes for realists in general: "The heart of a good Trollope novel
... is a firmly grasped character. Where Trollope's imagination has only
loosely seized his core character, there is utter failure. ... Trollope staked
all on a clear realization of character."[1] And the gallery of intensely developed, fully believable, and ultimately meaningful portraits, from Emma
Woodhouse and Jeanie Deans to Maggie Tulliver and beyond to Lambert
Strether, is a chief glory of the genre.

By contrast, characterization is usually seen as the metaphysical novelists' weakest suit, and their personages have frequently been dismissed as
unreal, insufficiently developed, gratuitous, and uninteresting. None of
these judgments is irresponsible, but they sometimes stem, like other objections to the genre, from an imperfect understanding of the writers' aims.
In the present chapter we shall consider all these apparent deficiencies of
characterization along with a few of the principles of metaphysical fiction,
principles which may go some distance towards a justification or, at least,
towards an understanding of the difficulties involved.

1. *Anthony Trollope: Aspects of His Life and Art* (Bloomington, Ind., 1958),
p. 184.

I: THE IDEALIZING PRINCIPLE

There are still some readers of Dickens who prefer his caricatures to the more fully developed character portraits of the realists, but other readers, including many who recognize much of his greatness and who wish sincerely to come to terms with his art, still balk at the unreality of his two-dimensional figures. Dickens might himself have sympathized with the problem; he was unable to be convinced by Hawthorne's Pearl.[2] And Hawthorne, in his turn, would surely have understood Dickens' criticism, for he had to "confess" in "Feathertop: A Moralized Legend," that his scarecrow protagonist reminded him "of some of the lukewarm and abortive characters, composed of heterogenous materials, used for the thousandth time, and never worth using, with which romance writers (and myself, no doubt, among the rest) have so over-peopled the world of fiction."[3] The problem goes far beyond Dickens and Hawthorne, however. As Richard Chase wrote, "The American novel [by which he meant romance] abounds in striking but rather flatly conceived *figures*—from Natty Bumppo, Hester Prynne, and Captain Ahab on down to Henry Fleming, Frederic Henry, Joe Christmas, and Thomas Sutpen—but with certain exceptions mostly to be found in the novels of James, Dreiser and Faulkner, it has been poor in notable and fully rounded *characters*."[4] Marius Bewley puts the case even more strongly:

> Because the American tradition provided its artists with abstractions and ideas rather than with manners, we have no great characters, but great symbolic personifications and mythic embodiments that go under the names of Natty Bumppo, Jay Gatsby, Huckleberry Finn, Ahab, Ishmael—all of whom are strangely unrelated to the world of ordinary passions and longings. . . . The great American novelists can, in their way, give us Lear, and make a decent attempt at Hamlet; but Othello, and even Romeo, are beyond their range.[5]

There are a number of reasons for this apparent failure, the first of which has already been hinted. Character is simply not primary in the romance; it is an element, a partial illustration or embodiment, an afterthought of an author who lives, as Trollope said of Bulwer, not with his characters, but "with his work, with the doctrines which at the time he wished to preach."[6] The odds are that a protagonist out of realistic fiction,

2. Letter to Forster, July 1851. "The Child is out of nature altogether." *The Letters of Charles Dickens*, II, 335.
3. *The Complete Works of Nathaniel Hawthorne*, II, 260.
4. *The American Novel and Its Tradition* (Garden City, N.Y., 1957), p. 40.
5. *The Eccentric Design: Form in the Classic American Novel* (London, 1959), p. 293.
6. *An Autobiography*, 2 vols. (Edinburgh and London, 1888), II, 73.

who was chosen from actual life because he seemed basically compelling and who is followed single-mindedly through his adventures in the novel, will be more real, more complex, more fully developed, more interesting in and of himself than, say, one of the many hypocrites whom Dickens invented or appropriated to help express the theme of *Martin Chuzzlewit*.

It is possible to compare the method of the realists to inductive and the method of the romancers to deductive thinking, but the analogy is only approximate and can be misleading. If followed in respect to characterization, for instance, it would suggest that the realistic novel works when it manages to abstract a worthy general truth by faithfully imitating the experience of a particular man, and that the romance is successful when it fleshes a general truth with the particular of an entirely realized and believable character. Thus, from the end products, it would be both impossible and pointless to distinguish between realistic and metaphysical novels. Each kind of fiction would finally consist of an important idea fully embedded in an objective experience. But the analogy is neater than it is true. Realists sometimes genuinely disbelieve in ideas, and romancers, for reasons we shall discuss, often do not want to make their abstractions any more concrete than they absolutely have to. Even when the romance character is taken from nature, because the author finds an apt model there, the attempt is not full portraiture, but what R. L. Stevenson was to call the "simplification of some side or point of life, to stand or fall by its significant simplicity."[7] Thus, when Hawthorne met the original of Pecksniff, he thought that Dickens had done the man an injustice,[8] and Pearl of *The Scarlet Letter* is not really a good likeness of Una Hawthorne, the bare-bottomed toddler, so charmingly and realistically described in the journals,[9] even though the little girl was already significantly simplified in her father's mind when he named her after a character from *The Faerie Queene*. The romancer uses his characters; he does not render or develop them much more than his thematic purposes require.

This attitude toward characters is part of what Bulwer meant by the idealizing principle, which has nothing to do with the prettification of sensuous nature but rather with its signification. Quilp is an idealized character, so is Claggart, and so are some physically and morally beautiful characters like Donatello and Billy Budd. The principle in question derived most immediately from German thought. Schiller believed that "the characters in the Greek tragedy are more or less ideal masks, and not actual

7. "A Humble Remonstrance," *The Works of Robert Louis Stevenson: South Seas Edition* (New York, 1925), XIII, 157.

8. *The English Notebooks* (ed.) Randall Stewart (New York, 1941), p. 313.

9. *The American Notebooks* (ed.) Randall Stewart (New Haven, 1932), p. 203.

individuals." [10] Even with Shakespeare, he felt, "the subject [sometimes] . . . forced him to fix his attention more upon a poetical *abstractum*, than upon mere individuals." [11] Hegel developed this insight into an aesthetic, stating that art was "the sensuous presentation of the Absolute," and that by taking what has otherwise been soiled and torn by "the contingent elements of external existence," and comparing it with "the harmony that is essential to its notional truth," art "rejects that in the world of appearance which it is unable to combine in such a unity, and for the first time, through this *purification*, reveals the Ideal." [12] Hegel believed that characters must have rich and complete natures, and he cautioned against "simplification . . . carried so far that any character appears as though it were pared down to a mere shadow-like semblance of any form of pathos," but at the same time he stressed the necessity of making "some essential trait of character stand out in bold relief," [13] and he utterly rejected the accurate imitation of nature as a worthy goal for art. [14]

Once again, it was Bulwer who made this German thought generally available to English and American writers. He was, moreover, familiar, as were the other romancers, with the full literary tradition which justified idealized characters. The importance of Spenserian romance as an influence on Hawthorne cannot be overstressed, and, as we have heard Bulwer say, the metaphysical novel in general "often invests itself in a dim and shadowy allegory which it deserts or resumes at will, making its actions but the peculiar incarnations of some peculiar and abstract qualities whose development it follows out." [15] All the romancers knew the passage from Cervantes in which Don Quixote defends the writers of ancient epics and medieval romances for "representing their heroes not as they really were, but such as they should be, to remain examples of virtue to ensuing ages." [16] They were also familiar with Fielding's statement from *Joseph Andrews*:

> I describe not Men, but Manners; not an Individual, but a Species. . . . I have writ little more than I have seen. The Lawyer is not only alive, but hath been so these four thousand Years, . . . When the first mean selfish

10. *Correspondence between Schiller and Goethe from 1794 to 1805*, trans. L. Dora Schmitz (London, 1877), Apr. 4, 1797, I, 304.

11. *Ibid.*, Apr. 7, 1797, I, 306.

12. *The Philosophy of Fine Art* (trans.) F. P. B. Osmaston (London, 1920), I, 95.

13. *Ibid.*, I, 212.

14. *Ibid.*, I, 317–318.

15. "On the Different Kinds of Prose Fiction with Some Apology for the Fiction of the Author," in *The Disowned* (London, 1835), I, xvi.

16. *The Ingenious Gentleman Don Quixote de La Mancha*, 2 vols. (trans.) Samuel Putnam (London, 1953) Part I, Chap. 25.

Creature appeared on the human Stage, who made Self the Centre of the whole Creation; would give himself no pain, incur no Danger, advance no Money to assist, or preserve his Fellow-Creatures; then was our Lawyer born![17]

Thus the metaphysical novelists recognized the idealized or simplified character as an injunction from German romantic aesthetics, but also as the heritage of the major forms of narrative which had come down to them: epic, romance, and satire. All these genres, as the metaphysical novelists read them, were types of allegory. Bulwer even claimed Shakespeare as a "poet who has never once drawn a character to be met with in actual life—who has never once descended to a passion that is false, or a personage who is real!"[18]

An important result of this allegiance on the part of the metaphysical novelists is that if we read their fiction as the realists have trained us to do, for the pleasure and instruction that is to be had from identifying with a complex, real, and fully rounded character, then we are almost certain to be disappointed. Perhaps we shall conclude with Henry James that allegory is one of the lighter exercises of the imagination.[19] Or we may argue, as was not unusual in the nineteenth century, that our favorites are realists after all, though with certain inexplicable lapses in taste and technique which we must try to excuse. George Levine has written, "The nineteenth-century novel tended to place character at the center of meaning."[20] Therefore, when we read any piece of fiction with the expectation that it is a novel, we almost inevitably focus our attention on the characters, and if we find that Stephen Dedalus, for instance, is a more interesting person than, say, David Copperfield, we are apt to conclude that Joyce's vision was the more profound or that Dickens must have held back the really significant incidents from his own young manhood.

Joyce's title promises a self-portrait. Dickens' title page, which reads in part, "*The Personal History, Adventures, Experience, & Observations of David Copperfield the Younger of Blunderstone Rookery (which He never meant to be Published on any Account)* by Charles Dickens," suggests a *fictional* autobiography or memoir in the tradition of Fielding, Le Sage, or Sterne.[21] The title character will certainly be important to Dick-

17. Book III, Chap. I, "Matter Prefatory in Praise of Biography."
18. "Introduction to *Zanoni.*"
19. *Hawthorne* (New York, 1879), p. 61.
20. *The Boundaries of Fiction* (Princeton, 1968), p. 8.
21. The similarities between *David Copperfield* and *Tom Jones* have long been noted. It is perhaps worth mentioning that Dickens' novel followed close after the great success of Bulwer's *The Caxtons*, which is an autobiography of its fictional author and a clearly acknowledged imitation of *Tristram Shandy.*

ens' book, but the first sentence warns us not to be too quick in concluding what his function is to be. He may not even be the protagonist. "Whether I shall turn out to be the hero of my own life, or whether that station will be held by anybody else, these pages must show." To be sure, Dickens ascribed to David some striking incidents from his own life, and, as Freudian critics have noted, the narrator's initials are indeed the author's reversed.[22] Sylvère Monod, moreover, believes that "psychological autobiography . . . plays such a considerable part in *Copperfield* that Dickens might also have called the book 'The Growth of a Novelist's Mind' in emulation of Wordsworth's subtitle for *The Prelude*."[23] All this is true. Monod's suggestion, as we shall see when we come to discuss the structure of the metaphysical novel, is particularly valuable. But the emphasis he imposes contributes to a limited reading of Dickens' work, for to treat the story exclusively as a record of personal growth is to neglect most of the side plots and minor characters, and this leaves us with only the portion of the book which previous critics have usually found to be least satisfactory.[24]

Monod, who is one of the most perceptive of Dickens' scholars, should not be singled out for blame; *David Copperfield* has seldom received a comprehensive reading. Most of the critics have concentrated on characters, but, I believe, without a full understanding of their functions. The older critics, led by Chesterton, valued the eccentrics, the gallery of flat figures who, it was supposed, were so fascinating that Dickens could not resist them as they burst into his imagination. According to such a reading, David's life is a necessary and inoffensive scaffold on which the shenanigans of Micawber and the rest could be staged. But if we take these minor characters more seriously, without denying their humor of course, it is possible to see how each of them represents a mistaken alternative to the sort of *Bildung* the book as a whole is recommending, to see, that is, how each is a thematically inspired, representative, or quasi-allegorical figure. They are flat, not because Dickens couldn't round them, or even primarily because Dickens knew caricatures were funnier or more terrifying than realistic portraits, but because they represent David's undeveloped impulses, each of which, if he settles for anything less than full harmony, he is in dreadful danger of becoming.

22. This point is emphasized in Steven Marcus' *Dickens from Pickwick to Dombey* (New York, 1965), p. 289.

23. *Charles Dickens as Novelist* (Norman, Okla., 1967), p. 317.

24. Monod gives *Bleak House* a similar half-reading in "Esther Summerson, Charles Dickens and the Reader of *Bleak House*," where he states that the third-person part would "have made a very fine novel, remarkably economical in method, if there had not been interspersed with it the first person narrative." *Dickens Studies*, V (1969), 17.

Angus Fletcher, writing on allegory in general, maintains that the hero of that genre "is not so much a real person as he is a generator of other secondary personalities, which are partial aspects of himself":[25]

> Redcross imagines Sansfoi and his brothers; Sir Guyon imagines Mammon and his cave; Sir Calidore imagines the Blatant Beast—in this sense the sub-characters, the most numerous agents of an allegory, may be generated by the main protagonists, and the finest hero will then be the one who most naturally seems to generate sub-characters—aspects of himself—who become the means by which he is revealed, facet by facet.[26]

The sub-characters of *David Copperfield*, which is both an allegory and a novel of development, perform a multitude of possible and unsatisfactory careers, and the hero responds to them so strongly because he recognizes each of their lives as potentially his own. Murdstone disciplines a poor wife to death as David is himself tempted to do with Dora. Micawber, Murdstone's opposite, stands as the extreme of a benign helplessness which has characterized David from his youth. Uriah Heep lusts after the woman whom the as yet callow David will eventually marry, while Steerforth does the dirty business of seducing his childhood sweetheart for him.[27]

Such vicarious lives are common throughout Dickens. Poor Dick dies instead of Oliver Twist, and Orlick, by his failures in life and love, is punished for crimes Pip wanted to commit. On the one hand, the device is a means for widening the scope of a first-person narrative by allowing us to follow the hero and his substitute embodiments down a number of tracks simultaneously instead of limiting us to a single set of adventures. Here the adventures of the minor characters remind one of the several interpolated subplots of *Gil Blas*. Or again, these alternate lives may be

25. *Allegory: The Theory of a Symbolic Mode* (Ithaca, N.Y., 1964), p. 35.
26. *Ibid.*, p. 36.
27. This interpretation is partly supported by Harvey Peter Sucksmith, who sees Micawber as, in one respect, "a comic projection of David." *The Narrative Art of Charles Dickens: The Rhetoric of Sympathy and Irony in His Novels* (Oxford, 1970), p. 190. Christopher Mulvey supports it also in his essay, "*David Copperfield*: The Folk-Story Structure" in *Dickens Studies Annual, Volume 5* (ed.) Robert B. Partlow, Jr. (Carbondale, Ill., 1976), pp. 74–94. Mulvey writes, "Steerforth and Heep . . . one corrupted through luxury, the other corrupted through poverty . . . are alike in that they take ways David might have taken. They represent two shameful directions that the 'personal history of David Copperfield' might have pursued" (p. 77). Carl Bandelin writes that by inducing Steerforth to visit Yarmouth, "David is [unconsciously] 'arranging' for Steerforth to commit in deed the transgression which he himself commits only in wish. Steerforth is thus David's surrogate in his quest for Emily's attention." "*David Copperfield*: A Third Interesting Penitent," *SEL*, XVI (1976), 605.

regarded, as Barbara Hardy argues, as potential doubles of the hero, who bring about his conversion by providing him with bad examples. "Dickens' characters," Professor Hardy writes, "are changed less by seeing what they have done than by seeing what they are, and in the exaggerated form of 'the glaring instance.' "[28]

Under the second explanation, the technique in question derives again most immediately from German Romantic psychology, which had described the mind in terms of an essential duality, and from German Romantic fiction which had illustrated this theory by means of the *Doppelgänger*, either a pair of characters who between them divide a single identity or one character who lives the two parts of his mind at alternate times. I have discussed this subject at some length in a previous work,[29] and we shall take it up again in a later chapter of the present study, but the point which is essentially relevant to our present discussion is that doubles are only half-men. They are not many-faceted Odysseuses or full-souled Anna Kareninas. The method of the German Romantics was to analyze the mind by reducing it to component parts, each embodied in a separate character, or in the halves of a separable character; and if these parts had been allowed to grow into realistic, that is to say, into complete characterizations, the aim would have been subverted. The developed characters of the realistic novel, for example, Dorothea Brooke and Paul Morel, contain contradictory impulses, of which at least the minor characters of the metaphysical novel are discrete and simplified embodiments.

Thus, a treatment of *David Copperfield* as a psychological autobiography, an interpretation which leaves out the minor characters and the subplots, does not do enough. Such a study provides an important corrective to the understanding of Dickens and the metaphysical novel, making it no longer possible for critics entirely to dismiss David as a significant character. But as an attempt to give a complete picture of the book, such an approach is like a study of *Le Roman de la Rose* that concentrates valuably on the speaker as a realistic character, but without noting the allegorical embodiments, whose interactions tell us, after all, most of what we know about his mind. Such idealized presences, taken together, are an essential part of the work's method, and to neglect them, as to enjoy them exclusively, is equally to miss the totality of the vision.

The earlier critics found it easy to dismiss the hero because the central intelligence of romantic fiction, not only of *David Copperfield*, but also of such works as *Wilhelm Meister* and *Finnegans Wake*, is seldom an obviously striking character in-and-of himself. For one thing, many of the

28. "The Change of Heart in Dickens' Novels," *Victorian Studies*, V (1961), 67.

29. *Robert Louis Stevenson and Romantic Fiction* (Princeton, 1966).

most interesting facets of his personality are acted out by his several *Doppelgänger* embodiments, by the projected subcharacters, as Fletcher calls them. In addition, since the romancer's attempt is to describe man's metaphysical rather than his psychological situation, his central character must be an epic everyman, who displays the universality of Dante's narrator and Milton's Adam. Schiller is specific on this point in one of his letters to Goethe:

> It is indeed a delicate and difficult circumstance for the novel that, in as far as the character of Meister is concerned, it should not conclude . . . with decided individuality. . . . The character is individual, but only as regards its limitations, and not as regards its substance.[30]

Perhaps the essence of the realistic hero is his individual particularity. Ernest Tuveson has argued that this quality accounts, at least, for the power which fictional characters have to charm us, and he explains the post-Lockean shift in Shakespearean criticism, a change from a concern with morality to an interest in character, in terms of the influence of the new psychology:

> Above all, we desire to be carried out of our chambers of consciousness into another's, to *feel* his awareness of reality; and literature, better than any other medium, can make possible this vicarious experience by arranging the impressions so skillfully that we seem to be undergoing, from within another's dark room of perception, the sensations that go to make up another self.[31]

But the hero of metaphysical fiction, which rejects Lockean psychology, has a different function and cannot, therefore, attract the reader's attention by his singular personality. Melville undoubtedly puts the matter best when he makes his famous distinction between the "singular" or "novel" and the "original" character. Singular characters "imply but singular forms," he says. "There is discernible [in them] something prevailingly local, or of the age. . . . Something personal—confined to itself." On the other hand, "the original character, essentially such, is like a revolving Drummond light, raying away from itself all round it—everything is lit by it, everything starts up to it (mark how it is with Hamlet), so that, in certain minds, there follows upon the adequate conception of such a character, an effect, in its way, akin to that which in Genesis attends upon the beginning of things."[32] Once again, the metaphysical novelist, since he is seeking to

30. *Schiller-Goethe Correspondence*, Nov. 28, 1796, I, 265.
31. *The Imagination as a Means of Grace: Locke and the Aesthetics of Romanticism* (Berkeley and Los Angeles, 1960), pp. 31–32.
32. *The Confidence-Man: His Masquerade* (ed.) Hershel Parker (New York, 1971), Chap. 44.

remake our view of the world, cannot charm us with the sounds and sights and smells which we have already been taught to recognize and to value. And thus, in some metaphysical novels like *David Copperfield*, the "original" character, part of whose function it is to generate iconic or idealized projections of himself, is less striking and easier to overlook than the "novel" or "singular" or "odd" characters of realistic fiction.

In other types of metaphysical novels, where *all* the characters are idealized projections of the author's mind, an opposite sort of problem exists. Richard Chase writes of *The Scarlet Letter* that "Chillingworth, Dimmesdale and Pearl can be conceived as projections of different faculties of the *novelist's* mind."[33] Yet, conditioned by their experience with drama and the dramatic novel, critics automatically cast about for a protagonist among the individual characters, and arrive, as might be expected, at little general agreement. The same difficulty exists with *The House of the Seven Gables*, where all of the present-day Pyncheons can be interpreted as embodying discrete characteristics of their distant ancestor, the Colonel. Jaffrey represents his greed, Clifford his self-indulgence, Phoebe his humanity, and Hepzibah his pride. The remaining character, Holgrave, stands for imagination, the faculty which the Colonel rigorously excluded from his psyche.[34] Hawthorne has given us, therefore, a sort of *Everyman* without Everyman, in which all five characters together have the potential to make up a single mind.

It is, of course, possible for a story to have a central character even in such a situation, for it does not necessarily follow that an author, because he represents a mind composed of discrete faculties, regards each part as of equal importance to his work or that he gives it a similar emphasis. We shall see that *The House of the Seven Gables* is a Spenserian romance, closely modelled on a book of *The Faerie Queene*, and, since it is an allegory of the imagination, Holgrave can be regarded as central to it in the same way that Redcross is central to the allegory of holiness. The same situation pertains in Melville's *Mardi* where the first-person narrator has also been seen as only one-fifth of a hero[35] or interpreted as "an aspect of Melville. . . . Melville on the side of his will and idealism."[36] And yet Taji, although he is a clear example of a type we shall later discuss under

33. *The American Novel and Its Tradition*, p. 79. My italics.

34. This interpretation belongs to Darrel Abel, "Hawthorne's House of Tradition," *South Atlantic Quarterly*, LII (1953), 573.

35. Merlin Bowen, *The Long Encounter: Self and Experience in the Writings of Herman Melville* (Chicago, 1960), p. 140.

36. William Ellery Sedgwick, *Herman Melville: The Tragedy of Mind* (Cambridge, Mass., 1945), p. 41.

the heading, "The Disappearing Character," is certainly the protagonist of the story he tells.

The terms, "will and idealism," correctly describe the subject of the allegory in *Mardi*. The two faculties, moreover, are virtually inseparable in Melville and throughout the nineteenth-century metaphysical novel. Taji wills blindly and stubbornly towards the completion of an ideal quest which he has always been pursuing. "In the distance," he tells us before the end of the first chapter, "what visions were spread." Those critics who contend that *Mardi* begins like *Typee* and *Omoo*, as a realistic narrative of facts, ought to bear at least these two differences in mind: (1) that the narrator here is not jumping ship in some interesting South Sea port, but, against all rational advice, on the high seas, some thousand miles from the nearest land; and (2) that he defects in *Mardi* not, as in the earlier works, because the ship is physically intolerable, but because it represents a vaguely understood spiritual deficiency.

Taji's ideal is an instinctive, nonrational matter. It is he, of course, and not Melville, who claims to have "chartless voyaged." Taji never has any arguments on his side, only pride and stubborn will. Thus when he tells the experienced Jarl of his plan to jump ship:

> At last he very bluntly declared that the scheme was a crazy one; he had never known of such a thing but thrice before; and in every case the run-aways had never afterwards been heard of. He entreated me to renounce my determination, not be a boy, pause and reflect, stick to the ship, and go home in her like a man. . . . But to all this I turned a deaf ear; affirming that my mind was made up; and that as he refused to accompany me . . . I would go stark alone rather than not at all. (Chap. 4)

And the same sort of irrational instinct guides him when he murders Aleema to rescue Yillah. Yillah has made no signal to indicate that she desires to be saved, and Taji has been ordered from the canoe by a vastly superior force. "Fifteen to three," he mentally notes. "Madness to gainsay his mandate. Yet a beautiful maiden was at stake" (Chap. 41). A maiden, it should be recalled, whom the impetuous Taji has yet to see.

Throughout the "Voyage Thither" part of *Mardi*, Taji dominates his companions in a way that was quite new for a Melville narrator. Tommo does not control Toby, nor, much less, does Omoo govern Doctor Long Ghost. But Taji, representing the will, must dominate. Thus he, rather than the much more experienced Jarl, is the commander of the *Chamois*; Samoa and Annatoo, quick to believe in his divinity, render up the *Parki* to him; and Yillah easily accepts him as her lover and master. His primitive companions (even Jarl is a Viking), rudimentary embodiments of human skills and instincts,[37] are glad to give him the leadership. The result is that they drift off course, both morally and geographically, and by a considerable distance.

In the second part of the narrative, after the arrival at Mardi, the narrator tries to maintain his dominance. His first statement to the inhabitants is an assertion of his divinity: "Men of Mardi," he announces, "I come from the sun" (Chap. 54). And although gods are commonplace in his new surrounding, and the people he meets are more powerful, more intelligent, more cultured, more learned than he, it appears at first that Taji will somehow continue to lead. Thus, when he determines to search for the lost Yillah, his new companions quickly volunteer to join with him. " 'I myself am interested in this pursuit,' " said King Media. " 'Your pursuit is mine, noble Taji,' " Babbalanja, the philosopher, assured him. " 'Where'er you search, I follow.' So too, Yoomy [the poet] addressed me; but with still more feeling. And something like this, also, Braid-Beard [the historian, Mohi] repeated" (Chap. 65).

This appearance of subservience is not deceiving, although during most of the rest of the book Taji will seem to have little control over the direction of his quest and even less to say of it by way of comment. This is as it should be. The will, as we have seen, is instinctive and inarticulate. It only acts. The business of Taji's idealized Mardian companions, on the other hand, is to intellectualize his vague quest, to interpret it according to their separate disciplines, to envision Yillah in ways that can make sense to the various reflective faculties of the mind for which they stand. Thus Yillah is an emblem of beauty to Yoomy's poetic imagination, a remembrance of lost innocence to Mohi's historical temperament, the ideal of political justice to the divine and kingly reason of Media, and absolute knowledge to the speculative and mystical forces of the brain represented by Babbalanja. By contrast, Taji has no ideas, only impulses.[38] For him, Yillah is simply a name he attaches to a quest which he has been following at least since he signed aboard the *Arcturion*, ostensibly to hunt transcendental sperm whales, and it is a name which he continues to use even after he knows that the physical Yillah no longer exists.

By dividing the quest and making it more specific, the companions render Taji's endeavor more comprehensible, and since in spite of this, the search for each of the Yillahs is bound to fail, Melville is able to come to rational conclusions about the nature of questing. He discovers what romance had been preaching since *St. Leon*, *Wieland*, and *Frankenstein*,

37. For an analysis somewhat analogous to the interpretation implicit in this sentence see Philip Graham, "The Riddle of Melville's *Mardi*," *Texas University Studies in English*, XXXVI (1957), 93–99.

38. See Bowen, *The Long Encounter*, p. 141.

actually since Malory: that to quest is to commit a form of suicide, fascinating, tempting, instinctively appealing, and that the quest can never
bring human happiness because it represents a breaking of all human
bonds and a turning away from all human values. The questor ceases to
be a man when he proclaims himself a god, and he ceases to concern himself with the legitimate aims of man when he strives for objects which are
beyond the reach of mankind. This is the lesson which each of the second
group of companions learns in the course of *Mardi* and which Melville
urges the silent narrator also to learn, recommending that Taji give up the
fruitless search for Yillah and settle for the unheroic but rational tran-
quility of Serenia, the utmost man can reasonably expect from life.

Basically, the companions act out the same sort of vicarious experiences
for Taji as Micawber and the other projected subcharacters perform for
David Copperfield. Both books, insofar as they make use of vicarious lives,
are *Bildungsromane* of the German sort. The English and American novel
of development, especially as practiced by such masters of realism as
Jane Austen, the early George Eliot, and Henry James, subscribes to a
British notion, older even than Locke, a conviction that we learn only
through experience, by making our own mistakes. The German *Bildungsroman*, as for instance, *Wilhelm Meister* and Novalis' *Heinrich von
Ofterdingen*, is more mystical. Wilhelm and Heinrich do not have many
experiences. In such a book, the hero's chief business is not to act, but
to read or hear the stories of the other characters. His initiation resembles
a sort of Masonic ritual in which the neophyte is made to stand before each
of a series of symbolic stations and at every stop to absorb the lesson of
some mystic statement or apologue. M. H. Abrams demonstrates how the
structure of Hegel's *Bildungsbiographie, Phenomenology of the Spirit*
(1807) represents "the Christian journey of the spirit through suffering
in quest of redemption and rebirth." As Hegel writes in his introduction,
the action

> may be regarded as the way of the soul, which travels through the sequence
> of its forms, like stations [*Stationen*] marked out for it by its own nature,
> in order that it may purify itself into pure spirit in reaching, through the
> complete experience of itself, the knowledge of what it is in itself.[39]

Similarly, Novalis' artist-hero instructs:

> There are two ways, by which to arrive at a knowledge of the history of
> man; the one laborious and boundless, the way of experience; the other
> apparently but one leap, the way of internal reflection. The wanderer of the
> first must find out one thing from another by wearisome reckoning; the

39. M. H. Abrams, *Natural Supernaturalism: Tradition and Revolution in
Romantic Literature* (London, 1971), p. 229.

wanderer of the second perceives the nature of every thing and occurrence directly by their very essence, views all things in their continually varying connections, and, can easily compare one with another, like figures on a slate.[40]

Thus, the romancer believes that personal trial and error is not the only or even the best way to wisdom—this is why he troubles to write books— and thus the stories narrated by Babbalanja, Mohi, Media, and Yoomy should be important not only to themselves but also to Taji and ultimately to the reader.

Mardi is a *Bildungsroman* of the will, in which the will, unfortunately, fails to achieve harmonious development with the rest of the psyche. The initiation does not succeed, and Taji, after all the ceremonial attempts to save him, emerges obviously dominant again and still engaged in his suicidal quest. He is ready now to commit "the last, last crime." As previously, Taji is incapable of arguing his position with anything more than slogans—"Better to sink in boundless deeps than float on vulgar shoals." But then, he doesn't have to argue. Action is his forte. And when the fruitless, idealized talkers desert at last, leaving him his "own soul's emperor," he is free to abdicate, to follow his mad quest to literal death (Chap. 195).

If we prefer to regard Taji as an aspect of Melville himself rather than as part of an unrendered but understood composite mind, then *Mardi* may be read as an exhaustive but unsuccessful attempt by the author to curb his own stubborn will and force it to accept the essential though unpalatable facts of his existence. These facts are (1) that truth is only relative, (2) that society is imperfect, (3) that love will not last, and (4) that all men must die. Babbalanja, Media, Yoomy, and Mohi respectively make a grudging peace with these necessary conditions in Taji's name, as had Annatoo, Jarl, Yillah, and Samoa, the embodiments of the conditions in the voyage thither. But though they present all the right arguments, they cannot make Taji or Melville sign the treaty.

In *Moby-Dick*, Melville mounts a similar argument against questing, and with a similar set of idealized characters.[41] Only this time the *Bildung* works, and, at least in the American edition, there is a positive ending. At the beginning, however, Ishmael is as potentially suicidal as the narrator of *Mardi*—he speaks of pistol and ball in the very first paragraph—and he is even more vague about the object of his quest or the causes of his anxieties. Like Taji, he leaves it to the others—Ahab, Starbuck, Stubb,

40. *Henry of Ofterdingen* [*Heinrich von Ofterdingen*] Cambridge, Mass., 1842), Pt. 1, Chap. 2.

41. Both Newton Arvin, a Freudian, and M. O. Percival, a Kierkegaardian, argue this position, Arvin in *Herman Melville* (London, 1950), p. 171, and Percival in *A Reading of Moby-Dick* (New York, 1967), p. 127.

Bulkington, etc.—to define the enterprise according to the various principles for which they stand. He goes along whether the voyage is a search
for revenge, for profit, for excitement, or the elemental seeking after death.
Chapter I presents as many arguments as the narrator himself can muster
to justify his going to sea. He protests rather much, and the best of his
motives seems cancelled after he meets Queequeg. "I felt a melting in me.
No more my splintered heart and maddened hand were turned against
the wolfish world. This soothing savage had redeemed it."[42] But the redemption does not in the slightest alter his plans to go whaling nor does
it prevent him (or even his redeemer) from enthusiastically joining Ahab
in his quest for the white whale. Ishmael is somewhat more speculative than
Taji, but he understands his own motives just as imperfectly. He quests instinctively, like the hydrotropic inhabitants of Manhattan whom he describes in the fourth paragraph of his narrative.

Again like Taji, Ishmael, since he also represents the will, assumes an
easy and, if *Moby-Dick* were a realistic novel, an unmerited dominance in
the early chapters. Queequeg, even more than Jarl, is the experienced
sailor, the King's son, the mystic teacher. He is the one who should lead,
especially in the important business of choosing a ship. Using Yojo as his
excuse, however, Queequeg defers. And here again this early centrality
of the speaker is unusual in Melville, who had gone back to an unassuming
narrator in *Redburn* and *White-Jacket*. Still following the pattern of *Mardi*,
moreover, Melville does not permit this dominance of the narrator to continue. After the *Pequod* is under way and the quest has begun, Ishmael is
permitted to retire somewhat into the background, and new characters,
embodiments of more intellectualizing faculties of the mind, are brought
forward. Neither Ahab nor Starbuck nor Fedallah has to cast about for
reasons to justify his whaling voyage. Each knows exactly what he is
searching for, just as Babbalanja and Yoomy could be more specific than
Taji as to the object of their Oriental travels. Once again, Melville is dissecting the motives behind questing so that they can be exposed and, which
is more important, in the hope that the more essential part of the ego,
represented by Ishmael, can be redeemed. And, of course, the initiation is
successful this time, which makes *Moby-Dick* a much more optimistic
work than *Mardi* and, perhaps, more of a romance, and the only one of
Melville's books which I can with confidence classify as a metaphysical
novel in the fullest sense.

Certain differences between *Mardi* and *Moby-Dick* are worth considering. At first glance it appears that the roles have simply been reversed.
Ishmael, like Babbalanja, settles for the marked-down vision and con-

42. *Moby-Dick* (eds.) Harrison Hayford and Hershel Parker (New York,
1967), Chap. 10. All citations will be to this edition.

sents to go on living. He clings to a lifebuoy, in spite of his realization that no ultimate truth about the nature of reality is available to man. Ahab, like Taji, stubbornly, suicidally, heroically refuses any such compromise. Ishmael lets himself fall out of Ahab's doomed boat, as Yoomy and Mohi jumped finally from Taji's prow. As Taji follows the dead Yillah beyond "the circumvallating reef" to his inevitable death, so Ahab attaches himself to the diving Moby Dick, his quest and his coffin. And it is not only Ahab who remains true to his quest in *Moby-Dick*. Starbuck, Queequeg, and the others also die at their stations; only Ishmael survives; whereas in *Mardi*, Taji is the only casualty of the main allegorical journey. Unless man deserts them, quests of any sort end in death, for even when, like Starbuck's quest, they seem modestly and piously enough inspired, they represent, as we have said, the desertion of life values.

Looking at the differences another way, we can suggest that perhaps the *Bildung* fails of achievement in *Mardi* just because the rational and humanistic forces elect to save themselves. They cure their own insanities and thus, relying only on rational arguments, leave Taji as mad as ever. In *Moby-Dick*, on the other hand, where the questors remain firm until their deaths, they provide for Ishmael, not a group of Job's comforters, but a set of *Doppelgänger* who, as we have heard Barbara Hardy argue in the case of Dickens, can convert the hero by appearing to him as "glaring examples." The psychological implication is significant, although it is as old, at least, as Aristotle. It suggests that the way to cure an insanely suicidal will is not to tame the humanistic elements which had previously encouraged its madness, not to Christianize Babbalanja or to make him rational, but to allow Ahab to act out the drama of his self-destruction. Ishmael is redeemed at the end of *Moby-Dick*. If Ahab, like the Captain of the *Arcturion*, had come to his senses and given up the hunt for the sperm whale, then perhaps Ishmael, still lacking his catharsis, would also have had to set out for Mardi and beyond. As Melville was to show in "Bartleby, the Scrivener," logical arguments cannot substitute for personal sacrifice in such a case, nor can good, rational advice take the place of mystic commitment.

The suggestion just presented is meant as one part of an answer to Richard Chase's argument that since the Ishmael and Ahab stories are not sufficiently related to one another in any cause-and-effect way, Melville's purpose in including them both must have been to provide us with two opposite and equally unsatisfactory answers to an unsolvable question.[43] We shall always be confused in reading metaphysical novels if we look for ordinary causes and effects. Romancers, as I have been trying to establish, did not believe in experience as an efficient cause of redemption. Very few

43. *American Novel and Its Tradition*, p. 91.

of the characters of romance are ever converted by what happens directly to them.

Nor is it fair, although this is probably Barbara Hardy's intention, even to reduce the process of change of heart by "glaring example" to a simple matter of "There but for the grace of God go I." The characters discussed in the foregoing pages have often been presented as though they were, indeed, simple allegorical embodiments, but my treatment of David Copperfield as both German *Bildungsbiographie* and English novel of development should indicate (and I shall try to make the point more clearly in the chapter on structure) that the metaphysical novel is essentially a mixed form. Leslie Fiedler recognizes this fact when he comes to discuss the characters of American romantic fiction, but he calls the mixture a product of confusion:

> In the history of the novel, the two modes, analytic and projective, have both flourished, the analytic developing through Flaubert and James to Virginia Woolf, Proust, and Joyce, the projective [in which "character, setting and incident alike are 'true,' not in their own right but as they symbolize in outward terms an inward reality"] moving on through Poe and the Surrealists to a modern climax in Kafka. In many writers, however (in Melville, for instance, and Dostoevski, in Dickens and Balzac and Faulkner), projective and analytic modes are mingled often confusedly; for such authors are the heirs to a confusion at the heart of the gothic about its own method and meaning. Precisely because the early practitioners of the tale of terror were only half aware of the symbolic nature of the genre, they did not know what kind of credence to ask for in their protagonists—presenting them sometimes as fully motivated characters in the analytic sense, and at others, as mere projections of unconscious guilt or fear. Such an heir of the gothicists, for instance, as Melville was betrayed into giving his symbolic Captain Ahab (who stands for "sultanic" hybris, i.e., for one aspect of the mind) a mind of his own; though the Parsae, who plays Satan to Ahab's Faust, is treated as a simple projection of an inner logic rather than a psychology.[44]

On the other hand, I have been arguing that it is not necessary to see the metaphysical novelists in so limited a framework. The Gothic novel was only a small part of the heritage they used in an attempt to put together a new mode of fiction, purposely combining elements from the various forms of realism and allegory in order ultimately to express a mythic vision. The *Doppelgänger* concept itself, which was used in England by such serious writers as Godwin and Mary Shelley, is a product of a mystic psychology, developing also from Richter, Tieck, Novalis, and Hoffman, who took fairy-tale logic with full seriousness. In the hands of

44. *Love and Death in the American Novel*, p. 125.

Dickens, Melville, and Hawthorne, the concept provided a means by which the idealized character could be used, not only to contradict the realistic world view, but to transcend, as well, the cold logic of allegory.

II: THE UNDEVELOPING CHARACTER

In the dramatic novel, the development of the thought is inextricably related to the development of a central character. Sometimes, indeed, both the author and the reader first discover the theme by following the character's growth. Realists have trained us, therefore, to read fiction by first identifying with a protagonist and then travelling with him through a series of incidents which shape his destiny. We are usually permitted to take, or we insist on keeping, a certain aesthetic distance from the character —otherwise fiction might be as uninstructive as life itself is to most of us— but we are at least encouraged to believe that we are learning the meaning of the experience at the same time and by the same process that he learns it.

Such training is bad for the reading of metaphysical novels. It is not easy to identify fully with the hero of metaphysical fiction because he is abstract or unrounded, therefore unlike ourselves, and because, as we shall see, he is passive, therefore unlike our preferred conception of ourselves. But even if we insist on following this unreal and not very attractive protagonist in spite of his dramatic inadequacies, he will not bring us far in the direction of a general truth. Unlike the hero of the realistic novel, he has not led his author to a vision and he cannot be expected to do more for us. Since even he does not learn from his own experiences, there is little of educational value to be gained from a close identification with him. He is oftentimes converted or redeemed, but usually through a sudden recognition or by out-and-out fairy-tale magic, never by the hard grind of personality against experience, for the metaphysical novelist, who achieves his a priori visions in dreams or while talking to his notebook or number plan, does not believe in experience as a redemptive force. Consequently, his characters, even those who are not static, do not really develop.

The fine difference between a changing and a developing character is one of the essential distinctions between the romance and the realistic novel, and it is perhaps the most important reason behind the general belief, only recently challenged and always with a certain trepidation or bravado, that realism is the profounder form.

Why is it [asks George Orwell] that Tolstoy's grasp seems so much larger than Dickens'—why is it that he seems able to tell you so much more *about yourself*? It is not that he is more gifted or even in the last analysis more intelligent. It is that he is writing about people who are growing. His characters are struggling to make their souls, whereas Dickens' are already finished and perfect. In my own mind Dickens' people are present far more often and far more vividly than Tolstoy's, but always in a single, unchangeable attitude, like pictures or pieces of furniture.[45]

Orwell's mind has, to some extent, played a trick on him. Dickens' people, from Pickwick to Eugene Wrayburn, do indeed grow; David Copperfield, Esther Summerson, and Arthur Clennam undergo very complicated and subtle changes; and even minor characters like Dick Swiveller and Micawber are far from unchanging in anything but their external mannerisms. Nevertheless, Orwell is right when he says that Dickens does not often describe a *process* of character growth.[46]

Bulwer gave up the attempt to portray characters in the minute acts of development as early as 1830:

> We do not intend, reader, to indicate, by broad colours and in long detail, the moral deterioration of our hero; because we have found, by experience, that such pains on our part do little more than make thee blame our stupidity instead of lauding our intention. We shall therefore only work out our moral by subtle hints and brief comments.[47]

This is the abject confession of a weakness, especially glaring in Bulwer, but shared to some extent by virtually all the writers of whatever form of romance. Since he does not give himself up to his hero in the manner of the realist, who allows the character a freedom to grow in the direction that his well-defined personality and the pressure of the incidents dictate, the romancer is in trouble when the time comes to make his character turn the significant corners of his development. Usually the romancer gets out of his predicament as best he can by neglecting to render what a realist would call the obligatory scenes. Instead, he usually indicates the changes by rendering very striking before-and-after pictures. Melville, for instance, does not show Ahab in the act of change; instead he gives a series of vignettes which mark the various stages of his psychological career. The narrative technique is similar to that of a progress by Hogarth rather than that of a motion picture. With Hawthorne, the great change occurs in Dimmesdale while we are watching Hester; in Hilda, while the author is concerning us with Kenyon. We judge the change largely by its result; that is to say, after it has occurred. Thus Taylor Stoehr has written that Hawthorne's novels "are rather like collections of tales strung together as a series of tableaux showing the characters in a variety of physical and moral pictures vis-à-vis one another. One almost wants to say that nothing

---

45. "Charles Dickens," *Dickens, Dali, and Other Studies in Popular Culture* (New York, 1946), pp. 68–69.
46. *Ibid.*, p. 69.
47. *Paul Clifford*, Chap. VIII.

happens *in* the novels; all the action takes place behind the scenes and in the wings."[48]

Of course, no writer who tells a story can render everything that happens. Much of the action, even in the most temporally unified of Greek tragedies, had to be consigned to the offstage regions. And a realistic novel or a romance, which deals with larger stretches of time, has, naturally, greater opportunities and greater necessities for exclusions. But the writer can, at least, decide which events he wishes to leave out and what material he absolutely must render. If he elects to concentrate on the moments during which the character is actually undergoing change, then the action will seem to be continuous, no matter how short the work or how many years it is supposed to encompass. *Macbeth* is a classic example here. If we contrast it with an epic drama on a somewhat comparable theme, Goethe's *Faust I*, which is much lengthier, yet covers considerably less time, we can see how the romancers' technique of presenting a series of relatively static pictures makes the action seem sporadic and interrupted and therefore much less the description of a process. Faust undergoes more change than Macbeth but seems a static character in comparison because of Goethe's short scenes and thematic interludes. Margaret, who moves from innocence to depravity to redemption, changes more than Lady Macbeth does and is on stage for a longer period of time. Yet we do not feel that we have seen Margaret struggling to make her soul because her appearances are a series of relatively brief, after-the-fact exposures, whereas Shakespeare's heroine, in the first part of the play at least, seems to develop continually as we are watching her.

Margaret's seduction is presented in a scene which juxtaposes snatches of her conversation with Faust against exchanges between Martha and Mephistopheles, a technique later used by Flaubert, who could not bring himself to identify with Emma Bovary's bourgeois seductions. Such a presentation can be thematically significant and highly comic, but, since it breaks our bond with the character, it does not contribute towards psychological realism. The most significant step in Margaret's development, moreover, that which leads to the murder of her child, takes place while Goethe has distracted our attention, as Mephistopheles has distracted Faust's, by transporting us to the Harz Mountains. Shakespeare would certainly have regarded the infanticide as an obligatory scene, just as George Eliot did in *Adam Bede*. Goethe decided to exclude it, partly, it is possible, because he had not lived with his character sufficiently to be able to make her actually do such a thing. For when so sharp a corner needs to be turned in

48. " 'Young Goodman Brown' and Hawthorne's Theory of Mimesis," *NCF*, XXIII (1969), 397.

the full glare of presentation, as, for instance (returning to Flaubert, but at a more realistic moment), with the suicide in *Madame Bovary*, it is not sufficient that the character be provided with a convincing number of intellectual or even emotional motivations. The author must invest himself so completely in the character that he seems, in his own mind, to be acting with her. Olympian objectivity is not an advantage at such a time. Like Flaubert, he must taste the arsenic so strongly that he vomits.

But even if they could have succeeded in rendering the process of character development, neither Goethe nor the metaphysical novelists would have found the attempt worthwhile. In the first place, as our appreciation for James and Tolstoy indicates, the growing character is the most fascinating article in the realist's bag of tricks. James has written that "a character is interesting as it comes out, and by the process and duration of that emergence; just as a procession is effective by the way it unrolls."[49] In the dramatic, or realistic, novel, where the characters are central, the more interest the reader feels in them the better. But the metaphysical novel is a symphony, not a concerto, and its author must always be careful not to make any one element stand out so distinctly as to distract our attention from the general harmony. Thus Schiller writes, "The epic poet does well to keep from subjects which of themselves greatly agitate the passions, whether of curiosity or of sympathy, in which case the action, as the object, would create too much interest for it to be kept within the bounds of being a simple means."[50] The situation is the same with overly fascinating characters, and since readers find it easy to identify with developing protagonists, the metaphysical novelist is fighting, here as elsewhere, against a "natural" element of his medium. To give us a satisfactory experience with his genre, he must encourage us to live, as Trollope blamed Bulwer for doing, with the work rather than the character.

Moreover, we have heard both Goethe and Schiller say that progression is precisely what the writer of epic and epic fiction does not want. In the realistic novel, as in the drama, the character is the prime vehicle. To empathize with him means, by definition, for the reader to lose his own self-identity. When the realist gets his character developing, the journey through the plot has begun. But the epic novelist isn't taking us anywhere, and least of all is he taking us out of our own skins. He wants us to remain completely ourselves and fully awake so that we can inspect the idealized

49. "Preface" to *The Spoils of Poynton*, Volume X of The Novels and Tales of Henry James (Cambridge, Mass., 1907–09). Reprinted in *The Art of Fiction: Critical Prefaces by Henry James* (ed.) R. P. Blackmur (London, 1934), pp. 127–28.

50. *Schiller-Goethe Correspondence*, Apr. 25, 1797, p. 316.

flowers of his narrative garden thoughtfully. Therefore, our absorption in a character growing through a continuous action would be adverse to his purpose.

Beyond these important technical considerations, the metaphysical novelists had a compelling thematic reason for presenting changing rather than developing characters. The general belief that conversion is a matter of slow growth and gradual development is based on cause-and-effect associational psychology, or at least finds powerful support there. It is another heritage from John Locke, who, as Tuveson explains,

> in effect transferred the clear identity from the ego to the separate ideas, the simple impressions. . . . The personality itself is a shifting thing [after Locke]; it exists, not throughout a life time as an essence, but hardly from hour to hour. . . . Locke is a source of the phenomenon of modern thought which Joseph Wood Krutch has termed the "dissolution of the ego," wherein a "fluid" replaces a "hard core" individual personality.[51]

Since this was precisely the psychology and the psychological world view against which the metaphysical novelists were striving, we should not expect them to use the method of their antagonists. Character change in the metaphysical novel, like truth, must come through sudden vision. Thus, we can legitimately criticize the authors when their mystical conversions fail to convince us, but, unless we are ourselves absolutely convinced of the validity of Lockean thought, we ought not to complain at their refusal to render a psychology they not only rejected, but regarded as the principal curse of their century, a psychology which their own fiction was specifically written to defeat.

III: THE DISAPPEARING CHARACTER

Thus it seems that the continuously developing character was beyond the reach of the metaphysical novelist and foreign to his purposes. The digressive interruption, as we have seen, was his favorite technique both for masking the artistic weakness and for keeping the character in bounds. A chapter on ambergris allows Captain Ahab time to duck backstage and change his costume for a new tableau, and it also gives Melville an opportunity to reemphasize thematic material of which our dramatic interest in his striking character may have made us forgetful.[52]

The technique in question leads us to consideration of a third seeming disability under which the characters of romance labor. Not only are they flat and apparently static; they also tend to weaken our concentration on

---

51. *Imagination as a Means of Grace,* p. 29.
52. For a somewhat fuller account of this technique see my article, "Romantic Unity in Melville's *Omoo*," *PQ*, XLV (1967), 95–108.

them by disappearing at times from the narrative. This characteristic is one of the things which has led some scholars to believe that Melville's works are patchworks of changed intentions. Only moderately troublesome has been the kind of disappearance we have just described, in which an important character is neglected for a chapter or so in order that a proper time interval may seem to have elapsed between two stages of his development or deterioration. Scholars and general readers as well have been much more upset by minor characters, like Bulkington, who are dropped entirely, or narrators, like Taji and Ishmael, who seem to start out as central characters and then fade into semiobscurity when the more engaging Babbalanja and Ahab appear.

David Copperfield contains all three kinds of disappearing characters. The hero quick-changes his own character while he focuses our attention on such matters as Doctors' Commons, the Peggottys, or the Strongs. Meanwhile, minor characters, like the Micawbers and the Murdstones, are constantly disappearing, and although Dickens often brings them back into the story, they vanish each time as if forever. Some interesting characters, as, for instance, the terrible old man who buys David's coat, are used only once. Scott had spoken out against romances where "the hero is conducted through a variety of detached scenes, in which various agents appear and disappear, without, perhaps having any permanent influence on the progress of the story."[53] And Virginia Woolf applied this same sort of criticism to *David Copperfield*:

> Dickens made his books blaze up, not by tightening the plot or sharpening the wit, but by throwing another handful of people in the fire. The interest flags and he creates Miss Mowcher, completely alive, equipped in every detail as if she were to play a great part in the story, whereas once the dull stretch of road is passed by her help, she disappears; she is needed no longer. Hence a Dickens novel is apt to become a bunch of separate characters loosely held together, often by the most arbitrary conventions, who tend to fly asunder and split our attention into so many different parts that we drop the book in despair.[54]

The third type of disappearance occurs when David, like Taji and Ishmael, seems much more the uninvolved narrator and less the central character in the middle portion of the story than he does at the beginning. In the chapters before Canterbury, David is the victim-hero of his narration; later, as at the reconciliation of the Strongs or at the unmasking of Heep,

53. "Introduction" [1830] to *The Monastery* (London, New York, and Melbourne, 1888–98), p. xii.

54. "David Copperfield," *Nation*, Aug. 22, 1925. Reprinted in *Charles Dickens: A Critical Anthology* (ed.) Stephen Wall (Harmondsworth, 1970), pp. 273–76.

David recedes into a bystander whose presence appears unnecessary, sometimes, as when he hears Rosa Dartle upbraid Little Em'ly, even unlikely.

We have already offered some explanation of the disappearances caused by interruptions. The other kinds of disappearances are also accountable in terms of the intentions of the metaphysical novel. Let us begin with the vanishing minor characters. In 1838 Macready restored the most famous of all disappearing characters, the Fool in *King Lear*, to the acting version of the play. A review, concentrating on this aspect of the production, was published in *The Examiner* on February 4. For some years, the article was attributed to Dickens. Now the writer has been established as John Forster, who, as he was Dickens' unofficial editor and the closest thing Bulwer had to a friend and literary advisor, is also a central figure in English metaphysical romance. Forster, Bulwer, and Dickens, moreover, were all close to Macready in 1838, so that the theories surrounding the restoration of the Fool, as they are expressed in the review, must have been familiar to all of them.

Forster's point is simply that the Fool is associated with Cordelia and represents the link which connects Lear to her during the time she is necessarily out of the play, banished by her father. The review does not carry the argument so far, but it follows naturally from what Forster has said that the Fool may disappear from the action when Cordelia is ready to reenter it. And, of course, this is precisely what happens. The Fool makes his celebrated disappearance "at noon" in Act III, Scene vi, just after Lear has fallen asleep in the hovel. Before the King speaks again, Cordelia, his "Poor Fool," has returned from France.[55] Forster might also have mentioned, for it accords with his explanation, that in the brief meantime, Poor Tom, the third fool of the play and still another disappearing character, has taken the places of the other two.

What this critique suggests is a system whereby thematic characters with roughly equivalent values can substitute for one another when the exigencies of plot require. Thus when the story takes the form of a journey, a central character can pass from one thematically oriented character to another as in *The Old Curiosity Shop*, where Nell walks down her long gallery of grotesques on her way to death. In *Martin Chuzzlewit*, when Dickens decided to send his hero across the ocean, the English hypocrites had to be left behind. Luckily, the author was able to find replacements in America.

Such a procedure is not suitable for the dramatic or realistic novel, where the emphases are on continuity and on the central character himself, not

55. Forster was not, of course, aware of the modern theory that Cordelia and the Fool were played by the same actor, a theory which, if valid, strengthens his argument.

on what he sees. To flood the story uneconomically with characters who appear briefly and then leave the action or are left behind by it, soon to be replaced by prototypes, splits our attention, as we have heard Virginia Woolf say, and distracts from character development, which is the primary business of the realist.

But the romancers found advantages in their substituting characters. For one thing these figures provided another means of keeping the central character from distracting the readers' attention away from the theme. And then, briefly appearing characters are more obedient; they don't usually stay around long enough to develop wills of their own which insist on carrying the theme off into unexpected directions, thus modifying or contradicting the author's a priori vision. If they nevertheless threaten in this way, they can always, since they *are* replaceable, be dropped, either for a few chapters or, in extreme cases, altogether. Moreover, the substituting characters should not be precisely interchangeable. In *Bleak House*, for instance, where Turveydrop, Skimpole, and Mrs. Jellyby are lateral displacements of one another, illustrating the theme of irresponsible parenthood, each gives a significantly different focus and thus makes the study more complete.

In the realistic novel, once again, which examines a character rather than a subject, such thematic completeness is unnecessary, and when a novelist finds it necessary to drop or deemphasize a character, as for instance, staying with irresponsible parents, Kate Croy's father in *The Wings of the Dove* or Lucy Ashton's father in *The Bride of Lammermoor*, he gains nothing by finding a substitute. Lionel Croy was probably dropped, anyway, because the *problem* he represents threatens to preempt our interest in his daughter's difficult situation. Dickens might have been just as quick to suppress him, but for his dramatic rather than his thematic danger, and, unlike James, he would have found another interesting, but perhaps less prepossessing, bad father to take his place.

Sometimes Dickens uses his substituting characters not only as a means of exploring his themes more fully but also as a technique for making his meaning more glaringly apparent. Thus, when Krook in *Bleak House* substitutes for his colleague, the Lord Chancellor, we can hardly miss the comments on the latter's essential ignorance and on the basic irrationality of his august proceedings. Similarly, in *Hard Times*, when Louisa recognizes an echo of her father's philosophy—What does it matter?—in the seducer Harthouse's indolent deviltry, the Gradgrind system is thoroughly exposed.

Three parallel and substituting characters of *Little Dorrit* serve to express Dickens' complicated theme more clearly, perhaps, than the actions of any of the major characters. Let us begin with Henry Gowan, whose amiable cynicism seems at first far less diabolical than James Harthouse's and hardly at all germane to the prison metaphor which dominates the book. Gowan describes himself pleasantly as "a disappointed man," a man like most others, but without illusions. His attitude towards life and towards his art is strikingly similar to the no-nonsense position of Thackeray, which, as we have seen, Dickens found objectionable.

> Clennam, I don't like to dispel your generous visions, and I would give any money (if I had any), to live in such a rose-coloured mist. But what I do in my trade [he is a painter], I do to sell. What all we fellows do, we do to sell. If we didn't want to sell it for the most we can get for it, we shouldn't do it. Being work, it has to be done; but it's easily enough done. All the rest is hocus-pocus. Now here's one of the advantages, or disadvantages, of knowing a disappointed man. You hear the truth. (Bk. I, Chap. 34)

Later, Amy Dorrit speculates with her acute intuition that the painter's bluff skepticism may be a form of neurosis. "I have sat wondering," she writes to Clennam, "whether it could be that he has no belief in anybody else, because he has no belief in himself" (Bk. II, Chap. 11). But it is still difficult at this point for us to conclude anything sinister about Gowan's attitudes.

When we see, however, a further distortion of the same world view reflected in the paranoid mind of Miss Wade, our reaction changes. This madwoman begins her "History of a Self-Tormentor" with a sentence which, except for the tone, might well have been spoken by Gowan. "I have the misfortune," she writes, "of not being a fool." And her own perception of the disappointed painter goes far beyond Amy's:

> He was like the dressed up Death in the Dutch series; whatever figure he took upon his arm, whether it was youth or age, beauty or ugliness, whether he danced with it, sang with it, played with it, or prayed with it, he made it ghastly.

Gowan's attitudes were "acceptable" to this obviously insane and dangerously mischievous woman, moreover, "because they echoed my own mind, and confirmed my own knowledge" (Bk. II, Chap. 21).

So represented in an unbalanced mind of a substituting character, Gowan's skepticism takes on a darker coloring, but Dickens is not through with his equations. Having traced the attitude to madness, he is ready now to follow it to criminality. "You are not more than ordinarily honourable, perhaps?" Miss Wade asks the murderer Rigaud, in whom she hears still another echo of her mind.[56]

> I announce myself, "Madame, a gentleman from the birth, and a gentleman to the death, but *not* more than ordinarily honourable. I despise such a weak

56. Alexander Welsh has suggested that Rigaud is also a double of Arthur Clennam. *The City of Dickens* (Oxford, 1971), p. 135

fantasy." Thereupon she is pleased to compliment. "The difference between you and the rest is," she answers, "that you say so." For she knows Society. (Bk. II, Chap. 28)

And thus, by means of his substituting and parallel characters, Dickens has shown the full implications of Henry Gowan's amiable and rational skepticism, and he has related it to the principal metaphor of *Little Dorrit*. He has demonstrated, progressively, how this world view makes a prison of the talents, a prison of the mind, and a prison of the moral sense. At the same time, Dickens relates Gowan's lack of faith in human nature to the more general mental and moral illness of England—Mr. Merdle's complaint—which has created the prison society in which all the characters seem forced to live.

Melville was also strongly influenced by *King Lear* and was especially interested in the Fool.[57] There is no evidence that Melville knew Forster's essay or that he especially noted the technique of substitutions in Shakespeare or Dickens, but it is certain that he used this device frequently in his own romances. Disappearances are so common in Melville that it is a wonder critics of *Moby-Dick* make such a fuss about Bulkington, whose absence would probably have gone unremarked if Melville had not drawn specific attention to it in "The Lee Shore," the "six-inch chapter" which dismisses him.

Bulkington's only other appearance occurs in Chapter III, when Ishmael observes him at the Spouter Inn. "The man interested me at once; and since the sea-gods had ordained that he should soon become my shipmate (though but a sleeping-partner one, so far as this narrative is concerned), I will here venture upon a little description of him." The description is only one paragraph long, and yet it is often argued that Bulkington was originally intended for the protagonist of *Moby-Dick* until Melville changed his mind about the kind of book he wanted to write. Then, since Bulkington was no longer needed, Melville is supposed to have written "The Lee Shore" to dismiss him. He is supposed also to have gone back to Chapter III to add the "sleeping-partner" parenthesis so that no one would notice his change of intention. This is a possibility, of course, but a rather unlikely one. Melville, who was writing his sixth full-length romance, must have known enough about his craft to realize that the easiest and best way of disguising such an alteration was not to add the parenthesis *and* the chapter, but to delete the paragraph, or, if he could not bear to part with so fine a thing, simply to cross out the subordinate clause in the paragraph which indicates that Bulkington may be heard of again.

57. See Charles Olson, *Call Me Ishmael* (New York, 1947).

He didn't cross it out because the Bulkington paragraph in Chapter III is an introduction to "The Lee Shore," not an amputated limb which "The Lee Shore" serves to tie off. And Bulkington is dropped at this point not because Melville changed his mind about him, but because he has served his purpose as a thematic stand-in for Ahab, whom Melville is at last ready to introduce.[58]

Such character abandonments were nothing new for Melville. In *Mardi* all of Taji's companions during the voyage thither are dispatched either by violent death or kidnapping before the book is half over. As we have seen, they make room for a new set of idealized characters, representing similar faculties of the mind at a more sophisticated level. Annatoo, the devil-plagued woman of mixed nature, is replaced by the idealistic philosopher, Babbalanja, with his skeptical demon. A scholar of the past substitutes for Samoa, a savage who could only embody the past. Instead of a Viking, we are given an actual king, Media, with real subjects and significant responsibilities. And the beautiful but inarticulate Yillah gives way to Yoomy, an ardent poet who sings her praises. Even closer to Bulkington, in temperament and in time of composition, is the Byronic Nord, White-Jacket's hermit friend and shipmate, who is introduced and dismissed in a single chapter. Nord isolates himself from the man-of-war world because he fears the scourge of authority, and since, as we are later to learn, this is the primary meaning behind the narrator's own voluntary isolation, Nord stands in for White-Jacket very much as Bulkington substitutes for Ahab.

Turning to the later works, Celio, a disappearing character from the first part of *Clarel*, is "Vine's double," as Charles Olson has pointed out.[59] And nothing in literature illustrates the technique of thematic substitution better than the many disguises of the Confidence-Man and the various manifestations of his victims, whose abrupt disappearances certainly do not represent any changed intention. Such characters cause less of a problem for the reader here than in *Moby-Dick*, for instance, because in *The Confidence-Man* Melville never provides any realistic grounds for standing on, and there is consequently less temptation for plot-mongers to cast about for a protagonist. Melville helps out also by giving us very early in the book something like a cast of disappearing characters, the guises which the Confidence-Man will assume in the course of his masquerade. The

58. Robert L. Peters writes, "No other character, with the possible exception of Father Mapple, better prepares us for the meaning of Ahab's tragic struggle with the whale. . . . Melville's analysis of Bulkington is like the early introduction of a major symphonic theme, or a *leitmotif*." *Explicator*, XVI (1958), Item 44.

59. *Call Me Ishmael*, p. 104.

spokesman is Black Guinea, one of the incarnations, and himself scheduled for a very quick disappearance:

> dar is aboard here a werry nice, good ge'mman wid a weed, and a ge'mman in a gray coat and white tie, what knows all about me; and a ge'mman wid a big book, too; and a yarb-doctor; and a ge'mman in a yaller west; and a ge'mman wid a brass plate; and a ge'mman in a wiolet robe; and a ge'mman as is a sodjer.

Most of these characters appear briefly on the decks of the *Fidèle* during the pages that follow, and those who do not appear may have been reserved for a sequel, which may be hinted at in the last sentence of the book: "Something further may follow of this Masquerade."[60] The revolving Drummond light of Melville's original mind brilliantly illuminates one of these substituting confidence-men until his thematic significance is expressed; then it passes on to the next. This technique may, as we have heard Virginia Woolf assert in the case of Dickens, "split our attention into so many different parts that we drop the book in despair," but such a criticism, coming from the author of *The Waves*, is less perceptive of the nature of the genre than one might have hoped.

We have anticipated a portion of our explanation of the vanishing major characters of the metaphysical novel when we spoke, in an earlier section of this chapter, of *David Copperfield* and of the near disappearances of Melville's narrators in the large middle sections of *Mardi* and *Moby-Dick*. Those readers who find such explanations more ingenious than convincing and who cling to the theory that the narrators disappear because the authors were unable to maintain an intention are referred to Dickens' number plans for *David Copperfield* and to the fact that Melville's hero also "disappears" during the long quest or pilgrimage sections of the narrative poem, *Clarel*. There exists, indeed, a complete pattern of similarities in *Mardi*, *Moby-Dick*, and *Clarel*, which settles, to my mind, the questions both of intention and of preconception. In all three, Melville interests us at first in a psychologically disoriented young hero, who finds himself in a strange place and describes the sights of it somewhat realistically. During these introductions all of the heroes find companions who are summarily dispatched (Celio, Bulkington, Annatoo) or allowed to

60. Hershel Parker notes that the names seem to be "intended as a complete list of the successive disguises of the Confidence Man, but no amount of casuistry can quite make it jibe with the text as it stands. Presumably Melville later altered his plan but not the list." *The Confidence Man: A Norton Critical Edition*, p. 10. *Pace*!

fade in importance and ultimately to disappear before the end of the book (Nehemiah, Jarl, and Samoa) or at least are less emphasized (Queequeg), and each hero falls in love or, in the case of Ishmael, participates in a marriage ceremony. Then, without warning, the loved one is called away —into Jewish mourning, which a Christian cannot penetrate, or into Ramadan, or into the mystic flesh cult of Hautia—and the hero is left alone to choose new companions for his quest-pilgrimage. Now, in all three of the stories, the hero fades into the background and remains visible at times only to observe the more exciting adventures of his new companions or to hear their digressive though thematically relevant statements and conversations. Meanwhile, each pilgrimage pursues its seemingly unhurried and philosophical way towards its shrine. Clarel's company journeys to the place of the Nativity in Bethlehem; the crew of the *Pequod* hunts the white whale; and Taji's companions sail deviously towards the whirlpool. When they arrive, the narratives are suddenly speeded up into furiously dramatic scenes, followed by brief codas in which the original protagonists become central once again and where they learn that, at the moment when their quests were being accomplished, the loved ones were lost irrevocably: Ruth, Queequeg, Yillah are all dead. When an identical pattern, however bizarre-seeming, recurs in the three most ambitious works of a single author, there is a certain perversity in critics who refuse to attempt a significant interpretation or to listen with patience to the attempts of others.

But perhaps it is better at this point to avoid the emotional question of Melville's structural intent and to concentrate our treatment of vanishing major characters on *Wuthering Heights*, which is almost universally regarded nowadays as both carefully planned and executed.[61] Robert Kiely calls it "one of the few perfect novels in nineteenth century English":

> Others may be more complex, more expansive, but *Wuthering Heights* belongs to that small group of books which convey the impression of an

61. There is a minority view expressced by Albert J. Guerard, who believes that while "the theoretical conception governing its structure is clear enough," *Wuthering Heights* "occasionally loses control of its major attitudes and emphases" ("Preface" to *Wuthering Heights*, New York, 1960. Reprinted in *Twentieth Century Interpretations of Wuthering Heights* ((ed.)) Thomas A. Vogler, Englewood Cliffs, 1968, p. 63).Q. D. Leavis, after scolding Americans for their bright ideas and while proving to everyone's satisfaction that *Wuthering Heights* is greater not only than the novel *Jules et Jim*, but even its film version, opines that Emily Brontë had some trouble getting free of a false start" ("A Fresh Approach to 'Wuthering Heights,'" in *Lectures in America* by F. R. Leavis and Q. D. Leavis, London, 1969, p. 88).

utterly self-sufficient world where style and content really are the same and where the reader can think of nothing useful to add nor superfluous to delete.[62]

And yet, because of its vanishing characters, this perfect novel is seldom treated as a totality. Almost all the criticism concentrates on the first half and on the very end;[63] even Kiely's extended discussion touches on the young Catherine and Linton Heathcliff only once,[64] and it never mentions even the name of Hareton Earnshaw.

Dorothy Van Ghent's famous and incalculably valuable discussion of *Wuthering Heights* argues that the first part is a kind of frog-prince story with an unhappy ending. The fair maiden neglects to kiss the dark youth, and he remains, therefore, unredeemed.[65] Heathcliff, as Cathy proclaims, is *herself*, and it is therefore a part of her own nature which she rejects when she turns away from her wild and instinctive playfellow, converting him into a Gothic monster. Although Cathy does not recognize it, Edgar Linton is also a part of her psyche.[66] When, after Heathcliff's return, Cathy rejects Edgar, transforming his common humanity into a sickly paralysis, she has lost all the psychological integrity of the original Catherine Earnshaw, and she seems to die of what is diagnosed in the book as a "permanent alienation of intellect."[67] Thus, in the terms we have been using, the heroine "disappears" before the story is quite half over. Hollywood and most critics have refused to read further.

The second part of *Wuthering Heights* is also a fairy tale built on doubles psychology. This time, however, the *Doppelgänger* work in two ways. Hareton Earnshaw and Linton Heathcliff are not only parts of the second Cathy in the same manner that Heathcliff and Edgar were parts of the first; each of the second generation actors is also a double of his older counterpart and therefore a substitute for a vanished character. Nelly ob-

62. *The Romantic Novel in England* (Cambridge, Mass., 1972), p. 233.

63. An important exception is U. C. Knoepflmacher, who treats the Catherine-Hareton relationship extensively when he discusses *Wuthering Heights* in *Laughter and Despair: Readings in Ten Novels of the Victorian Era* (Berkeley, Los Angeles, London, 1971). Knoepflmacher concludes, however, that this second plot is "clearly subordinated to that of the first set of lovers. Heahtcliff's tragedy cannot be dispelled" (p. 105).

64. *The Romantic Novel in England*, p. 244.

65. *The English Novel: Form and Function* (New York, 1956).

66. As Mary Visick writes, he is "a less extraordinary person; but he still retains enough of his Gondal past [as Lord Alfred] to make him a counterweight to Heathcliff." *The Genesis of Wuthering Heights* (Hong Kong, 1958), p. 58.

67. *Wuthering Heights* (eds.) Hilda Marsden and Ian Jack (Oxford, 1976), p. 160.

serves that Linton Heathcliff "might have been taken for my master's [Edgar Linton's] younger brother,"[68] and Hareton acknowledges Heathcliff as his own "devil daddy."[69] Nor is the second situation a watered-down version of the first, as has been argued.[70] On the contrary, Linton Heathcliff presents a grotesque, sometimes an embarrassing exaggeration of Edgar Linton's puling weakness and crybaby selfishness, and the illiterate Hareton Earnshaw, who throws rocks at strangers and hangs kittens from the backs of chairs, marks a considerable advance in depravity over the young Heathcliff. Linton and Hareton strike us as less extreme than their elders only when we make the easy mistake of comparing them with Edgar and Heathcliff *after* the latter have been rejected by their Cathy and have undergone their magical distortions.

The second Cathy, as her name suggests, is her mother's substitute, and, in the true fairy-tale tradition, she is given the opportunity to succeed where her elder counterpart has failed. Lockwood discovers in one of the early chapters that the first Cathy, trying out her marriage possibilities, had written herself "Catherine Earnshaw-Heathcliff-Linton." Her daughter, who was born Catherine Linton, who made herself Catherine Heathcliff by her first wedding, and who is soon to become Catherine Earnshaw by her second, literally marries her way back to the lost integrity. She accepts where her mother had rejected, despite the fact that Heathcliff, turned ogre now, makes acceptance much harder for her than it was for his Cathy and fully expects and believes he wants her to fail. Heathcliff, to revenge his own rejection, has made a spoiled invalid of his son before forcing Cathy to marry Linton, certain that such a marriage must be distasteful to her. But she foils Heathcliff by loving her cousin—"Why should you wish to force me to do what I'll willingly do of myself?"[71]—and her love redeems Linton, at least to some extent, causing him to feel a degree of pity for the first time in his life. Then Heathcliff throws her together with Hareton, whom he has systematically trained into a more brutish representation of his own distorted youth. "Now, my bonny lad, you are *mine!*" Heathcliff tells the boy immediately after Hindley's death, "And we'll see if one tree won't grow as crooked as another, with the same wind to twist it."[72] Again he is certain that Cathy, her mother's daughter, cannot accept such a monster; again he is taking his revenge for the rejection which he

68. *Ibid.*, p. 245.

69. *Ibid.*, p. 135.

70. See especially Richard Chase, "The Brontës: A Centennial Observance," *Kenyon Review*, IX (1947), 487–506.

71. *Wuthering Heights*, p. 332.

72. *Ibid.*, p. 230.

himself suffered; and again young Cathy foils him by loving where she ought to spurn. This time both she and Hareton are fully redeemed.

To this point, the psychology, fairy-tale though it is, does not appear so very mystical. Love and acceptance humanize us; rejection alienates us to grotesque monsters. If we can come to terms both with our common humanity, in all its embarrassing weakness, and with our disturbingly wild instincts, then we achieve harmonious selfhood. But the second Cathy redeems more than herself and her two lovers. Here is where the vanished characters come back. When she marries Linton Heathcliff, Cathy also seems to effect a cure for Edgar Linton's paralysis. Edgar, whose death coincides with the marriage, is represented as happy, after the long wait, to join his wife in the grave. "He died blissfully," Nelly says.[73] Heathcliff experiences a similar release when he is forced to recognize that Cathy and Hareton are in love. He ought to be enraged at the failure of his spiteful scheme; he ought, as he knows, to crush the lovers, who still remain within his power; but, although he does not understand the reason, with the acceptance of his double or substitute, his monsterhood has left him. Thus, Heathcliff anticipates his coming death and the consequent reunion with his loved one eagerly and with exhilarating bliss. Elliott Gose has written, "Heathcliff stops his revenge because he sees the spirit of Catherine in the face of Cathy and of Hareton. He wins not mere death but presumably union with the spirit of Catherine."[74] Even the dead Cathy, flanked in the grave by her two dead lovers, is reported to have found peace at last.

Thus the second generation, by a process which cannot be termed either conventional or rational, has redeemed not only itself, but also its doubles in the older, alienated generation. And characters who seem to have disappeared from the narrative, either by falling somewhat into the background, like Heathcliff and Edgar, or, like the first Cathy, by death itself, are still primary concerns of the author. They can be transformed against their conscious wills, without their participation, even after death, through the agencies of their doubles, the substituting characters.

Such magical transformations of vanished characters occur significantly also in Hawthorne, another romancer who planned his works with precision. Most of Arthur Dimmesdale's mystic development takes place when we cannot see him. Hilda literally disappears during a long and crucial portion of *The Marble Faun*. She is softened into womanhood not

73. *Ibid.*, p. 344.
74. *Imagination Indulged! The Irrational in the Nineteenth-Century Novel* (Montreal and London, 1972), p. 63.

only by long stretches of unpresented, nor even summarized, action, but by important onstage activity from which she is absent, and to which she seems to have no causal connection. The great personal sacrifice of Miriam and Donatello, symbolized in the complex ceremonial action at the carnival, makes a possible bride of the nearly bloodless Puritan, who has been quarantined meanwhile in a Raphaelesque world of ideal forms.

The change in Phoebe of *The House of the Seven Gables* is more gradual than Hilda's, but similar. Hawthorne reminds us from time to time throughout the work that the mystic and psychological influences of the old house and its occupants are making Phoebe less of an abstraction, more of a woman. But the most dramatic part of her transformation occurs during the few days when she leaves the house and the world of the story to visit her mother. She returns to the Seven Gables "graver, more womanly, and deeper-eyed, in token of a heart that had begun to suspect its depths" (Chap. 19). Hawthorne writes that "her experiences" have brought about the change, but he does not mean, as a realist would, that she has been altered at the grindstone of personal conflict or molded on the wheel of human association. During her most recent scene with Holgrave, just before her absence, all the right circumstances, including even the magic of transfiguring moonlight, were present, and yet the two lovers failed to come together. Both had to change before Pyncheon and Maule could be reconciled after two centuries. The penultimate step in Holgrave's transfiguration takes place during the dark hour when, alone in the house, he confronts the corpse of his hereditary enemy, Judge Pyncheon, and with his penetrating camera, looks into the abyss through the dead man's open eyes. Although this scene takes place offstage, Holgrave recounts parts of it and stresses their significance to his spiritual development. But, so far as we know, Phoebe has done or experienced nothing of relevance while she was at home with her mother, nor was anything done or said to her during this interval which would account for the completion of her necessary change into womanhood. Before she could become a fit wife for a Maule, things had to happen at the house from which she was absent and to its other inhabitants. The judge had to die there and complete the procession of condemned Pyncheon ghosts; Clifford had to break out of his isolation; proud Hepzibah had to learn to pray; and Holgrave had to undergo his dark night of the soul as he watched over and photographed Jaffrey's dead face. All these events prepared the house to receive Phoebe and finally to be transfigured by her; but they also played their nonrational part in transforming *her* from an idealized sunbeam into a living woman, so that she *could* perform the necessary miracle. And Alice Pyncheon, like Catherine Earnshaw of *Wuthering Heights*, is redeemed long years after her death by the actions of a later generation in which, of course, she takes no active part. Only when the judge dies do her posies bloom, and only in the last sentence of the book, after the engagement of Phoebe and Holgrave, does her ghost float "heavenward."

The House of the Seven Gables is worth a longer consideration at this point because it presents so many of the problems created by the characters of the metaphysical novel. Professor Darrel Abel, who offered an interesting explanation of what the book is attempting before there was much understanding of the general aims of the American romance, summed up the difficulties in which other critics had traditionally found themselves:

> They are unable to polarize its elements. It apparently lacks a single consecutive action and a constant set of characters. The narrative leaps over generations with apparent arbitrariness. The characters appear to have been prodded from repose, not into life and action, but merely into momentary and aimless liveliness; they appear to be posturing and gesturing rather than acting out the inner necessities of their individual natures according to the exigencies and opportunities of an actual environment. The story appears to progress casually, even haphazardly, rather than to advance towards a crisis determined by factors inherent in a given situation.[75]

In other words, the characters of *The House of the Seven Gables* are flat, static, and elusive, like the characters of romance in general. It is hard, as we have noted earlier, to decide which of them is the protagonist, and it is difficult to believe that some of them, Phoebe, for instance, are of flesh and blood. Surely all the main characters change, but readers trained in the cause-and-effect world of Locke and the realistic novel are at a loss to explain specifically what transforms them. Why, moreover, except that it is convenient to the story, should Jaffrey die precisely when he does, and why should his death make such a spiritual difference in the lives of the others? Isn't it simply a case of Hawthorne's forcing a happy ending on a gloomy situation? This, indeed, has been the conclusion to which most of the Hawthorne critics have come.

Before answering these objections, Abel invokes "Coleridge's 'golden rule' of criticism: *Until you understand a writer's ignorance, presume yourself ignorant of his understanding,*"[76] and he cautions that in so far as "realism means acceptance of the world of appearance as the 'real' world, Hawthorne was not a realist."[77] Thus the house itself, he writes, is not so

75. "Hawthorne's House of Tradition," p. 562.
76. *Ibid.*, p. 563.
77. *Ibid.*, p. 565.

much a realistically observed setting for dramatic action as it is a symbol for "the whole nature of man."[78] Abel then goes on to present the fruitful allegorical interpretation at which we glanced earlier in the chapter, when we considered the four living Pyncheons as discrete faculties of the old Colonel's mind and Holgrave as the reembodied imagination of his wizard ancestors. Here then are our idealized *Doppelgänger* and our disappearing and substituting characters once again.

The analysis is mechanical, but that would not have concerned Hawthorne, who would, indeed, have been glad to make the point that only after the death of Pyncheon Greed, as embodied by Jaffrey, can Phoebe, who stands for Pyncheon Humanity, accept the love of Holgrave, thus permitting Maule Imagination to become a part of the fully integrated and harmonious personality at last. My only difficulty with the interpretation is that I cannot see Jaffrey as a representative of only one part of the Pyncheon personality, especially when Holgrave, Hepzibah, and Phoebe recognize him as the complete, albeit diminished reincarnation of the original Pyncheon. Greed may be his leading characteristic, as it was the Colonel's, but, especially in the chapter called "The Pyncheon of To-day," the Judge reflects the other characteristics of his ancestor, as well— his heartiness, his voluptuary self-indulgence, his pride, his disdain for the imagination. If we wish to keep to the valuable allegory already suggested, therefore, it makes more sense to regard the Judge not, like his cousins, as a simplified single part of the Pyncheon character, but as a full representation of the unharmonious personality that must die before the new configuration, which includes the imagination, can come into being.

Such a modification facilitates a Spenserian reading, more in line with the highly suggestive interpretation of another critic, Buford Jones, who does not see the Seven Gables as the conglomerate of all its inhabitants, but as "an emblem of Judge Pyncheon's whole moral nature."[79] According to this reading, Hawthorne's allegory was based on the House of Pride episode from *The Faerie Queene*.[80] Clifford, Hepzibah, and especially Hol-

---

78. *Ibid.*, p. 571. In stressing this body-house analogy, which is spelled out in great length in the text of Hawthorne's romance, Abel is followed by Maurice Beebe, "The Fall of the House of Pyncheon," *NCF*, XI (1956), 1–17; Buford Jones, "The *Faery-Land* of Hawthorne's Romances," *ESQ*, No. 48 (1967), 109–124; and Donald Junkins, "Hawthorne's *House of the Seven Gables*: A Prototype of the Human Mind," *Literature and Psychology*, XVII (1967), 193–210.

79. "The *Faery-Land* of Hawthorne's Romances," p. 116.

80. Two other critics have emphasized Hawthorne's dependence on Spenser. Susan Mary Archer makes the case generally in her dissertation, "Hawthorne's Use of Spenser" (Univ. of Penn., 1967) and Hazel Thornburg Emry in "The House of Pride: Spenser's and Hawthorne's," *PQ*, XXXIII (1954), 91–94, notes the specific borrowing which Jones interprets at length.

grave, the debilitated Redcross Knight, are prisoners in Jaffrey's House of Pride, whom Phoebe (Una) rescues and ultimately transports to the House of Holiness (Jaffrey's suburban villa). Jones reads the plot structure as "a battle," in which "the forces of Pride and Holiness are set against each other, with the latter winning the struggle."[81] Thus Phoebe gives Holgrave the power to defeat and escape Jaffrey, the representative of that Pyncheon sin and pride which has usurped the Maule patrimony over the centuries.

The many pieces of evidence adduced to prove Hawthorne's borrowings from Spenser make, to my mind, an incontrovertible general case, and the reading is especially attractive because it supplies us with the polarity for which critics have so long and so fruitlessly been searching. But to establish this polarity, both Spenser's allegory and Hawthorne's use of it have been somewhat oversimplified, and an undue emphasis, it seems to me, has been given to the House of Pride episode in the works of both writers. By following and expanding this reading, however, we can see another way—a Spenserian way, adapted by Hawthorne—in which the romance makes use of its disappearing characters.

The Redcross Knight himself is one of the most important disappearing characters in English literature. Of course we are dealing here with a figure from a fragment, but Redcross, like the Fool in *Lear*, vanishes before the completed action of *The Faerie Queene* is half over, never to reappear. Moreover, critics have frequently recognized that Spenser employs substituting characters of the type described in our treatments of Dickens and Melville. Thus, Despayre has been traditionally understood as a more serious representation of Sansjoy, and Orgoglio as a more dangerous Lucifera. Moreover, Archimago and Duessa are shape-shifters, who appear in various disguises to plague the heroes.

The House of Pride episode is a part of this pattern of temptations by substituting and overlapping demons. It occupies Spenser through two cantos and Hawthorne through more than two chapters, but for neither writer is it the most serious or dangerous test the hero must undergo. Buford Jones' reading implies that Una rescues Redcross from the House of Pride, but, in fact, Spenser's hero is strong and cautious enough to save himself this one time. And so is Holgrave strong enough to free *himself* from the seven-gabled House of Pride when its owner is Hepzibah (Lucifera) rather than Jaffrey (Archimago), and when it stands only for wordly, self-destructive pride.

At this point Holgrave, like the second Cathy of *Wuthering Heights*, succeeds where his own prideful ancestors had failed. Cast out of the House of the Seven Gables, though they were its builders, and given dom-

81. "The *Faery-Land* of Hawthorne's Romances," p. 115.

inance only over the seemingly worthless province of dreams, the Maules have responded to Pyncheon pride with a destructive pride of their own. And this disability, Hawthorne tells us, has been the ultimate cause of the family's submersion:

> Their companions, or those who endeavored to become such, grew conscious of a circle roundabout the Maules, within the sanctity or the spell of which —in spite of an exterior of sufficient frankness and good-fellowship—it was impossible for any man to step. It was this indefinable peculiarity, perhaps, that, by insulating them from human aid, kept them always unfortunate in life. (Chap. 1)

Moreover, like Heathcliff, the Maules have been driven to distort and further alienate themselves by acts of spiteful revenge. Thus, Matthew Maule has perversely used his sacred power of the constructive imagination to destroy Alice Pyncheon, and the resulting guilt has transformed him into "the darkest and wofullest man that ever walked behind a corpse" (Chap. 13).

Holgrave, the present-day representative of the imaginative Maules, also suffers from the family disease of proud reserve, as evidenced by his shamefaced assumption of a false name and by the bitter, almost sophomoric sarcasm with which he treats the Pyncheons when he writes a story about them. He castigates his ancestral enemies, as Matthew had done, with the imaginative or artistic faculty, his sole heritage, and again like Matthew, he hates himself for his prideful reaction. As he admits, "the lunacy of the Pyncheons is . . . contagious," and he has written his story of Alice Pyncheon, he says, as "one method of throwing it off" (Chap. 12).

This exercise of the imagination does much to cure Holgrave of his crippling neurosis. It facilitates his self-rescue from the House of Pride, in fact, when it gives him the strength not to repeat his ancestor's prideful sin of gaining mastery over and violating the soul of an exposed and helpless Pyncheon woman, Phoebe, whom his reading of the story in the back garden has rendered nearly hypnotized. Thus Holgrave, like Redcross, has single-handedly overcome the temptation of the House of Pride.

I do not mean to deny the importance of this test in Spenser or in Hawthorne. Obviously the salvation of both heroes depends upon success in these crises. But it remains that Redcross and Holgrave make their own escapes unaided by Una or Phoebe, each through his "privie posterne" door; and, which is more important, neither knight is fully redeemed at this point. Holgrave is far from cured of the more profound aspects of Maule pride even after his escape in the back garden. He remains an isolated spectator of the Pyncheon tragedy. And in Spenser, Una does not appear at the moment of Redcross' flight from the House of Pride to lead him to the House of Holiness. First he must endure his encounters with Orgoglio and Despayre, who are much more dangerous to him than poor, foolish Lucifera.

Judge Pyncheon does not figure significantly in the House of Pride section of Hawthorne's romance. Comically proud Hepzibah has a life estate in the Seven Gables, and she exercises a tenuous mastery there until Chapter 15, "The Scowl and Smile," when Jaffrey enters with the east wind and asserts his power. If we do not count the photographic reproductions of him, the Judge appears only five times in the entire action of the romance. First, like Archimago, he frowns and smiles at Hepzibah from behind a tree. Later, dragonlike, he pricks Clifford's descending soap bubble with his nose. Three times he appears in the house, and in each case there is a clear and developed parallel to an episode in Book I of *The Faerie Queene*.

On his first penetration into the house, he lecherously threatens Phoebe, as Sansloy attacks Una. Here Jaffrey's sensuous and lustful qualities are stressed, his "fleshly effulgence," his "dark, full-fed physiognomy (so roughly bearded, too, that no razor could ever make it smooth)." When he tries to kiss his cousin, "the man, the sex, somehow or other, was entirely too prominent," and lest we take Jaffrey at his word concerning the chastity of his gesture, Hawthorne settles the matter by comparing his case with that of Ixion, who tried to rape Hera, the goddess of domesticity (Chap. 8). Phoebe, of course, is as little tempted as her prototypes in Spenser or in Greek mythology, and her attacker, since he is a consummate shape-shifter, threatens violence only for a moment before he craftily transforms himself back into the pleasant mask of Archimago.

> But, as it happened, scarcely had Phoebe's eyes rested again on the Judge's countenance, than all its ugly sternness vanished; and she found herself quite overpowered by the sultry, dog-day heat, as it were, of benevolence, which this excellent man diffused out of his great heart into the surrounding atmosphere;—very much like a serpent, which, as a preliminary to fascination, is said to fill the air with his peculiar odor. (Chap. 8)

Hawthorne does not say that Phoebe has won a victory over Jaffrey at this point, but it is significant perhaps that he does not reenter the house until she has left it. Nor is the threat which he poses to Clifford seriously raised again until there is talk of her going away. Then Holgrave describes Jaffrey in terms which hint at his next Spenserian incarnation:

> I can perceive, indeed, that Judge Pyncheon still keeps his eye on Clifford, in whose ruin he had so large a share. His motives and intentions, however, are a mystery to me. He is a determined and relentless man, with the

genuine character of an inquisitor; and had he any object to gain by putting Clifford to the rack, I verily believe that he would wrench his joints from their sockets in order to accomplish it. (Chap. 14)

The foregoing reference to the Inquisition is almost a standard feature of the tradition of the Gothic romance from which Hawthorne so frequently drew. It is also significant, though, that Spenser's Giant Orgoglio is associated with the Roman Catholic faction. And when Jaffrey appears after Phoebe's departure, both he and Hawthorne refer often to dungeons, to God, to formal religion, to the Judge's "prayers at morning and eventide, and graces at mealtime." He has previously been presented as a small man, but now, perhaps to emphasize the giant aspect, Jaffrey's bulk is stressed. "A foot was heard scraping itself on the threshold, and thence somewhat ponderously stepping on the floor." Both he and Orgoglio are compared to castles. And Jaffrey's forehead is described now as "the stony brow of a precipitous mountain" (Chap. 15).

In *The Faerie Queene*, the Redcross Knight is imprisoned by Orgoglio after he has drunk from an enervating fountain (Maule's Well?) which Spenser associates with the goddess Phoebe. He is rescued from the dungeon through the *deus ex machina* efforts of Prince Arthur, whom Una moves to kill the giant of spiritual pride. Judge Pyncheon is struck down by what readers have regarded as a Christian *deus ex machina*. And perhaps God interceded at the unconscious behest of the absent Phoebe, since she is the only churchgoing and successfully prayerful character in the book—one of God's angels, as Uncle Venner calls her—and since God is associated in this particular chapter with the "sunbeam," Phoebe's symbol (Chap. 16).

The result of Jaffrey's death is that Clifford is set free, at least temporarily, from the dungeon of his mind. Holgrave is also released when Hepzibah, apparently at the precise moment of the Judge's death, unbolts the door to the gable in which he has been shut away, thus permitting a Maule to penetrate to the heart of the house; to take, in fact, sole living possession of the mansion which was wrongfully built on his ancestral ground.

But the disappearing Jaffrey Pyncheon, though dead, has still not finished with his enemies. Clifford, for all his misleading sense of release, does not leave the Seven Gables a free man. Rather he flees Jaffrey, who once again, and for the last, the most terrible time, has shifted his shape. "Come, come; make haste;" Clifford whispers to Hepzibah, "or he will start up like Giant Despair in pursuit of Christian and Hopeful, and catch us yet" (Chap. 16). Clifford's allusion, of course, is to Bunyan's allegory, not Spenser's, but it is also meaningful in terms of the parallels to *The Faerie Queene* which we have been following, for in the canto after the death of Orgoglio, "Sir Trevisan flies from Despayre, / Whom Redcross Knight withstands."

By his death, which is regarded as God's vengeance and the fulfillment of the Pyncheon curse, Jaffrey is transformed, as Hawthorne reminds us a number of times,[82] into an allegorical representation of Death. The House of the Seven Gables is now neither the House of Pride nor Orgoglio's Castle; with a golden bough hanging before its door, the mansion has become Hades, the House of Death. This is the ironic inheritance which, with the unbolted gable door, the departing Pyncheons have left for the last remaining Maule, after excluding him for two centuries. And the "dark, cold, miserable hour" Holgrave spends with Jaffrey's corpse, like the Redcross Knight's encounter with Despayre, is his most terrible temptation. "I am all astray," Holgrave says.

> The presence of yonder dead man threw a great black shadow over everything; he made the universe, so far as my perception could reach, a scene of guilt and of retribution more dreadful than the guilt. The sense of it took away my youth. I never hoped to feel young again! The world looked strange, wild, evil, hostile;—my past life, so lonesome and dreary; my future, a shapeless gloom, which I must mould into gloomy shapes! (Chap. 20)

In Spenser, Redcross is driven to the verge of suicide by such thoughts as these, but he is rescued by Una, who "snatcht the cursed knife, / And threw it to the ground." Similarly Holgrave is saved by the returning Phoebe. "You crossed the threshold," he tells her, "and hope, warmth, and joy came in with you! The black moment became at once a blissful one." And after their love is declared, "They transfigured the earth, and made it Eden again, and themselves the two first dwellers in it. The dead man, so close beside them, was forgotten. At such a crisis, there is no Death; for Immortality is revealed anew, and embraces everything in its hallowed atmosphere" (Chap. 20).

Now it is, in both Spenser's romantic epic and Hawthorne's metaphysical novel, that the redeeming heroine can lead her rescued knight to the House of Holiness for final purification, so that Redcross can fulfill himself by becoming St. George, the slayer of dragons, and Holgrave can become a true Maule again, the planter of trees and the builder of houses "for another generation" (Chap. 20). Here I find myself in complete agreement with Professor Jones, who writes that "contrary to much recent criticism, the departure of Holgrave, Phoebe, and the others from the House of Seven Gables contains no overtone of pessimism implying the eventual creation of another house of pride [or, I would add, another Castle of Orgoglio or House of Death]. In assuming proprietorship of

82. *The House of the Seven Gables*, pp. 295, 302, 305, 307.

Judge Pyncheon's 'elegant country-seat,' they are, in Spenserian terms, merely reclaiming a part of the lost patrimony that sin and pride had usurped."[83]

This point concerning the optimism of *The House of the Seven Gables* is a crucial one in our consideration of the characters of romance. Everyone agrees that, after his dissatisfaction with the gloomy ending of *The Scarlet Letter*, Hawthorne set out to write a cheerful book. But a sentence from a letter to his publisher—"It darkens damnably towards the close, but I shall try hard to pour some setting sunshine over it"[84]—has encouraged critics to conclude that "after more than three months of writing and 'within two or three or four weeks of completion,' Hawthorne perceived that the logic of his story was leading to a somber ending. What he poured over it may be called sunshine, perhaps, but it was no part of his original plan, if, indeed, he had planned his conclusion at all."[85]

Such a critique assumes that *The House of the Seven Gables* is a realistic novel, and that its story, along with its characters, was free to follow its own internal logic until Hawthorne illegitimately intervened at the last moment. The additional parallels to Spenser which I have pointed out should help to combat such a reading. Hawthorne's characters could not have escaped his intention because they were allegorical representations long before they were human beings. Like *The House of the Seven Gables*, Spenser's epic "darkens damnably" during the Orgoglio and Despayre cantos, but there was never a real possibility that Una would not overcome the various embodiments of pride or that Phoebe would not pour her sunshine, which was prepared from her first entrance, over the gloom generated by the shifting shapes of Jaffrey Pynchon's life and death.

Critics have failed to sense the logic of both Hawthorne's and Spenser's conclusions because the endings are not guided by causal necessity. But psychological allegory and, perhaps, the workings of the human brain, are governed by a different sort of inevitability. Phoebe and Una can save not so much by what they *do* as by what they *are*—Love and Faith. Hypocrisy and Pride may seem more powerful and more believable to us in a skeptical age, but in the magical world of romance they can be defeated, and not by struggle, but by simple displacement, by a change of mental attitude.

This may not be the sort of thing which happens in the real world, at least not in the Lockean way in which most of us have agreed to perceive it, but romancers were trying to render another reality, the interior universe

---

83. "The *Faery Land* of Hawthorne's Romances," p. 118.

84. Quoted by William Charvat, "Introduction," *The House of the Seven Gables*, Centenary Edition, II, xxii.

85. *Ibid.*

of the brain, where, as they believed, an altogether different sort of logic prevails. In this romance world, characters are not fully rounded people, but flatly conceived faculties of the mind; oftentimes "unrealistic," but still archetypically real; frequently capable of being transformed, but not of progressive development; sometimes apparently forgotten, but never really absent, nevertheless.

·IV·

Two Characters: the Passive Hero and the Woman Who Exalts

He never looked at me at all. I just stopped the truck and him
already running back to go around to the door where she was
sitting. And he came around the back of it and he stood there,
and her not even surprised. "I done come too far now," he says.
"I be dog if I'm going to quit now." And her looking at him
like she had known all the time what he was going to do before he even knew himself that he was going to, and that
whatever he done, he wasn't going to mean it.
    "Aint nobody never said for you to quit," she says.
                        —WILLIAM FAULKNER, *Light in August*

I: THE PASSIVE HERO

Still another difficulty with the characters of romance is that they tend,
especially the heroes, to be passive. This quality has generally been regarded as a fault by bustlingly active Victorian critics and their successors,[1]
but we should not forget that the passive hero was central to the poetry
of Keats and Byron and a stock-in-trade of romantic fiction, whether it
was published serially or not. Goethe had seen this inactive "hero" both
as a heritage from eighteenth-century English fiction and as a requirement
for the nonprogressive epic in prose, the aesthetics of which he and
Schiller were soon to work out.[2] Thus Goethe wrote:

> In the novel, opinions and occurrences are above all to be presented; in
> the drama, characters and action. The novel must move slowly, and the views
> of the main character must, in one way or another, obstruct the unraveling
> of the whole. . . . The hero of the novel must be passive, or at least not
> highly effectual; we demand of the dramatic hero impact and deeds. Grandi-
> son, Clarissa, Pamela, the Vicar of Wakefield, even Tom Jones are, if not
> passive, yet retarding characters, and all occurrences are in a sense molded
> upon their dispositions.[3]

1. In *Charles Dickens as Serial Novelist* (Ames, Iowa, 1967), pp. 142–172,
Archibald C. Coolidge explains how the passive hero helped Dickens solve the
unity problem imposed by the serial form of publication.
2. See Chap. II, pp. 57–59.
3. *Wilhelm Meisters Lehrjahre* (trans.) Thomas Carlyle, Book 5, Chap. 7.

A few years later, Hazlitt wrote a playful essay on "Why the Heroes of Romance are so Insipid," concluding that it is largely a matter of plot necessity: the hero must not be too active or the villain would never get a proper chance to make his mischief.

But even Hazlitt recognized one fictional hero, Scott's Edward Waverley, as passive for a legitimate, thematic purpose. If he had lived another generation he would have acknowledged many more, for in the metaphysical novel the passive hero is the closest approach to an archetypal embodiment of nineteenth-century man. Bartleby is perhaps the clearest example, but none of Melville's narrator heroes, except Taji, are strong actors. They avoid heroism by virtue of their indolence, as in *Omoo*, their inexperience, as in *Redburn*, or their fear, as in *White-Jacket*.

The narrator of Melville's greatest work begins his story by instructing or requesting the reader to call him Ishmael, and in the first paragraph, when he speaks of pistol and ball and of knocking people's hats off, he seems bent on justifying the Byronic, the Old Testament, and the Islamic connotations of his assumed name. But the pretense is quickly dropped. The Biblical Ishmael was an outcast, a patriarch, and a bitter activist, whose hand was lifted against every man. Schiller and Byron introduced the figure to romantic literature with heroes who rebel against an establishment which has treated them unjustly. But Melville's hero has not been cast out by American society, unless it was by his stepmother, who punished him once when he was a boy. He is surely isolated, but it appears to have been by his own choice that he has preferred a life on the passive and meditative ocean over active confrontation with the world, and he specifically likens his preference to Cato's suicide. He is not the elder son, rejected by his father and denied his place in God's Covenant; rather, as Father Mapple's sermon is supposed to indicate, Melville's "Ishmael" is God's elect, the poet-prophet, who tries to escape his divine mission by assuming the disguise of his theological contrary, by skulking about the piers like Jonah and taking ship to the opposite end of the world.

Melville's hero pretends, tongue-in-cheek, to be incensed at "those stage managers, the Fates," who have put him down "for this shabby part of a whaling voyage, when others were set down for magnificent parts in high tragedies," but Father Mapple understands what has motivated him to become a common seaman:

> And now how gladly would I come down from this mast-head and sit on the hatches there where you sit, and listen as you listen, while some one of you reads *me* that other and more awful lesson which Jonah teaches to *me*, as a pilot of the living God. How being an anointed pilot-prophet, or speaker of true things, and bidden by the Lord to sound those unwelcome truths in the ears of a wicked Nineveh, Jonah, appalled at the hostility he

should raise, fled from his mission, and sought to escape his duty and his God by taking ship at Joppa. (Chap. 9)

For all these reasons, the narrator of *Moby-Dick* does not deserve to be called Ishmael. He appropriates the name as a disguise to mask his desertion and as a justification for the passive resignation from responsibility which he attempts.

From *Omoo* onward, this false Ishmael of Melville's usually befriends a more legitimate outcast or a more seriously isolated figure. Doctor Long Ghost cannot go home from Tahiti, Harry Bolton is crushed in body after being broken in spirit, Jack Chase, as we learn from the dedication to *Billy Budd*, has been entirely lost sight of, and Queequeg drowns. They have all been literally denationalized. Elsewhere in American fiction voluntary outcasts and expatriates befriend Negroes, Jews, American Indians. In England they sometimes form similar bonds with members of the lower classes, thus establishing spiritual alliances between what Disraeli called "the two nations." Such friendships, since they provide foil, should help us to distinguish between the true and false Ishmael, but they also contribute one of the most plausible justifications for the latter's self-exile. It is as though Isaac (Faulkner finally used the name and all its implications in *Go Down, Moses*), experiencing a guilty repugnance when he learns that his despised elder brother has been cast out for his sake, resolves therefore to reject his own inheritance in the Covenant God made with his father.

The motif is strongly expressed in a number of nineteenth-century masterpieces. Ivan Karamazov, refusing his share of God's grace because it is purchased with the suffering of children, vows to surrender his ticket to life, resolves to kill himself. Gregers Werle of Ibsen's *The Wild Duck* exiles himself because of his father's sins and catastrophically befriends the man he thinks his father has most seriously wronged. Of American romances, Melville's again make the point most clearly. The hero of *Pierre* thinks of himself as an exiled Titan, perhaps even a forsaken Christ, but in fact he voluntarily renounces his Crown-princedom in Eden because of an injustice his father may have done to his alleged half-sister. The legitimate son of tender conscience thus sacrifices himself for the bastard.

In England, Dickens is the great exponent of this same motif. Walter Wilding of "No Thoroughfare" (1867), written with Wilkie Collins, is wealthy because, when he was a baby, he was mistaken for the legitimate heir. He succumbs to the utmost grief and despair when he discovers that he has "innocently got the inheritance of another man." Thus, Walter resolves, "He must be found. How do I know that he is not at this moment in misery, without bread to eat? He must be found!"[4] Ultimately Wilding

4. *Christmas Stories*, (London, 1956), p. 561.

dies of this grief and from the resulting condition, which in our own century would be called an identity crisis. "It is impossible," he says, "that I can ever be myself again. For, in fact, I am not myself."[5]

Collins developed this theme elsewhere, though less significantly, in *The Woman in White* and *The New Magdalen*. Dickens had treated it supremely in *Little Dorrit*, where Arthur Clennam, as it turns out, would have better claim to be called Ishmael than Melville's hero has. His mother, like the Biblical Hagar, has been banished, and her questionable marriage set aside. His own exiled young manhood has been severely crippled. Both mother and son, moreover, are the victims of a self-righteous Sarah, Mrs. Clennam, who believes she is acting as God's agent in punishing the fallen woman and her bastard. Thus Arthur Clennam's credentials as an outcast of society seem excellent. But he knows nothing of his real situation or his true history when we see him floundering in his lassitude, unable to save Pet Meagles from Henry Gowan, incapable of loving Amy Dorrit, powerless to act meaningfully in his own behalf, and pressed down with the conception of himself as Nobody, the unworthy man who has never lived. Like Richard Carstone of *Bleak House*, Arthur cannot take firm hold anywhere because nothing in his society is settled, but in his case the feeling of tentativeness is aggravated by a nagging anxiety that he may have no moral right even to his modest and unimproved position in that society, that his place may have been gained at the expense of someone else, perhaps of Little Dorrit. "The shadow of a supposed act of injustice . . . had hung over him since his father's death . . . vague and formless" (Bk. I, Chap. 27). Thus, after his lost youth and his consequent late entrance into English life, it is impossible for Arthur to get started in any meaningful direction:

> there was the subject seldom absent from his mind, the question, what he was to do henceforth in life; to what occupation he should devote himself, and in what direction he had best seek it. He was far from rich, and every day of indecision and inaction made his inheritance a source of greater anxiety to him. As often as he began to consider how to increase this inheritance, or to lay it by, so often his misgiving that there was some one with an unsatisfied claim upon his justice, returned; and that alone was a subject to outlast the longest walk. (Bk. I, Chap. 16)

In his own mind, therefore, Clennam is not a victim of oppression who has the right to be active for himself or in behalf of his fellow outcasts. Rather, feeling himself guiltily associated with the class of oppressors, he is robbed of all motive power. "I have no will," Arthur confesses, "that is to say . . . next to none that I can put in action now" (Bk. I, Chap. 2).

Hawthorne's Holgrave, from *The House of the Seven Gables*, seems

5. *Ibid.*, p. 563.

even more of an Ishmael than does Clennam. Holgrave's entire family has been disinherited, and each generation of it has, Ishmael-like, savored this wrong as the controlling truth of his life. The first Maule died with a defiant curse. Young Matthew Maule used the disinheritance to justify the psychological rape he committed on Alice Pyncheon. And the entire line has been driven by the social injustice into a prideful isolation, deeper, perhaps, than the situation would seem to warrant! The disinheritance has made Holgrave himself, who travels in the disguise of an assumed name, even more unsettled than Arthur Clennam or any ship-jumping Melvillean Ishmael. In his twenty-two years he has been a schoolmaster, a salesman, an editor, a pedlar, a writer, a dentist, a ship's supernumerary, a tourist, a farmer, and a lecturer.

> His present phase, as a Daguerreotypist, was of no more importance in his own view, nor likely to be more permanent, than any of the preceding ones. It had been taken up with the careless alacrity of an adventurer, who had his bread to earn; it would be thrown aside as carelessly, whenever he should choose to earn his bread by some other equally digressive means. (Chap. XII)

Holgrave's essential characteristic, like that of all his ancestors, is his imagination, the "only inheritance" of the Maules. Artistic creation is his proper sphere. But he does not practice this calling any more seriously than he does the others. Instead, the potential writer of tragedies seems content to remain a mere spectator or critic:

> "Undoubtedly," said the Daguerreotypist, "I do feel an interest in this antiquated, poverty-stricken, old maiden lady; and this degraded and shattered gentleman—this abortive lover of the Beautiful. A kindly interest too, helpless old children that they are! But . . . it is not my impulse—as regards these two individuals—either to help or hinder; but to look on, to analyze, to explain matters to myself, and to comprehend the drama which, for almost two hundred years, has been dragging its slow length over the ground, where you and I now tread. If permitted to witness the close, I doubt not to derive a moral satisfaction from it, go matters how they may. (Chap. XIV)

Holgrave is thus a familiar figure in Hawthorne's fiction—the dilettante artist as cozy critic and irresponsible Paul-Pry. He appears elsewhere in "Sights from a Steeple," *The Blithedale Romance, The Marble Faun*, and even the unfinished *Septimius Felton*, where the hero seeks the elixir of life because, as he complacently believes, he is "dissevered from" humanity.

> It is my doom to be only a spectator of life; to look on as one apart from it. Is it not well, therefore, that sharing none of its pleasures and happiness,

I should be free of its fatalities, its brevity? How cold I am now, while the whirlpool of public feeling is eddying around me! It is as if I had not been born of woman![6]

And, indeed, Hawthorne had been fascinated by indolent heroes from as early as *Fanshawe* (1828).

But of all Hawthorne's "Ishmaels," Holgrave is especially useful to compare with Arthur Clennam of *Little Dorrit* because both men seem to blame their isolation and perhaps the resulting lassitude on the social system, on the world of experience. It is partly for this reason that the novels in which they appear have been seen as closer to realism than anything else the two authors have written. If Arthur Clennam shows perseverance and energy in anything, it is in his vigorous attack on the Circumlocution Office, and, while Holgrave is casual about most matters pertaining to his life, he seems at least to be in earnest when he preaches that society needs to be constantly reformed to save us from falling into the paralyzing power of "Dead Men":

> I doubt whether even our public edifices—our capitols, state-houses, court-houses, city-halls, and churches—ought to be built of such permanent materials as stone or brick. It were better that they should crumble to ruin, once in twenty years, or thereabouts, as a hint to the people to examine into and reform the institutions which they symbolize. (Chap. XII)

Thus, in spite of their essential lassitude, which they share with Melville's false Ishmael, Clennam and Holgrave seem less disposed than he to run away from the battle. Their hands are indeed raised in combat, if not against all men individually, at least against the aggregate of mankind, his social fabric.

On the other hand, the two heroes are comparable once again in that, after a brief and ineffectual skirmish, each ultimately abandons his war against society. Arthur never formally renounces his social convictions, but he admits to Ferdinand Barnacle that the Circumlocution Office bears no responsibility at least for the mess he has made of his own life. And when he leaves the Marshalsea with Little Dorrit at last, we feel confident that he is through with his career of tilting at social windmills. Holgrave, of course, goes much further, announcing himself in the last chapter "a conservative" and confessing, when he proposes marriage to Phoebe, that while "the world owes all its onward impulse to men ill at ease, the happy man inevitably confines himself within ancient limits." His fulfillment as an artist, says the erstwhile spectator, who had shouted for the universal destruction of public edifices, will be "to set out trees, to make fences—

6. *The Complete Works of Nathaniel Hawthorne*, XI, 250–51.

perhaps, even, in due time, to build a house for another generation" (Chap. XX).

Readers have traditionally taken Arthur Clennam's retreat from the great battle to indicate Dickens' realistic understanding that society is too big and too powerful to be successfully attacked, that the best one can hope is to find some private shelter from its evil. And we have seen that critics tend to dismiss Holgrave's volte-face as part of Hawthorne's weak attempt to "pour some setting sunshine" over the end of a properly pessimistic tale. The thrust of my own interpretations would suggest a different conclusion: namely, that in each case the separate armistice which the hero signs with his society indicates that as a part of his redemption, he has come to understand that the real cause of his paralysis lies deeper than he had at first imagined and closer to home, that it resides in his own world view and can be corrected only there. I would insist, against the advocates of the stylish dark Dickens, that the ending of *Little Dorrit* is far from pessimistic, even in a comparison with the ending of *Bleak House.* If, as virtually every reader has noted, imprisonment is the controlling metaphor of the first eighteen numbers of the book—psychological and financial as well as physical incarceration—then the final double number is characterized by a succession of stunning jailbreaks. Affery's love for Arthur strengthens her resolve to break loose from her fear of physical violence. Pancks, motivated by moral outrage, discovers the courage to cancel his economic bondage to Casby. Tattycoram, faced with the "glaring instance" of Miss Wade, finds the spiritual grace to break out of her psychological imprisonment. Flora frees herself from the past. Even Mrs. Clennam, when faced by Blandois' narrated version of her own history, becomes powerful enough to overcome her symbolic, psychosomatic paralysis. And, most important, Arthur Clennam, with the help of Little Dorrit, escapes, not only from the Marshalsea, but, more significantly, from his inner prison of guilt and self-doubt. Everything in this conclusion betokens release, and both the tone and phrasing of the final sentences seem intended to echo the ending of *Paradise Lost.* The path for Arthur and Amy amid the sunshine and shade of the roaring streets is also a solitary way, and while some readers may regard their love as a comedown from the Edenic dreams the author has craftily encouraged them to indulge, it will lead ultimately to something more than the quiet joys of two frightened children. It is, indeed, the "usefulness" of their "modest" lives that Dickens emphasizes in the concluding paragraph.

Angus Wilson complains that "the plan" of *Bleak House,* "so logical and complete, by which the Jarndyce lawsuit corrupts all who touch it (save Mr. Jarndyce, a nonesuch), is quite upset when we discover that Lady

Dedlock's fall from virtue has nothing to do with her being a claimant in the case."[7] But Chancery is no more the source of evil in *Bleak House* than is the Circumlocution Office in *Little Dorrit*. The first page of *Bleak House* establishes the view that evil is primordial. Chancery is just an inadequate way of treating the chaos, and the great danger of all social institutions lies only in the fact that they have managed to gain so much public confidence. Looking to Chancery, a powerless specific, the sufferers neglect more effective though less glamorous cures, such as Esther Summerson offers, and thus the corrupting disease goes unchecked. The decay continues until we threaten to slide back at last into the original disorder. Dickens' charge against the Lord Chancellor is not that he created Tom-all-Alone's, but that neither he nor the world around him is ready to acknowledge the fact that he is institutionally powerless to prevent it. Dickens' ultimate charge, though a sympathetic one, is against his characters and his readers, who would turn, like Esther's mother, to the passion and the pride for solutions which only love and humility are capable of rendering.

Richard Carstone does not learn this lesson until he is on his deathbed. Clennam, on the other hand, appears to have recognized in time the truth in Ferdinand Barnacle's irritatingly complacent pronouncement that "the Genius of the country . . . tends to being left alone," and the Circumlocution Office "is not a wicked Giant to be charged at full tilt; but only a windmill, showing you, as it grinds immense quantities of chaff, which way the country wind blows" (Bk. II, Chap. 28). Dickens was himself a tireless and often frustrated attacker of specific social abuses, but, as the Leavises have written, he saw "people as at once the products and the symptoms of their society and the producers of it."[8] The paralysis of the system, therefore, is the symptom and the sum of the lassitudes in its Barnacles, its Merdles, its Gowans, its Dorrits, and, which is most significant to Arthur because here alone he can act effectively, in its Clennams. Thus, like Melville's Ishmael, who slinks away from the struggle, Clennam and Holgrave, who rush into it prematurely, sporadically, and ineffectually, must overcome their own basic passivities before they can hope to redeem the world.

Such an interpretation gains support when we consider that the large majority of apathetic young men in the metaphysical novel, unlike Clennam, Carstone, and Holgrave, do not even begin by blaming society for their paralyses. Miles Coverdale joins a socialist experiment, but he is no rebel. James Steerforth and Eugene Wrayburn are snobs, who trade on their positions in the establishment; still they are as unhappy as Holgrave

7. *The World of Charles Dickens* (New York, 1970), p. 234.
8. F. R. Leavis and Q. D. Leavis, *Dickens the Novelist* (London, 1970), pp. 280–81.

and Clennam about the indolent fever from which they all suffer. Sydney Carton is another example of the unrebellious yet unfulfilled man, as, on the comic level, are Dick Swiveller and Micawber.

In *The Last Days of Pompeii* Bulwer suggested that the superstate, which he saw, more than twenty years before *Little Dorrit*, as a vast prison, was responsible for the ignoble lassitude of his hero:

> He felt, it is true, the impulse of nobler thoughts and higher aims than in pleasure could be indulged; but the world was one vast prison, to which the sovereign of Rome was the Imperial jailer; and the very virtues, which in the free days of Athens would have made him ambitious, in the slavery of earth made him inactive and supine. For in that unnatural and bloated civilisation all that was noble in emulation was forbidden. (Bk. II, Chap. 4)

Bulwer also drew occasional portraits of the authentic Ishmael. One can instance Beck, the pauper outcast of *Lucretia*, who was perhaps a source for Jo in *Bleak House*, and Paul Clifford, who declares unrelenting warfare on society in the manner of Schiller's Karl Moor. But the unfulfilled heroes in most of Bulwer's romances tend to be well-placed in life and are too indolent even to be much discontented with the inequalities of the system.

In the 1837 preface to *Ernest Maltravers*, Bulwer writes that "It would have led, perhaps, to more striking incidents, and have furnished an interest more intense, if I had cast Maltravers, the Man of Genius, amidst those fierce and ennobling struggles with poverty and want to which genius is so often condemned. But wealth and lassitude have their temptations as well as penury and toil." Here was a problem more immediate to the writer's own situation and to that of most of his readers. Thus Bulwer seems to be speaking of himself and of his own work when he has Ernest comment on the "second-rate" *Memoirs of Madame d'Épinay*:

> Some persons seem born with the temperament and the tastes of genius without its creative power; they have its nervous system, but something is wanting in the intellectual; they feel acutely, yet express tamely. These persons always have in their character an unspeakable kind of pathos. A court civilisation produces many of them, and French memoirs of the last century are particularly fraught with such examples. This is interesting—the struggle of sensitive minds against the lethargy of a society, dull, yet brilliant, that *glares* them, as it were, to sleep. It comes home to us; for . . . how many of us fancy we see our own image in the mirror! (Bk. II, Chap. 1)

The emphasis, to be sure, is still on man and social institutions, but the society is not a wicked giant here, nor a dead hand; it is the simple though terrifying reflection of the individual and his own inadequacies.

The character and the situation recur throughout Bulwer's fiction. The title character of *Godolphin* is described in the preface as "the man of poetical temperament, out of place alike among the trifling idlers and the bustling actors of the world."

> Wanting the stimulus of necessity, or the higher motive which springs from benevolence, to give energy to his powers and definite purpose to his fluctuating desire; not strong enough to break the bonds that confine his genius, not supple enough to accommodate its movement to their purpose ... he can triumph in no career.

More than twenty years later, Harley L'Estrange of *My Novel* is almost identically trapped in his prison of world weariness:

> "I have sat in the Strangers' Gallery, and heard your great speakers; I have sat in the pit of the opera, and seen your fine ladies; I have walked in your streets; I have lounged in your parks, and I say that I can't fall in love with a faded dowager, because she fills up her wrinkles with rouge."
>
> "Of what dowager do you speak?" asked the matter-of-fact Audley [Egerton, M.P.].
>
> "She has a great many titles. Some people call her Fashion, you busy men, Politics: it is all one,—tricked out and artificial. I mean London Life. No, I can't fall in love with her, fawning old harridan!"
>
> "I wish you could fall in love with something."
>
> "I wish I could, with all my heart." (Bk. V, Chap. VI)

And Harley is equally weary of himself:

> If it were in the power of an animal magnetizer to get me out of my own skin into somebody else's! That's my fancy! I am so tired of myself,—so tired! I have run through all my ideas,—know every one of them by heart. (Bk. V, Chap. X)

Even in *Kenelm Chillingly*, written at the end of his long career, Bulwer repeats the same motif. Kenelm is a sort of Don Quixote with the education and tact and kindness of a Sir Charles Grandison, and yet he too suffers from the moral paralysis we have been tracing. "I have been doing my best to acquire a motive power," he says, "and I have not succeeded. I see nothing that I care to strive for, nothing that I care to gain" (Bk. IV, Chap. II).

It is worth pausing for a moment over *Kenelm Chillingly* because in this sententious and long-winded philosophical romance, Bulwer is more specific than elsewhere in assigning the cause of the malaise. It resides, he feels, in the spirit of the age—"the Age in which we have the misfortune to be born—an Age of Progress ... an Age of Prigs" (Bk. II, Chap. XXI). His is also, as Kenelm comes ultimately to understand, an age of realism.

"I have been educated in the Realistic school, and with realism I am discontented, because in realism as a school there is no truth. It contains but a bit of truth, and the coldest and hardest bit of it, and he who utters a bit of truth and suppresses the rest of it, tells a lie." (Bk. III, Chap. XII)

As an aesthetic, realism makes for weak and false art; as a philosophy, Chillingly believes, it has robbed him and the youth of England of their ideals, chilling (Bulwer's pun) all their warmth of heart, and laughing them out of all potential greatness. Thus, realism, for Bulwer, is the wasteland blight which has rendered England spiritually impotent.

The passive hero, therefore, was a thematic necessity in the metaphysical novel. His troubled lassitude offered the best symbol for the typical nineteenth-century moral paralysis, diagnosed by Alfred de Musset in 1835 as *la maladie du siècle présent*.[9] He is Coleridge's Hamlet, Goethe's Faust, Byron's Harold, Arnold's Empedocles, Carlyle's Teufelsdröckh at the Centre of Indifference. He wants desperately to break out, to find his Arnoldian vent in action, but the spiritual forces of his era seem to prevent him. The business of the metaphysical novel is to alter these forces by changing the world view, but the terrible passivity, though it is undramatic, must first be fully reported before it can be dealt with.

II: THE WOMAN WHO EXALTS

Since he cannot help himself, the passive hero usually finds his salvation in the metaphysical novel through the agency of another character, whom modern commentators have found even less satisfying. We proceed, therefore, to the household Virgin, the hearthside Madonna, the domestic angel with her sunny smile and little basket of keys, who figures so strongly in the fiction we have been considering. Hawthorne's Phoebe and Melville's Lucy are prime examples, but Dickens is so famous for this character, or so notorious, according to one's point of view, that she constitutes the highpoint of his art, or else she epitomizes his worst fault. Nell, Mary, Florence, Agnes, Esther, Sissy, Amy, Lucie, Biddy, Lizzie—these are the encapsulated heroines, as Barbara Hardy has called some of them. They represent, or resemble, and this is perhaps part of our difficulty in accepting them, the one clear article of an almost conventional religious faith to be found in the metaphysical novel.[10]

Of course, the domestic angel was not particular to our writers. She was

9. *La Confession d'un Enfant du Siècle* (ed.) Robert Doré (Paris, 1937), p. 24.

10. James R. Kincaid has written, "*The Old Curiosity Shop*, for all its hatred of Little Bethel, uses evangelical rhetoric and clearly expects something like a religious conversion to Nellyism." *Dickens and the Rhetoric of Laughter* (Oxford, 1971), p. 78

a heritage from, among many other places, the Gothic novel, where the quiet hearthside was often established as a positive pole against the diabolic attractions of the superhuman quest. Godwin's *St. Leon* and Mary Shelley's *Frankenstein* serve as good examples. In the former, the hero discovers the *elixir vitae* and feels himself "henceforth forever debarred" from genuine marriage. "An immortal can form no real attachment to the insect of an hour."[11] This is a tragic consequence because "Man was not born to live alone. He is linked to his brethren by a thousand ties; and, when these ties are broken, he ceases from all genuine existence."[12] *Frankenstein* makes the point even more strongly. Victor constantly vacillates between the affectionate circle of his friends and family and the debilitating, evil isolation of his laboratories. Whenever he is away from the hearthside, his mind turns either to Promethean thoughts, in which he envisions himself as the creator of a new race of men and so produces his Monster; or else he sees himself as the preserver of the old race, and so murders his female creation, ending the Monster's last chance at healthful domestic affection. Thus solitude always depraves. Institutionalized society, moreover, is presented as unjust, as instanced by the trial of Justine and the fate of the DeLaceys. Each time Victor returns to the hearthside, though, domestic affection cures the wounds inflicted by his ambitiously questing psyche or by self-interested society. Yet Victor recognizes his obgligations only to his own satanic pride or to mankind at large. His personal and solitary quest to create human life without the sexual cooperation of a redeeming female is literally a sin against the idea of family, and it is not surprising therefore that the offspring he succeeds in producing should physically destroy all his own loved ones and that Victor should call it his Vampire.[13]

The domestic Madonna who tended this redeeming hearthside is also prominent throughout the nineteenth century and in virtually every school of literature. George Eliot's Romola is "The Visible Madonna" (Chap. XLIV). She is regarded by the plague-stricken populace as "The Holy

11. *St. Leon: A Tale of the Sixteenth Century* (London, 1799), III, 132.

12. *Ibid.*, III, 97.

13. Turning to a much less important work in the same tradition, Charlotte Dacre's *Zofloya; or, The Moor* (London, n.d.), we can see how widespread the theme was. There the consummate villain, Count Ardolph, is most strongly characterized by the warfare he wages against the family as an institution: "The species of crime, the dreadful and diabolical triumph which gratified his worthless heart the most, was to destroy, not the fair fame of the innocent unsullied female—not to deceive and abandon a trusting yielding maid—no, he loved to take higher and more destructive aim—his was the savage delight to intercept the happiness of wedded love—to wean from an adoring husband the regards of a pure and faithful wife—to blast with his baleful breath the happiness of a young and rising family —to seduce the best, the noblest affections of the heart, and to glory and to exault in the wide-spreading havoc he caused." (p. 5)

Mother" (Chap. LXVII), and Dorothea Brooke of *Middlemarch* has, as Lydgate perceives, a "heart large enough for the Virgin Mary" (Chap. 76). Significant also, and interesting in their variety, are Rossetti's "Blessed Damozel," Patmore's *The Angel in the House*, Hopkins' tall nun, James' Milly Theale, and Browning's Pompilia. This ideal character can be found virtually anywhere in nineteenth-century literature, even in the dead-level realism of *Mark Rutherford's Deliverance*, where the narrator's love for the child Marie is described as "love of God Himself as He is—an unrestrained adoration of an efflux from Him, adoration transfigured into love, because the revelation had clothed itself with a child's form."[14]

But the main thrust of realistic fiction was to present characters first of all as people. Archetypal meanings emerged from these characters in realistic works because, no matter what the intention, it is difficult for an intelligent mind to regard anything for a considerable length of time without generalizing about it. If the associational psychology of the realists has validity, then the seemingly mystic process by which the novelist first discovers his meaning while he is in the act of writing must come down to this: that he unconsciously fits the raw experience he is imitating into certain symbolic patterns which, although he may not have previously recognized them, have become deeply imbedded in his mind. Thus significant realism is a sort of accidental allegory, serving to embody and preserve the common myths of its period, which, because they *are* generally accepted, we call reality. Since she was still one of the most powerful myths of the times, the redeeming woman occurs in realistic fiction, but her power was clearly diminishing during the course of the nineteenth century, and she is therefore not always central in such works and not always successful.

The romancer, on the other hand, is concerned with myth at a more conscious level. The metaphysical novelists in particular, who wished to alter the "reality" of their century, did not merely reflect the fading concept of the redeeming woman; they employed it purposefully and insisted that it still had or could retain all its power. Such an adherence strikes most twentieth-century readers as superstition, and it went somewhat against the grain of common thought even in its own time—this is why it had to be insisted upon—but it does not necessarily follow, as many critics seem to assume, that the writers had to struggle to maintain their own belief in the idealized female.

For the metaphysical novelists, symbolic meaning lay very close to the surface of life; sometimes the meaning seems almost to have floated above it, to have been more real to them than life. Such, at least, was the case with the myth of the redeeming female. Hawthorne named his daughter

14. William Hale White, *Autobiography and Deliverance: Mark Rutherford* (New York, 1969), p. 269.

Una and nicknamed his wife Phoebe long before he thought of writing *The House of the Seven Gables*, and his love letters would indicate that he may have valued Sophia more as a redeeming spirit than as a flesh-and-blood woman. Melville called his wife "Orianna," his "Fairy Queene," and "Madonna of the Trefoil," the Virgin of the humble clover.[15] Unlike these Americans, Dickens had to search for his redeemer outside of his marriage, but he didn't have very far to look for his Virgin, and even her name was correct. As his early letters amply show, Dickens thought he lived in a world of dragons and angels; he tended to idealize most of the people around him, but no one more than his sister-in-law, Mary Hogarth. "So perfect a creature never breathed," he wrote to Thomas Beard shortly after Mary's sudden death in May, 1837.[16] In other letters Dickens called her "the light and life of our happy circle"[17] and "the grace and ornament of our home."[18] The words "grace" and "life" are especially significant, and we find them repeated in three more letters, each of which describes Mary as "the grace and life of our home."[19] Nor did this conception fade quickly from Dickens' mind. Four years later, when he had to give up his secret plan of eventually being buried next to Mary, he wrote, "I don't think there ever was a love like that I bear her. . . . I cannot bear the thought of being excluded from her dust,"[20] and in 1844 Dickens had a dream or dream vision in which Mary appeared to him dressed in "blue drapery, as the Madonna . . . in a picture by Raphael."[21]

Dickens' reference to Raphael identifies still another source for the domestic angel of Victorian romance, perhaps the most significant of all, for Raphael's name and the idea of the Madonna were virtually synonymous in the nineteenth century. Raphael is himself somewhat out of style nowadays, and the dominant force he still exercised in the nineteenth century is usually overlooked, especially by students of literature, even those who have been quick to take the hint about Dutch Realism, offered in *Adam Bede*. We are likely to forget, though, that for a great many writers of the period, including George Eliot, but especially among the metaphysical novelists and other romancers, Raphael maintained his more than three-

15. See Leon Howard, *Herman Melville: A Biography*, p. 141, and Melville's "Prefatory Dedication" to *Weeds and Wildings with a Rose or Two, Collected Poems of Herman Melville* (ed.) Howard P. Vincent (Chicago, 1947).

16. May 17, 1834. *The Pilgrim Edition of the Letters of Charles Dickens*, I, 259.

17. To an unknown correspondent, June [8], 1837. *Ibid.*, I, 268.

18. To George Cox, May 8, 1837. *Ibid.*, I, 258.

19. To George Thomson, May 8, 1837, *Ibid.*, I, 257; to W. Harrison Ainsworth [May 8, 1837], *Ibid.*, I, 257; and to Richard Johns [May 31, 1837], *Ibid.*, I, 263.

20. To Forster, Oct. 25, 1841. *Ibid.*, II, 410.

21. To Forster, Sept. 30, 1844. *The Letters of Charles Dickens*, I, 269.

century-old place as the greatest of all visual artists, and his Madonna stood as the ultimate, most powerful, artistic creation.

Raphael was especially necessary to the value-seeking spokesmen for metaphysical thought because, as a recent art historian has written, "his confidence in humanity was greater than that of any artist since the fourth century B.C."[22] Thus, Carlyle and Emerson equated Raphael with Shakespeare as an illustrator of wisdom, while Goethe worshipped him along with Mozart. He was the representative artist for all three of these sages of romantic thought, as he was for Hegel, who saw Raphael as the prime example of the idealizing artist.[23]

The nineteenth-century work of romantic fiction that makes perhaps the most obvious use of Raphael's Madonna is Victor Hugo's *Notre-Dame de Paris*, which begins with a production of Pierre Gringoire's play, "The Wise Decision of Madame Virgin Mary." The flesh-and-blood Madonna of the work is, of course, Esmeralda, whose Ralphaelesque qualities are especially emphasized. She is compared to the Virgin throughout, up to the very moment of her death, and when she stands at the gallows for the first time "she resembled what she had been, as a virgin of Masaccio resembles a Virgin of Raphael's—weaker, thinner, more delicate."[24] Esmeralda saves Gringoire's life, she redeems Quasimodo, who had previously loved Big Marie, the bell of the Cathedral, and she spurns Claude Frollo, the alchemist priest, who worships the power of blackness.

The first gallows scene, referred to above, may have been an influence on the opening chapters of *The Scarlet Letter*. In both scenes the weak lover looks down on the prisoner from a balcony and wills her to keep silent; in both scenes the Faustian alchemist, with his hellish bargain, is in the crowd. And, of course, Hawthorne's heroine is also compared at this moment to the Madonna. "Had there been a Papist among the crowd of Puritans, he might have seen in this beautiful woman, so picturesque in her attire and mien, and with the infant at her bosom, an object to remind him of the image of Divine Maternity, which so many illustrious painters have vied with one another to represent" (Chap. II).

The parallel is tempting, and it is tempting also to suggest that Hawthorne's association of the Virgin with the element of sunshine, as exemplified everywhere in his depiction of Phoebe in *The House of the Seven*

22. Kenneth Clark, *The Nude: A Study in Ideal Form* (Garden City, N.Y., 1956), p. 274.

23. *The Philosophy of Fine Art* (trans.) F. P. B. Omaston (London, 1920), I, 213.

24. *Notre-Dame of Paris* (trans.) J. Carroll Beckwith (London, 1895), Bk. VIII, Chap. VI.

Gables, and the similar association in the character of Esther Summerson of *Bleak House* are both derived from *Notre-Dame de Paris*, where Esmeralda, "bathed in sunshine," worships the soldier, "her lord Phoebus,"[25] and is herself loved by a Promethean alchemist, who says, "Gold is the sun; to make gold is to become God."[26]

But one must always be cautious in tracing the sources of romance, for the mythic patterns are bewilderingly intermixed and the ultimate roots are in commonly available myths. Certainly, at least, the metaphysical novelists did not need the specific influence of Hugo to put them on to these motifs or to introduce them to Raphael's Madonna. Indeed, the advocacy of Raphael during a period when his art was coming seriously under attack from Ruskin and others was an important aesthetic position with most of the metaphysical novelists.[27] The particular association of sun worship and virginity, moreover, had been an interest of romance at least since Heliodorus. And Raphael, whose great accomplishment, according to Berenson, was to Hellenize the Bible,[28] drew significantly upon the ancient romances. His Psyche and his Galatea can be seen as variants of his Holy Virgin, at least insofar as they all represent idealized womankind. For the nineteenth century, therefore, Raphael established both Christian and classical antecedents and connotations for the Madonna figure.[29] The Chris-

25. *Ibid.*, Bk. VIII, Chap. VI.

26. *Ibid.*, Bk. V, Chap. I.

27. For Bulwer, Raphael was always the figure to set most strongly against the realists, with their tawdry and ephemeral aims. For Dickens, he was "the Great Master" whose accomplishments rendered the Pre-Raphaelites as ridiculous among painters as would be a Pre-Galileo Brotherhood for scientists ("Old Lamps for New Ones," *Household Words*, June 15, 1850, p. 266). Hawthorne's two European notebooks and Melville's *Journal of a Visit to Europe and the Levant, October 11, 1856—May 6, 1857* (Howard C. Horsford ((ed.)), Princeton, 1955) show that these writers paid more attention to Raphael's works than to those of any other painter or sculptor. There was a book about Raphael in Melville's library, and Hawthorne's home was decorated, from the early days of his marriage until his death, with engravings of Raphael's paintings. (Two of the tableaulike moments in *The Blithedale Romance*, the last scene at Eliot's Pulpit and the scene in the Lyceum Hall when Coverdale whispers in Hollingsworth's ear, are, I would venture, quotations from an engraving of *The Transfiguration*, which Hawthorne owned.) "Until we learn to appreciate the cherubs and angels that Raphael scatters through the blessed air in a picture of the Nativity," Hawthorne wrote relative to the debate between ideal and realistic art, "it is not amiss to look at a Dutch fly settling on a peach, or a bumble-bee burying himself in a flower ("The French and Italian Notebooks by Nathaniel Hawthorne" [ed.] Norman Holmes Pearson [diss. Yale, 1941], II, 389). Raphael's *Madonna della Sedia* was for him "the most beautiful picture in the world" (*ibid.*, II, 373).

28. *The Italian Painters of the Renaissance* (New York, 1931), p. 39.

29. Alexander Welsh writes that "the redemptive figure who tends the [hearth]

tian influence, moreover, is also of a mixed sort, for it developed—again through Raphael, but this time in his Sienese phase—from medieval cults of the Virgin which went some distance beyond the tenets of orthodox Christianity.

When we consider the Madonna figure of the metaphysical novelists, then, we are dealing with a significant symbol, not just an embarrassing convention. The redeeming woman was a pervasive force in the daily lives of these writers, who tried to gain their own salvation through her flesh-and-blood embodiments. She was the supreme subject of the painter they held in highest respect. And she carried spiritual connotations from the periods of history and the movements of thought with which they were attempting to combat modern rationalism. Our own impatience with her as a literary figure may suggest that the metaphysical novelists lost this battle, but from the point of view of their own times, they were employing the most potent symbolic embodiment available to their century. Even John Stuart Mill and Auguste Comte would not have argued this point with them.

Alexander Welsh, who has written the best study of the nineteenth-century Madonna figure, believes that her "powers are concentrated against death."[30] My own reading of the century suggests that while the fear of annihilation was powerful, especially in Melville and Dickens, writers expressed an equally strong concern with a sort of death-in-life, a moral paralysis, the loss of effective motivation. The great thing about the Madonna, about the female principle, for that matter, was not that she had power against some specific evil, but, as Henry Adams recognized, that she represented power itself, the generative or motive energy which the nineteenth century feared it had lost and was preoccupied, at all levels of philosophical thought and quackery, to regain. Thus the Saint-Simonians waited for a female Messiah. When a Rube Goldberg "Motive Power" machine was constructed at mid-century in Lynn, Massachusetts, a pregnant woman was brought in to give it official birth.[31] And females, preferably virgins, were often essential ingredients of the many experiments in animal magnetism, whose aim was to free man from the limitations of his conscious or rational mind, so that he might be able to realize his full potential.

"The search for pure power," as Angus Fletcher has written, "is at the heart of all allegorical quests,"[32] and we have seen that a lack of motive

---

fire is endowed with powers reminiscent of the domestic religion of Greece and Rome, of Christian salvation and more ancient wisdom." *The City of Dickens* (Oxford, 1971), p. 212.

30. *Ibid.*
31. See Slater Brown, *The Heyday of Spiritualism* (New York, 1972).
32. *Allegory: The Theory of a Symbolic Mode* (Ithaca, N.Y.), p. 338.

power is the chief symptom of the disease from which the hero of the metaphysical novel is a sufferer. The domestic angel restores him in several ways: partly by removing the shield of experience which had deadened his inner electrical circuits, partly by weaning him away from the mad, irrelevant, energy-wasting quests of his century, and partly by feeding him from the dynamo of her own love. These are the functions of Phoebe in relation to Holgrave and the functions of Hilda, "the handmaiden of Raphael," in relation to Kenyon. They were the benefits also which Hawthorne hoped to derive from his own wife. "Thy husband needs thy sunshine," he wrote Sophia on November 27, 1840 (and November is the month for the winter vision of romance), "for he is quite pervaded with the sullenness of all nature."[33]

Admittedly, with all the power that is ascribed to her, the domestic angel is often presented in terms which appear in our times to be more than somewhat condescending. Thus Hawthorne had written to Sophia during the previous winter: "You are a poem . . . a sort of sweet, simple, gay, pathetic ballad, which Nature is singing, sometimes with tears, sometimes with smiles, and sometimes with intermingled smiles and tears."[34] It was his "faith and religion not to mix her up with any earthly annoyance."[35] There can be no doubt, moreover, that Holgrave intends to treat his Phoebe in much the same manner, a manner which modern women are, of course, justified in resenting. Bulwer's love letters to his bride were actually written in baby talk. Lily, the heroine of his *Kenelm Chillingly*, is described as "neither child nor woman," and she speaks charmingly "with the naïveté of a child six years old." Lily has been protected from education by her guardian, who would have her happy rather than learned, and would form her into a sort of lyric, "weaving out poetry from her own thoughts and fancies" (Bk. VI, Chap. XVII). Such a character seems an insult to modern, educated women, but the point of *Kenelm Chillingly* is that education, especially modern education, is the disease that has blighted *both* the men and the women of England. Unspoiled Lily is sufficiently powerful to restore her indolent lover to a worthwhile career and to teach him that a meaningful life must be based on "fixed beliefs daily warmed into vital action in the sunshine of a congenial home" (Bk. VI, Chap. XIV). Near the conclusion of *My Novel*, a book which warned that the schoolmaster is loose in the land and which attempted systematically to disprove the aphorism "Knowledge is Power," the redeemed hero pronounces, "Blessed is the woman who exalts."

33. Quoted in *Love Letters of Nathaniel Hawthorne* (Chicago, 1907), I, 228.
34. Dec. 5, 1839. *Ibid.*, I, 108.
35. Letter to Margaret Fuller, Aug. 28, 1842. *Hawthorne and his Wife* (ed.) Julian Hawthorne (Cambridge, Mass., 1884), I, 254.

In both Hawthorne and Bulwer the power of these women is clearly supernatural. Phoebe's strength derives from "homely witchcraft" (Chap. V). Lily's pet name, taken quite seriously in a number of playful conversations, is Fairy. Nadia of *The Last Days of Pompeii* is "a very emblem of Psyche in her wanderings; of Hope, walking through the Valley of the Shadow; of the soul itself, lone but undaunted, amidst the danger and the snares of life" (Bk. V, Chap. IX). Sophy Waife, the heroine of *What Will He Do With It?*, is called Ladybird, and Bulwer finds opportunities to associate her with both Titania and Sabrina Fair. In *Night and Morning*, the heroine is finally described as "Florimel . . . the new and the true one" (Bk. V, Chap. 22).

Bulwer presents his uneducated, fairy redeemer most fully, and most sententiously, in *Ernest Maltravers* and its sequel, *Alice; or, The Mysteries*. In these works, an illiterate fifteen-year-old girl, who has never heard of God or thought about the Creation, ultimately saves the philosophical Maltravers from the paralyzing *mal du siècle*. And in the final chapter of *Alice*, Ernest gives her full recognition:

> Here have I found that which shames and bankrupts the Ideal! Here have
> I found a virtue, that, coming at once from God and Nature, has been
> wiser than all my false philosophy and firmer than all my Pride! You . . .
> alike through the equal trials of poverty and wealth, have been destined to
> rise above all triumphant; the example of the sublime moral that teaches us
> with what mysterious beauty and immortal holiness the Creator has en-
> dowed our human nature when hallowed by our human affections! YOU
> alone suffice to shatter into dust the haughty creeds of the Misanthrope and
> Pharisee! And your fidelity to my erring self has taught me to love, to
> serve, to compassionate, to respect the Community of God's creatures to
> which—noble and elevated though you are—you yet belong.

In Melville, because of the shipboard settings, the Madonna often appears in symbolic form rather than as an actual character. The two words which break the spell and rescue the hero-narrator from his lassitude and paralysis among the Typees are "Home" and "Mother," and they are replaced at the conclusion of *Omoo* by an American whaling ship, with a "motherly look," which carries him away from the cynically despairing Doctor Long Ghost and the rotting society of Tahiti. In *Moby-Dick*, the hero is rescued by another motherly whaler, named for an Old Testament woman who was generally interpreted as a prefigurement of the Virgin. "On the second day, a sail drew near, nearer, and picked me up at last. It was the devious-cruising *Rachel*, that in the retracing search after her missing children, only found another orphan."

Of the actual women characters in Melville's works, Fayaway is merely an exotic dream, but Arfretee and Mrs. Bell, both mother figures, appear briefly in *Omoo*. Yillah, of *Mardi*, seems to promise redemption to all her questors, if they could only find her, and had *Pierre* been a true romance, the alienated hero would, no doubt, have been saved by Lucy, who "in her own virgin heart remained transparently immaculate, without shadow of flaw or vein" (Bk. XXIII, Pt. IV). *Clarel* is another "unfulfilled romance" (Pt. X, Sect. i), and once again the redeeming female is present. Ruth's potential function is defined in the lines where Melville describes her mother:

> Clarel, bereft while still but young,
> Mother or sister had not known;
> To him now first in life was shown,
> In Agar's frank demeanor kind,
> What charm to woman may belong
> When by a natural bent inclined
> To goodness in domestic play;
> On earth no better thing than this—
> It canonizes very clay:
> Madonna, hence thy worship is. (Pt. X, Sect. xxxix)

It has been generally and, I believe, correctly assumed that Dickens' already idealized, dead sister-in-law became the model for his positive heroines, beginning with Rose Maylie, who appeared in the installment of *Oliver Twist* published in the month marking the first anniversary of Mary Hogarth's death.[36]

> The younger lady was in the lovely bloom and spring-time of womanhood; at that age, when, if ever angels be for God's good purposes enthroned in mortal forms, they may be, without impiety, supposed to abide in such as hers. She was not past seventeen [Mary's age at the time of her death]. Cast in so slight and exquisite a mould; so mild and gentle; so pure and beautiful; that earth seemed not her element, nor its rough creatures her fit companions. The very intelligence that shone in her deep blue eye, and was stamped upon her noble head, seemed scarcely of her age or of the world; and yet the changing expression of sweetness and good humour, the thousand lights that played about the face and left no shadow there; above all, the smile; the cheerful, happy smile; were made for Home; for fireside peace and happiness. (Chap. 29)

When he was preparing to render the death of Little Nell, Dickens wrote, "Dear Mary died yesterday when I think of this sad story."[37]

36. The heroine's names, both first and last, suggest that Dickens may have intended her as an anniversary tribute. We have already seen (Chap. I, p. 30) that he had been planning Rose from as early as the previous November.

37. To Forster, Jan. 8, 1841. *Pilgrim Letters*, II, 182.

The succeeding heroines, those who redeem the hero, were endowed with as much suggested magical and/or religious power as Dickens could manage without turning them into wholly allegorical and fleshless creations. Amy Dorrit sees herself as a figure in a fairy tale. Esther Summerson, besides her doubly symbolic name, has nicknames from folk literature. The heroine of *A Tale of Two Cities* is sometimes called Ladybird, like the character in Bulwer. Her real name, Lucie, which both Bulwer and Melville also used, means light and suggests associations with the most famous of the virgin martyrs, Dante's guide in the *Purgatorio.* Indeed, all the redeeming heroines of Dickens, from Rose to Lizzie, bear some saint's name or its diminutive.[38] On the other hand, there is no St. Estella, perhaps because Dickens did not originally plan to redeem the hero of *Great Expectations* through the love of the central female character.

David Copperfield is less—or at least less obviously—a religious allegory than *A Tale of Two Cities,* but Agnes Wickfield surpasses even Lucie as a consciously presented religious icon, an image of the Virgin.[39] Agnes comes from Canterbury, the religious capital of England, and "the house that held her," David writes, was "quite a sacred place" (Chap. 39). After the death of Dora, "she was like a sacred presence in . . . [David's] lonely house" (Chap. 54). David speaks of "her angel face" (Chap. 60) and calls her at various times, "the better angel of the lives of all who come within her calm, good, self-denying influence" (Chap. 18), his and Dora's "guardian angel" (Chap. 42), "my good angel" (Chap. 25), and "the better angel of my life" (Chap. 60). "All the little good I have done, and all the harm I have forborne, I solemnly believe I may refer to her" (Chap. 35).

So much could be dismissed perhaps as mere conventional sentimentality, such as might be found in dozens of bad Victorian novels, but Dickens wants to do much more than hyperbolically to point out the purity of Agnes' moral nature. To emphasize his conception of her as a religious icon, he insists on comparing her always with works of graphic art. Thus when David enters the Wickfield house for the first time he is confronted by a portrait of Agnes' dead mother. Moments later, when he sees Agnes herself, framed in the doorway of a panelled wall, he likens her to the figure in the painting. "It seemed to my imagination as if the portrait had

38. E.g., Nell for St. Helen or St. Eleanor.

39. J. Hillis Miller writes that David's relation to Agnes "is a late example of that transportation of religious language into the realm of romantic love which began with the poets of courtly love. . . . David has the relation to Agnes which a devout Christian has to God, the creator of his selfhood, without whom he would be nothing." *Charles Dickens: The World of His Novels* (Cambridge, Mass., 1958), p. 157.

grown womanly, and the original remained a child" (Chap. 15). Years later "the perfect likeness of the picture, a child likeness no more, moves about the house" (Chap. 18). During that first meeting David makes another comparison which likens Agnes to another work of graphic art, this time one with specific religious connotations:

> I cannot call to mind where or when, in my childhood, I had seen a stained glass window in a church. Nor do I recollect its subject. But I know that when I saw her turn round, in the grave light of the old staircase, and wait for us, above, I thought of that window; and I associated something of its tranquil brightness with Agnes Wickfield ever afterwards. (Chap. 15)

A few pages later, Dickens fixes the image in our minds. "The soft light of the coloured window in the church, seen long ago, falls on her always, and on me, when I am near her and on everything around" (Chap. 16). Nor will he ever let us forget it. "I began to think," David writes much later, "that in my old association with the stained-glass window in the church, a prophetic foreshadowing of what she would be to me . . . had found a way into my mind" (Chap. 44).

What Agnes comes ultimately to mean for David is also presented in a static way, suggestive again of a painting or a statue. Thus he describes her as she announces Dora's death—"That face, so full of pity, and of grief, that rain of tears, that awful mute appeal to me, that solemn hand upraised towards Heaven!" (Chap. 53). And Agnes, caught in this pose, becomes, quite literally, David's mental picture of her. "As you were then, my sister, I have often thought since, you have ever been to me. Ever pointing upward, Agnes, ever leading me to something better; ever directing me to higher things. . . . Until I die, my dearest sister, I shall see you always before me, pointing upward" (Chap. 60). Moreover, this is the image of Agnes which ends the book:

> Oh Agnes, Oh my soul, so may thy face be by me when I close my life indeed; so may I, when realities are melting from me like the shadows which I now dismiss, still find thee near me, pointing upward!

Readers have often complained that Agnes is an infuriatingly unreal character, that, especially in her disinterested attitude towards David's love for Dora, she goes beyond the pale even of saintly womanhood. It is not enough to say in Dickens' defense that she is not primarily intended to be real. Such readers are perfectly aware of this argument, and they are not satisfied by it. Barbara Hardy notes that the heroines of Dickens "are still sometimes defended on the grounds that their identity is symbolic rather than realistic and related to fairy-tale or myth rather than to the imitation of life."

It is obviously—very obviously—true that they are presented in fairy-tale and fabulous terms, but this only serves to draw attention to their sentimentality. Genuinely resonant mythological characters, such as Cinderella, Kafka's 'K' or Beckett's tramps, make their appeal by tapping our collective awareness, and do not need to be fussed over and advertised. Dickens' heroines are propped up by fairy-tale references (as real fairy-tale characters never are) and are also surrounded by emotional demands: they are too much admired, too much loved, too much pitied, too much held up as emotional stimuli. A symbolic character like Cinderella makes her point by the simplicity and singularity of the situation: if we try to imagine the teller of her tale asking for pity and admiration the difference between fairy-tale symbolism and Dickens' sentimental idealization should be plain.[40]

This contrast between Dickens' fairy-tale characters and the figures of legitimate fairy tales is certainly valid, and one can respond only by suggesting, while trying to ward off blows, that Dickens may have been working in a more demanding genre than was the teller of Cinderella, or even (dare one say it?) than Kafka or Beckett. They were seeking what Howells called "the effect of reality in visionary conditions"; whereas Dickens was trying, as we shall see in the next chapter, for "a visionary effect in actual conditions."[41] If Dickens could have been content to abandon the "real" world, or merely to describe it, Agnes would not, perhaps, have needed all the fussing over. But since he insisted on presenting that world, he had perhaps to use extreme methods to make us believe in or even to recognize its redeemer. True, Cinderella has also appeared in countless realistic novels where she has still been able to make "her point" with only "the simplicity and singularity of her situation," but it is always a different and a much darker point than she makes in the fairy tale. Agnes is the religious mystery of the real world in which she appears. She is like the statue of the Virgin which stands in the center of some politically cynical and physically sordid Italian city, equally as real and generally as influential as the filth and corruption which surround her, but requiring, perhaps, at least a modest pedestal.

"Given the premises of London life and of the earthly city," writes Alexander Welsh, the "home [this heroine establishes] represents nothing less than life in the midst of death."[42] Thus Agnes is described as the "one plain motive" in Mr. Wickfield's life (Chap. 15). Even Uriah Heep sees her in an allegorical way. "The image of Miss Agnes," he says, "has been in my breast for years" (Chap. 35). And for Micawber, "Miss Wick-

40. *Dickens: The Later Novels* (London, 1968), p. 10.
41. The quotations are from W. D. Howells, *Heroines of Fiction* (New York, 1901), p. 162.
42. *City of Dickens*, p. 143.

field . . . is, as she always is, a pattern, and a bright example. My dear Copperfield, she is the only starry spot in a miserable existence" (Chap. 49). For David she is the "One face, shining on me like a Heavenly light by which I see all other objects. . . . the dear presence, without which I were nothing" (Chap. 64).

The influence of Agnes on the four male characters just mentioned indicates a configuration which recurs in more or less complete form in a number of the works. Dickens' characters are usually orphans, but his Madonna figure is almost always accompanied by a father or a father substitute: Madeline Bray's father in *Nicholas Nickleby*, Nell's grandfather, old Martin Chuzzlewit, Mr. Dombey, Mr. Wickfield, John Jarndyce, Sissy Jupe's father, William Dorrit, Doctor Manette, Gaffer Hexam, Mr. Grewgious. And usually it appears to be the heroine's main business in the plot to attempt the salvation of this character, not from literal death, but from a sort of death of the spirit, a death-in-life.

A Tale of Two Cities is essentially a story of resurrections, of exhumations, sometimes comical, sometimes melodramatic, sometimes deeply psychological and spiritual. There are plenty of real corpses in the book, but the emphasis is on the living dead, and the most obvious of these is Doctor Manette, whom an unjust political system has converted from a warm human being into a number—One Hundred and Five North Tower.[43] Manette has been buried alive in the Bastille for eighteen years until Lucie, one of the most powerful of Dickens' heroines, comes "to restore [him] to life, love, duty, rest, and comfort" (Bk. I, Chap. 4).

She succeeds, but only temporarily. Manette has his relapses. And the fact seems to be that most of these fathers, despite the effort which is expended on them, are at best only partially to be redeemed. Sometimes they do not love or trust the Madonna sufficiently, but there is at least a suggestion in *David Copperfield* and *The Old Curiosity Shop* that it may be just as bad to love her too much when the love involves an exclusion of the rest of the world. Nell's grandfather and Mr. Wickfield nearly damn themselves by devoting their lives single-mindedly to the welfare of their redeemers. Their sacrifice is marred because they lack the important realization, which, as we shall see, both Wilkins Micawber and Sydney Carton share, that they are to be the true spiritual beneficiaries. To assume that service to the Virgin is ultimately for her sake, rather than for one's own, is, after all, another manner of demonstrating an insufficient faith in her power.

There is another wrong way to love the Virgin, as exemplified by Gride,

43. Similarly, the Gradgrind system in *Hard Times* tried to reduce Sissy Jupe to Girl 20, and the impersonal prison of David Copperfield tried to convert Littimer and Heep into numbered model inmates.

Quilp, Hugh of the Maypole, Pecksniff, Carker, Heep, Stryver, Orlick, Headstone, and Jasper. For though the heroine may be incorruptible, it is still possible to lust after her in a way that seems to pose a threat to her purity. These are men who have given themselves over to the financial, the material, the animal view of existence and who are consequently already dead in the spiritual sense and beyond the heroine's power. Dickens has somewhat more sympathy for the type than does T. S. Eliot, but surely Guppy of *Bleak House* is the original for the young man carbuncular. Yet with all the sympathy and fascination, there is little hope of redemption for the characters of this class. Only Lizzie Hexam of *Our Mutual Friend* is able to save her would-be seducer, but in a physical state which leaves him only somewhat less battered than Quilp and Carker.

The Madonna is also associated with one or two other men, possible lovers sometimes, and, at any rate, more generally capable of redemption. In *The Old Curiosity Shop* they are Kit Nubbles and Dick Swiveller. Kit, unlike Swiveller, does not consciously aspire to be Nell's husband, but his romantic love for her is beyond question. Little Barbara, whom he marries instead, is constantly made aware that she is a substitute as she listens to her husband's inspired retellings of the saint's legend of "good Miss Nell who died." Luckily, Barbara "was not of a wayward or capricious nature" (Chap. 69), and presumably she does not object. Similarly, the Marchioness, whom Dick takes as his substitute redeemer, is reminded of her function as Swiveller frequently remarks "at divers subsequent periods that there had been a young lady saving up for him after all" (Chapter the Last). Actually, Nell has practically no contact with either of these men during the critical stages of their lives, and her influence on them is a vague business at best, although perhaps no vaguer than in Christian cults of the Virgin. Nevertheless, the book leaves us feeling that Nell's life and death have somehow kept Kit straight and have brought about Swiveller's conversion.

> When Death strikes down the innocent and young, for every fragile form from which he lets the panting spirit free, a hundred virtues rise, in shapes of mercy, charity, and love, to walk the world, and bless it. Of every tear that sorrowing mortals shed on such green graves, some good is born, some gentler nature comes. In the Destroyer's steps there spring up bright creations that defy his power, and his dark path becomes a way of light to Heaven. (Chap. 72)

There is a direct line of development from Dick Swiveller to Wilkins Micawber to Sydney Carton. Dickens' vision of this character becomes so much more serious that the resemblance may not be immediately apparent, and it is also true that while the Virgin dies for Swiveller, Carton seems to die for the Virgin. Nevertheless, the same waste forces are present in all three, and all three benefit from the same redemption. Swiveller and Micawber become men; Carton, a god. Insofar as Dick and Sydney are concerned, the redemptions take place within an aura of mystery. Swiveller must experience purgation through a sickness almost unto death, which is a frequent precondition to conversion in Dickens (cf. *Martin Chuzzlewit, Dombey and Son, Bleak House, Little Dorrit, Great Expectations*), and the fairy-tale aspects of his adventures with the Marchioness, which include a lost slipper, are laid on pretty thick. Carton, of course, must pass through the full rites of a crucifixion on the guillotine, the modern cross as Dickens has designated it (Bk. III, Chap. 4). The conversion of Micawber is accomplished with less overt mystery, and perhaps this is one of the reasons it has gone down harder with readers than either of the others. Nevertheless, the redemption takes place under the influence of Agnes Wickfield, who, as we have just seen, is the most emphatically mystical character in the Dickens world, and whom we have heard Micawber identify as "the only starry spot in a miserable existence."

All three characters, like Pancks, Tom Pinch, and Newman Noggs, are slaves of the lamp to the evil forces of the stories they appear in. Dick becomes a tool in Quilp's money plot against Kit Nubbles, although he has enough natural insight to realize that Quilp is not a choice spirit. He saves himself when he rescues the Marchioness, the Virgin's substitute. Micawber is clerk to the spirit of rebellious undiscipline which pervades *David Copperfield*; more specifically, he is the servant of Uriah Heep in the latter's uprising against the Wickfields. When he exposes Heep, Micawber acts, as he believes, to save the Virgin from an unholy, forced marriage to the serpent, and that something should indeed "turn up" for him after such a rescue is not religiously inappropriate. Carton is Stryver's jackal; that is to say, he serves the modern spirit of self-interest, from whom he gains, as is logical, scant reward, either worldly or spiritual. Carton is, next to Manette, the most obviously buried of the living characters in *A Tale of Two Cities*. The victim of no specific external force except a vague disgust at the "desert all around," he is "the man of good abilities and good emotions, incapable of their directed exercise, incapable of his own help and his own happiness, sensible of the blight on him, and resigning himself to let it eat him away" (Bk. II, Chap. 5). Sydney is one version, perhaps the most Byronic, of the hero of metaphysical fiction we have recently discussed, the passive hero or apathetic young man. "I am like one who died young," he says. "All my life might have been" (Bk. I, Chap. 13). He doubts even the power of Lucie to reclaim him, but, given the opportunity, he finds through her the grace to break his allegiance to Stryver and the world, to sacrifice his physical life for the preservation of her sacred hearthside.

The other sort of generally redeemable man usually wins the Virgin's love quite easily and, perhaps therefore, tends to undervalue her spiritual power. For several reasons, he presents almost as many difficulties to the modern reader as she does. To begin with, he is less engaging than the pathetic old men, the lustful villains, and the near scoundrels we have just been discussing. He does not suffer from an exciting or charming inner turbulence, but only from a dull feeling of spiritual unworthiness. We have already encountered this character when we discussed Arthur Clennam, who thinks that somehow the money on which he lives belongs by rights to the impoverished Dorrits. In *Great Expectations* Pip's sense of sin is so powerful that Dickens was reluctant to allow him redemption even after guiding him through a seemingly exhaustive series of the mystical rites of purgation—Pip undergoes humiliation, poverty, and romantic heartbreak and passes through near deaths by fire, water and sickness. Yet in this one case, Dickens does not permit the slighted Virgin to wait for his imperceptive hero, but marries her instead to Joe Gargery, who needs no redemption.

We shall later suggest in relation to Pip's ambition to be a gentleman that *Great Expectations* is a story built on the fairy-tale motif of the bad wish fulfilled. The same structure also governs his vague feeling of unworthiness. In his youth he was unjustly made to feel guilty for things he could not control—his class, his age, his sex, the very fact of his being alive; by the end of Part Two, however, he has sufficiently earned his hatred of self. Thus Pip justifies his vague sense of sin and, like Arthur Clennam, experiences something almost like relief when he is able to convict himself on solid grounds. Both of them are too preoccupied with themselves to look for help where it is most easily to be found.

David Copperfield belongs also to this class of characters. He, too, was made to feel guilty by his elders—Mr. and Miss Murdstone, Mr. Creakle, even his mother, who told him, "I am so much grieved, Davy, that you should have such bad passions in your heart" (Chap. 4). In Dover, he thinks he began a "new life with a new name," but the habit of guilt follows him. No one holds him responsible for the seduction of Little Em'ly, but he appears to feel more remorse about it than does the actual seducer. Later he feels guilty towards his servants for leading them into crime by his lax mastership. Then he faults himself for trying to form Dora's nature as Murdstone had tried to form the character of his mother. Finally, although the guilt is too deep here even for overt expression, he takes responsibility for the death of his wife, for, surely, he had wished it.[44]

Charles Darnay is still another of these guilty heroes. Like his father-in-law, he is the victim of political situations, but he suffers more deeply

44. This last was, of course, a guilt which Dickens himself may have felt.

from a sense of inherited sin which forces him to flee France for England, changing his name from Evremonde (Everyman), and later causes his return to France, where he may face trial and find absolution from his ancestors' (original) sins. Like David in the case of Dora's death, Charles cannot share this, his most serious guilt, with anyone, not even his Virgin bride. But despite this serious evasion and the utter failure of his dramatic gestures, he does not escape redemption.

It is not the lot of these men to sacrifice their all and heroically to rescue the Virgin. They are the chosen suitors, the uneasy inheritors, the reluctant Isaacs of the nineteenth century, schooled in guilt and unprovided with any active means for expiation. They must simply accept the sacrifices which are made in their behalf—the inexorable death of a Nell, the awful patience of an Agnes. Think of Darnay, who must compete throughout his life with the ghost of Sydney Carton, who has assumed his name, his guilt, and his punishment. It is not an easy fate, and none of the heroes can reconcile himself to it without a struggle. Note how Arthur Clennam resists:

> No, darling Little Dorrit. No, my child. I must not hear of such a sacrifice. Liberty and hope would be so dear, bought at such a price, that I could never support their weight, never bear the reproach of possessing them. (Bk. II, Chap. 29)

Redemption should come through personal action in the world of experience. Arthur Clennam feels this as strongly as the modern critics, for the abandonment of a belief in dramatic or realistic action is as much a difficulty for the character of the metaphysical novel as for the reader. Arthur has spent his life waiting for the lifting of the psychological barrier which has kept him from such meaningful action. If he can't have that sort of fulfillment, then he is ready to settle for senseless punishment in the most humiliating of debtor's prisons. Yet neither form of heroism is allowed him, and he is virtually forced to accept the calm love of a motherly wife, a mystical conversion, Christian grace. He acquiesces in his salvation, but only as David Copperfield turned at last to Agnes, after all other possibilities had been exhausted. Experience has crippled him, but he retains enough mistaken faith in it to fight against so easy, so ignoble, so undramatic a bargain. "Better to sink in boundless deeps. . . ."

"The greatest Victorian art," George Levine has written, "tended . . . to be seriously flawed, to reveal a curious combination of great strength, intelligence, insight, alertness to complexity, and sympathy, with blatant inadequacies and naïveté."[45] Levine has also written:

45. *The Boundaries of Fiction* (Princeton, 1968), p. 6.

Whatever the time, faith in experience is one of the conditions of good fiction. George Eliot and Dickens go wrong precisely where they lose their faith in it and force themselves to believe in things which everything else in their created worlds seems to contradict, as for example, the loving reunion of Maggie and Tom at the end of *The Mill on the Floss*, or the incorruptible moral beauty of Esther Summerson in *Bleak House*.[46]

George Eliot's is a much more complex case than most critics have recognized, but leaving her aside, it is certainly not just to say that Dickens, any more than Melville or Hawthorne, *loses* his faith in experience. Rather he contradicts such a commitment, stating, as do all the metaphysical novelists, the paradox that only by abandoning one's exclusive belief in a world of personal action is it possible to qualify for a life of meaningful activity. To establish such a paradox, it was necessary for our writers to break away from the absorbing cause-and-effect world, to frustrate both the readers' and the characters' demands for dramatic solutions, and to engage us in a realm of the imagination, where, at least throughout the nineteenth century, the domestic Madonna could maintain a powerful reality and a sufficient strength for the archetypal passive hero.

46. *Ibid.*, pp. 71–72.

· V ·

A Suitable Remoteness: the Romantic
Side of Familiar Things

On some summer nights New York is as hot as Bangkok.
—SAUL BELLOW, *The Victim*

Henry James, in his highly influential but frequently misleading book on Hawthorne, apologizes blandly for the genre in which his author chose to write, a choice dictated by the unfortunate American setting. "It takes a great deal of history to produce a little literature . . . it needs a complex social machinery to set a writer in motion."[1] James goes on to say that "history, as yet, has left the United States but so thin and impalpable a deposit that we very soon touch the hard substratum of nature."[2] Hawthorne was forced, therefore, to write about human nature directly in romances, although he would have preferred, as James believes, to render it realistically: that is to say, as reflected in the experiential world of social interactions.

Hawthorne is himself somewhat responsible for this misunderstanding. We have seen that it was part of his policy to strike modest poses in his prefaces, to pretend he believed that he would more worthily be spending his time at any number of different occupations, one of which might have been the writing of realistic novels. But he is most specific in laying the blame on himself, not on his country. As a setting, Hawthorne keeps saying, America is fruitful ground for the realist. His own experiences in the Salem Custom House provided him with rich material for a novel, material which he failed to use only because, as he says, he failed to perceive its hidden meaning.

> The fault was mine. The page of life that was spread out before me seemed dull and commonplace, only because I had not fathomed its deeper import. A better book than I shall ever write was there; leaf after leaf presenting itself to me, just as it was written out by the reality of the flitting hour, and

1. *Hawthorne* (New York, 1967), p. 23.
2. *Ibid.*, p. 31.

vanishing as fast as written, only because my brain wanted the insight and my hand the cunning to transcribe it.[3]

On the other hand, Hawthorne believed that the American scene, though it provided ample subject matter for the realist, was definitely inadequate as a backdrop for romance. Thus he writes in the preface to *The Marble Faun*:

> No author, without a trial, can conceive of the difficulty of writing a Romance about a country where there is no shadow, no antiquity, no mystery, no picturesque and gloomy wrong, nor anything but a common-place prosperity, in broad and simple daylight, as is happily the case with my dear native land. It will be very long, I trust, before romance-writers may find congenial and easily handled themes either in the annals of our stalwart Republic, or in any characteristic and probable events of our individual lives. Romance and poetry, like ivy, lichens, and wall-flowers, need Ruin to make them grow.[4]

Henry James also notes the absence of "ivied ruins" in America, but the list of deficiencies he compiles emphasizes the social rather than picturesque failings of American life. His long catalogue begins by complaining that America has "no state, in the European sense of the word" and it climaxes by pointing out the lack of American Epsoms and Ascots.[5]

Hawthorne, it appears, was of the opinion that America had a sufficiency of such social properties and that they distracted from what he wanted to say. European romancers, he wrote in the preface to *The Blithedale Romance*, seem to have things better because "in the old countries, with which Fiction has long been conversant, a certain conventional privilege seems to be awarded to the romancer; his work is not put exactly side by side with nature; and he is allowed a license with regard to every-day Probability, in view of the improved effects which he is bound to produce thereby." And lacking both the ruins and the license in his own society, Hawthorne sought "a suitable remoteness"[6] from glaring reality by setting his romances in Brook Farm, in Italy, in colonial Boston, and in a seventeenth-century house.

The problem was much less exclusively American than Hawthorne believed. Ruins are more apparent to tourists than to inhabitants. At least English romancers were not aware of any such license as Hawthorne thought to be theirs, and certainly none was granted them by the critics, who insisted, almost unanimously, on realism of the most literal and

3. *Centenary Edition*, I, 37.
4. *Centenary Edition*, IV, 3.
5. *Hawthorne*, pp. 55–56.
6. *Centenary Edition*, III, 2.

commonplace variety.[7] It was not by accident that almost all the important Gothic romances had been set in faraway times and/or in remote places, and, on the whole, Charles Brockden Brown had been more successful in domesticating the form than William Godwin had been. When Ainsworth and Bulwer tried to write London Gothic in the 1830s, the critical outcry against them as vulgarians and subversives was so loud that both writers speedily abandoned their experiments.

As we noted in an earlier chapter of this study, Bulwer made a brief stand against the critics on this issue, claiming in *A Word to the Public* (1847), that "crime is a legitimate object of fictitious composition."[8] But the critics were unimpressed, and he beat a hasty retreat into the mildly domestic Caxton novels, muttering much later when he wrote *The Coming Race* that literature attempting to fulfill its traditional task of dissecting "those complex mysteries of human character which conduce to abnormal vices and crimes" will always be held in contempt by a society that complacently regards itself as Utopian.[9]

Nevertheless, in the posthumously published *Kenelm Chillingly*, Bulwer states the conditions under which even a Victorian can safely write romance and tragedy. It is largely a matter of finding a sufficiently remote setting:

> With the art of poetry, how imperatively, when it deals with the great emotions of tragedy, it must remove the actors from us, in proportion as the emotions are to elevate, and the tragedy is to please us by the tears it draws! Imagine our shock if a poet were to set on the stage some wise gentleman with whom we dined yesterday, and who was discovered to have killed his father and married his mother. But when Oedipus commits these unhappy mistakes nobody is shocked. Oxford in the nineteenth century is a long way off from Thebes 3000 or 4000 years ago. (Bk. V, Chap. IV)

This was a fact of literary life of which the old writers of Gothic romance had been well aware. An unfamiliar setting, either in time or place, provided a release from the usual requirements of commonplace reality. Thus Victor Frankenstein tells Walton, "Were we among the tamer scenes of nature, I might fear to encounter your unbelief, perhaps your ridicule; but many things will appear possible in these wild and mysterious regions."[10]

7. According to Carolyn Washburn, "the criteria which dominated the consideration of narrative prose fiction, 1832–1842. . . . [were] that a novel be true to life, probable, based on experience; and that it be moral. Both requisites . . . characterized the opinions of not only this decade but the whole period, 1832–1860." "The History, from 1832 to 1860, of British Criticism of Narrative Prose Fiction," (diss. Univ. of Illinois, 1937), p. 20.

8. Printed with *Lucretia; or, The Children of Night* (London, 1853), p. 305.

9. *The Coming Race* (Edinburgh and London, 1871), pp. 155–156.

10. *Frankenstein; or, The Modern Prometheus* (London, 1831), p. 17.

Nor could one imagine a Justice Fielding around the corner to spoil the reader's belief in the tyrannies practiced at Udolpho, although, of course, when an Italian like Manzoni wanted to use roughly the same setting, he had to secure his license by going backward in time.

Hyatt Waggoner suggests that in seeking his "suitable remoteness," Hawthorne wanted more than simple escape from the laws of probability:

> The best sort of [artistic] view would, he thought, be that which provided *distance*—in time or in space—so that the raw fact as such would not dominate, so that irrelevant multiplicity would be dimmed and softened by distance to allow the pattern, the meaning to emerge. Long views were best, just *because* the viewer could not see the details so well.[11]

The explanation is essentially correct, and it pertains not only to Hawthorne and the metaphysical novelists, but to the entire romance tradition, which, as I have previously maintained, was primarily interested in meaning. Surface complexities tend to obscure the depths of allegorical significance, and romancers felt that settings, like characters, had to be simplified lest they attract attention to themselves at the expense of the entire work. The local colorists were another army of the realist revolt and had also to be resisted.

There is still a third reason why the romancers sometimes preferred not to use the everyday world as setting. The metaphysical novelists, of course, were themselves in full revolt, not against literary conventions, but against the overmastering psychology of Locke and the materialists, who had created the everyday world, or, at least, which comes to the same thing, had established our conception of the everyday world. In her influential study of Germany, Madame de Staël had perceived Europe as suffering from a debilitating illness which had dulled the English imagination and perverted French taste. The cause of this disease, "the materialistic philosophy, gave up the human understanding to the empire of external objects, and morals to the personal interest; and reduced the beautiful to the agreeable." Kant's philosophy, she continued, "wished to re-establish primitive truths and spontaneous activity to the soul, conscience in morals, and the ideal in the arts."[12]

Bulwer, like Carlyle, recommended the imagination—especially as embodied in literature which developed from German idealism—as the most hopeful means of freeing his contemporaries from their enslavement to the world of material facts. The other metaphysical novelists were also strong antimaterialists. For Melville's Ishmael, as a recent critic has written,

11. *Hawthorne: A Critical Study* (Cambridge, Mass., 1963), p. 31.
12. *Germany* (Boston, 1879), II, 159.

> Knowledge does not result from bringing man face to face with a collection of pure facts. It involves, paradoxically, a turning away from the factual world, a retreat into an imaginary reality where the only visible objects are literary ones, products of the imaginative realm they inhabit. . . . Meaningful books are products of a mind which has turned away from the chaos and confusion of the world towards a contemplation of its own activity.[13]

In *Hard Times*, Dickens especially emphasized his long held conviction of the psychological necessity of fostering the imagination rather than allowing it to atrophy in the Gradgrind system, with its absolute reliance on "hard Facts." Thus he wrote of the workingclass: "When romance is utterly driven out of their souls, and they and a bare existence stand face to face, reality will take a wolfish turn, and make an end of you" (Bk. 2, Chap. 6). And Hawthorne had shown in *The House of the Seven Gables* how a psyche which values only commonsense factualism and despises imagination to the point of exclusion must literally drown in its own material blood.

How then was it possible for the metaphysical novelists to oppose a worldview while at the same time faithfully rendering the world which that view had created? The realistic novel with its emphasis on experience was itself a product of associational psychology and therefore had no difficulty in this respect. But the metaphysical novel, which depended on such things as occult conversions and fairy-tale psychology, was at a distinct disadvantage when it chose its settings from an everyday reality predicated on a disbelief in mysticism.

Conrad's Marlow points out how an absolutely remote setting can help solve this difficulty:

> Do you notice how, three hundred miles beyond the end of telegraph cables and mail-boat lines, the haggard utilitarian lies of our civilisation wither and die, to be replaced by pure exercises of imagination, that have the futility, often the charm, and sometimes the deep hidden truthfulness, of works of art?[14]

Our writers, therefore, had good reasons to head into never-land or at least into the far away. Moreover, in English Gothic fiction, Scott's historical novels, and the *Märchen* of German Romanticism, the beginnings of a viable tradition justifying such settings had already been established. It is therefore interesting that the metaphysical novel did not go much farther in the direction of fantasy and pure allegory than it did. But the highest forms of romance, since the times of the Milesian tales, have

---

13. Edgar Dryden, *Melville's Thematics of Form: The Great Art of Telling the Truth* (Baltimore, 1968), p. 84.

14. *Lord Jim: A Tale* (Edinburgh, 1900), p. 302.

always been impure mixtures. The characters of the genre, Frye says, are halfway between gods and humans.[15] Its allegory, both Bulwer and Faulkner have testified, is an off-and-on business;[16] its comedy, as we shall see, contains tragedy; and its favorite setting is not in an absolute, but in a suitable remoteness, "an available foothold," Hawthorne called it, "between fiction and reality."[17]

Mrs. Radcliffe and Walter Scott seemed to have fulfilled such a double requirement by placing realistic protagonists in unrealistic situations and remote settings. At the very beginning of the Gothic tradition, as Horace Walpole testifies, the attempt had been to reconcile the ancient romance of "imagination" with the modern novel of "common life" by conducting "the mortal agents of his drama according to the rules of probability; in short, to make them think, speak, and act, as it might be supposed mere men and women would do in extraordinary situations."[18]

But this was not an entirely satisfactory solution for the romancers of the middle of the nineteenth century, who were less interested in fully believable characters, and at the same time unwilling absolutely to abandon the contemporary and phenomenal world to their rivals among the realists. Almost all the important romancers at mid-century, and even some of the less important practitioners, were determined to make the modern scene available to romantic fiction. Ainsworth, in his attempt to English the Italianate Gothic fiction of Mrs. Radcliffe, wanted to see "how far the infusion of a warmer and more genial current into the veins of the old Romance would succeed in reviving her fluttering and feeble pulses."[19] Admittedly, Ainsworth was primarily interested in entertainments,[20] but more serious romancers wanted to show that although the prevailing world view tended to obscure the fact, man was actually living in what Wilkie Collins called "the midst of romance."[21] Thus Charles Reade's matter-of-fact romances tried to give his readers "the great tragi-comedy of humanity

15. *Anatomy of Criticism* (Princeton, 1957), p. 187.

16. We have already heard Bulwer on the "dim and shadowy allegory" which the metaphysical novel deserts or resumes at will. Faulkner's attitude towards allegory and symbolism, as expressed in a number of his statements recorded in *Faulkner in the University* (eds.) Frederick L. Gwynn and Joseph L. Blotner (Charlottesville, Va., 1959), pp. 68, 109, 121, is that they are tools which an author may find useful at one point of his story and unnecessary at another.

17. *Centenary Edition*, III, 2.

18. "Preface to the Second Edition," *The Castle of Otranto* (ed.) W. S. Lewis (London, 1969), p. 7.

19. 1849 "Preface" to *Rookwood* (Philadelphia, n.d.) pp. xxii–xxiii.

20. See George J. Worth, *William Harrison Ainsworth* (New York, 1972).

21. Quoted in Walter C. Phillips, *Dickens, Reade, and Collins: A Study of the Conditions and Theories of Novel Writing in Victorian England* (New York, 1919), pp. 125–126.

that is around and about them and environs them at every crossing, in every hole and corner." [22] Later in the century, the American naturalist-romancer, Frank Norris, making his "Plea for Romantic Fiction," put the case even more strongly:

> Romance does very well in the castles of the Middle Ages and the Renaissance Chateaux. . . . But let us protest against limiting her to such places and such times. . . . You will find her equally at home in the brownstone house on the corner and in the office building downtown. And this very day, in this very hour, she is sitting among the rags and wretchedness, the dirt and despair of the tenements of the East Side of New York. [23]

But a character in Kingsley's *Alton Locke* (1849) makes virtually the same plea: "Ay, Shelley's gran'; always gran'; but fact is grander—God and Satan are grander. All around ye, in every gin-shop and costermonger's cellar are God and Satan at death grips; every garret is a haill Paradise Lost or Paradise Regained." [24] And Carlyle had urged from the 1820s that poetry "must dwell in Reality, and become manifest to men in forms among which they live and move."

> This is what we prize in Goethe, and more or less in Schiller and the rest [of the German Romantics]. . . . The coldest skeptic, the most callous worldling, sees not the actual aspects of life more sharply than they are here deliniated. The Nineteenth Century stands before us, in all its contradiction and perplexity; barren, mean, and baleful, as we have all known it, yet here no longer mean or barren, but enamelled into beauty in the poet's spirit; for its secret significance is laid open. . . . For these men have not only the clear eye, but the loving heart. They have penetrated into the mystery of Nature. [25]

Bulwer was arguing a similar position from quite early in his career. In *Ernest Maltravers*, which was itself a serious effort to write an English, that is, a practical *Wilhelm Meister*, he had written, "when Shelley, in one of his prefaces, boasts of being familiar with Alps and glaciers and Heaven knows what, the critical artist cannot help wishing that he had

22. *Ibid.*, p. 126.
23. Reprinted in *The Theory of the American Novel* (ed.) George Perkins (New York, 1970), p. 246.
24. Chap. VII. A recent critic, Elliott B. Gose, writes of such romances that "as Victorians they were greatly concerned with the environment, both social and natural; as artists they were influenced by the Romantic preoccupation with the inner self. In several cases, they believed they had an obligation to reconcile the two." *Imagination Indulged! The Irrational in the Nineteenth-Century Novel* (Montreal and London, 1972), p. 57.
25. "State of German Literature [1827]," *The Works of Thomas Carlyle* (London, 1899), XXVI, 65–66.

been more familiar with Fleet Street and the Strand" (Bk. III, Chap. III). This statement, we can be sure, is not a call for simple, down-to-earth realism, for in his own preface of 1840, Bulwer emphasized that while he wanted to produce in *Maltravers* "life as it is," he did not mean by this "the vulgar and outward life alone, but life in its spiritual and mystic as well as its more fleshly characteristics." It was, he felt, a difficult combination he was trying for. Thus Bulwer wrote in the 1845 preface to *Night and Morning*, of "The vast and dark Poetry around us, the Poetry of modern Civilisation and the Daily existence shut out from us by the shadowy giants of Prejudice and Fear." But he felt that his own resolution and the courage of his followers, among whom in 1845 he especially counted Dickens,[26] were sufficient for the task. It was also, Bulwer was convinced, a necessary combination they were attempting, for if the metaphysical novel was going to save its readers from the materialistic world view, as he fully intended it to do, the writer could not altogether turn his back on the everyday reality which the materialists had imposed. "He who would arrive at the Fairy Land," he asserts in the same preface, "must face the Phantoms."[27]

Bulwer tried to find his suitable remoteness in two ways. On the one hand, he wrote what he believed to be a new kind of historical romance, the principles of which he expressed in the preface to the third edition of *Harold: The Last of the Saxon Kings*:

> There are two ways of employing the materials of History in the service of Romance: the one consists in leading to ideal personages and to an ideal Fable, the additional interest to be derived from the historical groupings; the other, in extracting the main interest of romantic narrative from History itself. . . . [The first, the way of Scott] is unquestionably the more popular and attractive. . . . I contented myself with the humbler task to employ Romance in the aid of History. I shut myself out from the wider scope permitted [to the fancy of Scott and his followers] . . . and denied myself the licence to choose and select materials, alter dates, vary causes and effects according to the convenience of that more imperial fiction which invents the Probable, where it discards the Real.

Bulwer's historical novels are heavily documented, far beyond the practice of Scott, with footnotes and end notes, all of which are intended to provide an air of near authenticity and a feeling that the past is only slightly less immediate than the present. These works contain what has recently been

26. The preface suggests that Pecksniff was inspired by a character in *Night and Morning*.

27. The metaphor's meaning is clear to readers of Bulwer's *Zanoni*, where would-be initiates must pass the fearsome Dweller of the Threshold if they are to leave the inadequate world of realism and enter the occult realm of the imagination.

recognized as "the most scholarly and complex use of history by any Victorian novelist."[28] The past, as Bulwer treats it, is much more everyday than Scott's, while his characters are less realistic, much more abstract. His is therefore a reversal of the old Gothic process, which placed realistic characters in ideal situations.

The other solution which Bulwer employed came really to the same thing, except that it dealt with an almost believable though slightly distorted contemporary world, peopled, once again, with ideal types. Thus began the school which, as we shall see in a moment, W. D. Howells negatively characterized as romantistic rather than truly romantic, but which was by far the more significant movement in terms of the history of nineteenth-century English and American narrative.

The link between these two techniques of Bulwer had already been forged by two of the most important Continental romancers of the 1820s and 1830s, Hugo and Manzoni. *Notre-Dame de Paris* and *I Promessi Sposi* are historical novels which seek the maximum in remoteness. Thus the pasts which they employ for settings are purposely distorted into wild, nightmare worlds. The first two books of *Notre-Dame de Paris* establish a milieu of gothic grotesquery with the dreamlike adventures of Pierre Gringoire. The romance begins with an episode which anticipates Kafka— Gringoire's maddeningly unsuccessful attempt to stage his play—and it continues through the wild Parisian night with the procession of the Lord of Misrule, the assault on Esmeralda, Gringoire's "trial" in the City of Thieves, his near hanging, and his strange marriage to Esmeralda. Throughout all this fevered madness flit the gypsy girl and the hunchback, beauty and ugliness. Manzoni's book, which was one of the most influential works of the early part of the century, follows in many ways the traditions of the Gothic novel and of Scott. The characters are realistically complex, and, in the early chapters, the rural setting is simplified and remote. When the hero moves into the cities, however, the remoteness is strongly intensified as the riot and plague scenes convert the setting into a backdrop from the city of dreadful night.

What both writers demonstrated is that the urban scene, largely neglected by the early romancers, is susceptible of grotesque distortion; what was left for the romanticists of the mid-century to discover, perhaps with the help of De Quincey, is that the city need not exist in the distant past to render up its potential remoteness. When Dickens wrote historical romances he also set them in grotesque, riot-torn and violent cities. The London of *Barnaby Rudge* is "a mere dark mist—a giant phantom in the air" (Chap. 31), and the Paris of *A Tale of Two Cities* is a scene of fan-

28. James C. Simmons, "The Novelist as Historian: An Unexplored Tract of Victorian Historiography," *Victorian Studies*, XIV (1971), 299.

tastic allegory. These are cities of the past, like Bulwer's Pompeii,[29] but modern New York, as described in Melville's *Pierre*, and modern London, as presented in Bulwer's *Lucretia* and in the large number of Dickens' works, are almost equally faraway and grotesque.[30] As David Masson, Dickens' contemporary, put it, starting with "a hint from an actual fact," he produces "a world of semi-fantastic conditions, where the laws need not be those of ordinary probability," and where "characters of a human kind verging on the supernatural, as well as characters actually belonging to the supernatural" can exist together.[31] And thus Dickens could produce what he called the "Romance of the real world,"[32] in which he could "purposefully" dwell, as he said in the preface to *Bleak House*, "upon the romantic side of familiar things."

W. D. Howells refused to grace the school we have been describing with so honorific a term as romantic. "Romance, as in Hawthorne, seeks the effect of reality in visionary conditions; romanticism, as in Dickens, tries for a visionary effect in actual conditions."[33] This sounds like a meaningful difference between the two writers, but it will not hold up for anything but the early works of Hawthorne. Howells goes on to say that "the [character] types of Dickens are always speaking for him, in fulfillment of a mechanical conception and a rigid limitation of their function in the drama. They are, in every sense, parts, and Hawthorne's creations are

29. Curtis Dahl has pointed out that Bulwer's descriptions of Pompeii are drawn from the catastrophic school of historical fiction, which has associations with such Romantic painters as John Martin. "Bulwer-Lytton and the School of Catastrophe," *PQ*, XXXII (1953), 428–442.

30. In *The Narrative Art of Charles Dickens: The Rhetoric of Sympathy and Irony in His Novels* (Oxford, 1970), Harvey Peter Sucksmith writes that "Dickens tries to face his own age. . . . [but he] discovers poetry in the contemporary city and takes the very image of a congested urban mass as the symbol of the flux of life" (p. 116). Donald Fanger describes the process by which Dickens managed this conversion of fact into vision: "By manipulation of externally imposed atmosphere, by creating those careful harmonies of a character with his surroundings, of an indoor scene with its lighting and landscape with the weather and time of day—by all such techniques of emotional underscoring, Dickens manages to involve his reader in [what Arnold Kettle called] "a world that is strikingly, appallingly relevant to our world." It is, in fact, our world transfigured by vision, sometimes comically, sometimes pathetically. The objects are all real and minutely observed. It is only their functions, their relations, that are different. Circumstantial realism, realism of topography, physical ambience, dress, custom, is present, but tinged romantically with the sense of strangeness and wonder that is Dickens' own contribution to fiction and to the varieties of romantic realism." (*Dostoevsky and Romantic Realism* [Cambridge, Mass., 1965], pp. 71–72).

31. David Masson, *British Novelists and Their Styles* (Cambridge and London, 1859), pp. 248–49.

32. "Hunted Down," *Reprinted Pieces*, p. 681.

33. *Heroines of Fiction* (New York, 1901), p. 162.

persons, rounded, whole."[34] This is the distinction we attempted a few pages ago between the way romance seemed to be heading in the days of the Gothic novel (real characters in an ideal world) and the way, as I believe, the metaphysical novel actually developed (ideal characters in a distorted real world). But one has trouble, certainly Dickens did, trying to read any of Hawthorne's allegorical figures as "*persons*, rounded, whole," and, except in, perhaps, *The Scarlet Letter* and in some of the stories, the worlds of Hawthorne seem no less and no more real than those of Dickens. In the notes for *The Ancestral Footstep*, Hawthorne describes his technique of romantic realism in terms which are certainly applicable to the Dickensian mode. Speaking of one of his settings, he plans that "it might have so much of the hues of life that the reader should sometimes think it was intended for a picture, yet the atmosphere should be such as to excuse all wildness. . . . The descriptions of scenery, etc., and of the Hospital, might be correct, but there should be a tinge of the grotesque given to all the characters and events. The tragic and the gentler pathetic need not be excluded by the tone and treatment."[35]

Hawthorne's agonies in "The Custom House" over the "better book" he should have written are generally interpreted either to prove that he really wanted to write Trollopean realism, as he said much later, or else they are dismissed as a mock serious bow which the romancer sometimes makes in the direction of drab realism before beginning his own more inspired work. If one has to choose between such alternatives, then the second is certainly the more attractive. When it comes down to a choice between "the narratives of a veteran shipmaster" and *The Scarlet Letter*, only the rankest Philistine would hesitate. But Hawthorne offers a third possibility:

> I might readily have found a more serious task [than recounting the ship-master's stories]. It was a folly, with the materiality of this daily life pressing so intrusively upon me, to attempt to fling myself back into another age; or to insist on creating the semblance of a world out of airy matter, when, at every moment, the impalpable beauty of my soap-bubble was broken by the rude contact of some actual circumstance. The wiser effort would have been to diffuse thought and imagination through the opaque substance of today, and thus to make a bright transparency; to spiritualize the burden that began to weigh so heavily; to seek, resolutely, the true and indestructible value that lay hidden in the petty and wearisome incidents, and ordinary characters, with which I was now conversant.

These sentiments are similar to the views we have heard expressed by the English romancers who were Hawthorne's contemporaries, and in

34. *Ibid.*
35. *Complete Works of Nathaniel Hawthorne*, XI, 491.

view of the fact that nearly all the books for adults Hawthorne wrote in the amazingly productive period following "The Custom House" attempt just such a spiritualization of the everyday world as is there described, it seems proper that, for once, we take him at his word. What he calls for is not the old kind of stark romance he had achieved in *The Scarlet Letter*, where believable though abstract characters speak out of a sort of stylized void, almost as in a Greek tragedy or a German *Märchen*, nor does he want mere picturesque realism. He says that he should have written the romance of the everyday, such as Dickens and Bulwer were writing, and such as he was himself very soon to write in *The House of the Seven Gables*.

It is indeed possible that Pecksniff was an even more immediate model for Judge Pyncheon than were the characters out of Spenser whom we discussed in a previous chapter. Another influence can be found in *The Old Curiosity Shop*, where a similar theme pertains: bright innocence, threatened by the gloomy, grotesque, materialistic world, ultimately overthrows or redeems it, by virtue not of her actions, but of her essence. In both works a pathetic old person who makes a failure out of keeping a prosaic shop could not survive without the heroine's cheerful and responsible aid. In both works a rightful heir is locked away. And in both, a materialistic relative, Jaffrey and Fred, threatens the sympathetic, more spiritual characters because he has deluded himself into the mistaken notion that they are rich. Jaffrey has also a source in Quilp, especially in the scene in which the latter makes sexual advances on Nell. Each villain, moreover, is developed in terms of the worldly serpent metaphor, and each heroine is almost literally an angel.

But leaving the matter of influence aside, and returning to the problem of romantic setting, I think it is possible that the two writers may have been thinking similarly when Dickens wrote *The Old Curiosity Shop* and Hawthorne, shortly before beginning *The House of the Seven Gables*, composed "The Custom House." Both works of Hawthorne speak of the power of evening and its illuminations to transfigure the actual world and make it a fit theater for romance. In *The Seven Gables* moonlight "softened and embellished the aspect of the old house. . . . The common-place characteristics—which, at noontide, it seemed to have taken a century of sordid life to accumulate—were now transfigured by a charm of romance" (Chap. 14). And it is this "charm," quite literally meant, which makes possible the redeeming love of Holgrave and Phoebe. My suggestion is that Hawthorne's idea about the power of imperfect illumination is rather like a thought developed near the beginning of *The Old Curiosity Shop*, where Master Humphrey justifies his nighttime rambles.

I have fallen insensibly into this habit, both because it favours my infirmity and because it affords me greater opportunity of speculating on the characters and occupations of those who fill the streets. The glare and hurry of broad noon are not adapted to idle pursuits like mine; a glimpse of passing faces caught by the light of a street lamp or a shop window is often better for my purpose than their full revelation in the daylight, and, if I must add the truth, night is kinder in this respect than day, which too often destroys an air-built castle at the moment of its completion, without the smallest ceremony or remorse. (Chap. 1)

And when Nell is discovered dead, we are reminded of how she looked in the glow of the fireside and the furnace and in the evening. "So," Dickens tells us, "shall we know the angels in their majesty, after death" (Chap. 71).

In "The Custom House" the effect of moonlight and firelight on the ordinary world is developed at much greater length:

Moonlight, in a familiar room, falling so white upon the carpet, and showing all its figures so distinctly,—making every object so minutely visible, yet so unlike a morning or noontide visibility, is a medium the most suitable for a romance-writer to get acquainted with his illusive guests.

Hawthorne then goes on to show how the most everyday aspects of domestic scenery—chairs, lamps, a child's shoe, a basket—"are so spiritualized by the unusual light, that they seem to lose their actual substance, and become things of intellect. . . . Thus, therefore, the floor of our familiar room has become a neutral territory, somewhere between the real world and fairy-land, where the Actual and the Imaginary may meet, and each imbue itself with the nature of the other." Then the warmer light of "the somewhat dim coal-fire . . . mingles itself with the cold spirituality of the moonbeams, and communicates, as it were, a heart and sensibilities of human tenderness to the forms which fancy summons up. It converts them from snow-images into men and women." Thus romance transforms the meaningless ordinary world into cold allegory and then renders it back as palpitating and significant life.

The Dickensian process of spiritualizing the real world by night-light distortions may have come consciously to Hawthorne's mind while he was writing "The Custom House," but it is certainly not necessary to insist on the specific influence. Both Wordsworth and Coleridge had written on the power of moonlight to transfigure reality, and such idealizations had been a necessary, if not fully realized, part of Hawthorne's aesthetics for some time past. The sculptor in "Drowne's Wooden Image" is a mediocrity because his figures are entirely earthbound. Yet when he achieves his masterpiece, it is not a work of pure spirituality—"it is as ideal as an antique statue, and yet as real as any lovely woman whom one meets at a fireside or in the street."[36] And Hawthorne claims the same power for himself when he observes the bathing girls in "Footprints on the Sea-Shore." As he says, "I know these girls to be realities of flesh and blood, yet, glancing at them so briefly, they mingle like kindred creatures with the ideal beings of my mind."[37]

Nevertheless, the most frequent mode of these early tales, as of *The Scarlet Letter*, is, as Howells has described it, one of realistic allegory, rather than of allegorized reality. Even in a story like "The Threefold Destiny," where the statement is that the end of the most mystic quest can be found in the love of the ordinary girl next door, Hawthorne's method is to present not "a story of events claiming to be real," but "an allegory, such as writers in the last century would have expressed in the shape of an Eastern tale, but to which I have endeavored to give a more life-like warmth than could be infused into those fanciful productions."[38] The technique is thus curiously at odds with the theme, and it was not until "The Custom House" that the two were reconciled. There, as we have noted, Hawthorne postulated not only that the allegory must be warmed to the semblance of reality but that it should have been abstracted in the first place from the everyday world. And it was henceforth that he seems consciously to have sought a suitable rather than an absolute remoteness in his settings.

The Marble Faun uses perhaps the most exotic of the post-"Custom House" backgrounds, but it presents a much more recognizable Italy than was evident in "Rappaccini's Daughter." The difference stems, in part, from the fact that in the meantime Hawthorne had lived in Italy and had a notebook of impressions to draw on for the romance, whereas, for the story he had only, like Mrs. Radcliffe, some romantic impressions. The difference can also be accounted for by his now confirmed and realized aesthetic principle that the purpose of the artist—he is speaking specifically of the sculptor—must be to "idealize the man of the day to himself,"[39] that it is, putting the matter most baldly, "his business to idealize the tailor's actual work."[40] Thus, under Howells' definition, Hawthorne after 1850 must be classified as a romanticist in the style of Dickens rather than a romantic.[41]

36. *Ibid.*, II, 354.
37. *Ibid.*, I, 511.
38. *Ibid.*, I, 527.
39. "The French and Italian Notebooks of Nathaniel Hawthorne," II, 247.
40. *Ibid.*, II, 341.
41. In this respect, Taylor Stoehr has written that the central struggle of Hawthorne's art was "to force his daydreams into a certain relation with everyday life

Most of the writers we have so far considered were city men, who had to provide a romantic coloration for those familiar scenes which represented everyday reality in the minds of their readers. Dickens' task at the beginning of *Bleak House* is to distance us from contemporary London and at the same time keep it recognizable. He proceeds by shrouding the real city in fog and by imagining "a Megalosaurus, forty feet long or so, waddling like an elephantine lizard up Holborn Hill." Other metaphysical novelists, those whose settings, if left untouched, would seem absolutely exotic, were of course faced with an opposite problem. Melville, for instance, had to factualize the world of his fiction for the sake of achieving a suitable remoteness.

In Melville, the ocean world always stands for the opposite of home; it is a foreign milieu which tempts the discontented and troubled narrators to utter alienation. Each of Melville's first three books begins with an abandonment of duty, the jumping of a more or less realistic whale ship in favor of some savage paradise, fresh or decayed. Always these escapes are journeys to ironic Edens, and, insofar as settings are concerned, the books tend strongly in the direction of allegory. The unreal quality of Melville's Pacific Island world is emphasized in the first chapter of *Mardi* when Taji looks out from the deck of the prosaic *Arcturion* toward the cloud-built archipelago of his quest:

> In the distance what visions were spread! The entire western horizon high piled with gold and crimson clouds; airy arches, domes, and minarets; as if the yellow, Moorish sun were setting behind some vast Alhambra. Vistas seemed leading to worlds beyond. To and fro, and all over the towers of this Nineveh in the sky, flew troops of birds. Watching them long, one crossed my sight, flew through a low arch, and was lost to view. My spirit must have sailed in with it; for directly, as in a trance, came upon me the cadence of mild billows laving a beach of shells, the waving of boughs, and the voices of maidens, and the lulled beatings of my own dissolved heart, all blended together.

Such visionary passages occur also in *Typee* and *Omoo* and, of course, in *Moby-Dick*, and they are always balanced by down-to-earth material—scientific observations and travel-book descriptions. It is a mistake, however, to take these factual admixtures as the true essence of Melville and to conclude that at the beginning of his career and at the beginnings of his most ambitious works, he intended to write realistic fiction. The accident of his brother's placing *Typee* with John Murray, who had, more or less, to certify the authenticity of all the works in his Colonial and

---

without giving up their essential strangeness." " 'Young Goodman Brown' and Hawthorne's Theory of Mimesis," *NCF*, XXIII (1969), p. 398.

Home Library, trapped Melville into the pretense that his first two romances were veraciously autobiographical. So far as the evidence from Melville's letters goes, however, he never tried to pretend with anyone other than his publisher. Murray kept asking for hard proof, and with good reason, since the incidents of *Typee* and *Omoo* derive at least as much from the author's reading and imagination as from his experiences. Both books, moreover, are controlled by theme rather than character, and their digressive structures suggest the romantic rather than the realistic tradition of fiction.

Melville wrote his anxious publisher that after the appearance of Toby's authenticating letter in the newspapers, *Typee* was being read in America as "a Romance of Real Life."[42] This statement was delivered tongue-in-cheek; nevertheless, it comes closer to describing Melville's intentions than the phrases "narrative of facts" or "true narrative" which appear in others of his letters to Murray. The juxtaposition of the ordinary world of the whalers and the exotic scenes of Polynesia provided Melville with what must have seemed to him the degree of remoteness essential to the Romance of Real Life, the aim of all the metaphysical novelists.

Still other writers, those who lived in and could authentically describe areas already sufficiently exotic, had perhaps less factualizing to do than Melville and less idealizing than Dickens or Hawthorne. Richter's Franconia and Faulkner's Mississippi already provided, like Hardy's semimythical Wessex, "horizons and landscapes of a partly real, partly dream country."[43] So, perhaps, did rural Yorkshire, but it is interesting that Emily Brontë found it necessary to distance it slightly in *Wuthering Heights* by placing the action in the time of her father's generation and to actualize it by first viewing the scenery through the eyes of a city man.

The purpose of all these writers was to establish a never-land in the midst of reality so as to create the "suitable remoteness" of which Hawthorne spoke and towards which all the metaphysical novelists strove. Their purpose, as we shall see, was to apply "romantic" solutions to "realistic" problems. Since remoteness is a concept which can exist only in the mind, moreover, and since reality, as we commonly accept the term, belongs to the realm of objective experience, this technique of the metaphysical novelists absorbs the outer world into the deepest recesses of the mind. It permits the author, therefore, to operate his story of the recognizable world by the dream logic of depth psychology rather than by the dictates of commonsense and Lockean materialism.

The purpose of scenic juxtaposition and distortion in the metaphysical novel, therefore, is harmony. But the sought-for reconciliation, we must

42. July 15, 1846, *The Letters of Herman Melville*, p. 38.
43. "Preface" to *Far from the Madding Crowd* (London, 1912), p. viii.

remember, is not between the ideal and material views of the world, but between the mind of man and the natural world in which man must live. Since the materialists had caused the alienation, their world had ultimately to be rejected along with their psychology, or rather, their world had to be transformed, made new, by means of a different psychology. The suitable remoteness of Hawthorne's settings was intended, once again, to offer "an available foothold between fiction and reality," and, as the metaphor suggests, the author meant to leave one of the two behind and below him. Thus the "theatre, a little removed from the highway of ordinary travel," which he tried to establish for *The Blithedale Romance*, is not the place where Locke and Fichte will come to terms, but where they must fight things out, and as we shall see, this confrontation created serious problems for the metaphysical novel.

·VI·
Structure

When a man has once broken through the paper walls of
everyday circumstance, those unsubstantial walls that hold
so many of us securely prisoned from the cradle to the grave,
he has made a discovery. If the world does not please you,
you can change it. Determine to alter it at any price, and you
can change it altogether. You may change it into something
sinister and angry, to something appalling, but it may be you
will change it into something brighter, something more agreeable, and at the worst something much more interesting.
—H. G. WELLS, *The History of Mr Polly*

I: THE LOOSE METHOD

Harry Levin writes that "the movement of realism, technically considered,
is an endeavor to emancipate literature from the sway of conventions."[1]
This manner of looking at the evolution of narrative form, which is amply
justified by the published attitudes of realists, assumes that there was once
a natural way of telling a story, a straightforward and realistic way, but
that over the years elaborating writers had made the road crooked. It is
based on an appealing view that nature is simple and so must art once have
been until sophisticated artists cluttered it with complicated styles and
techniques. Yet one can distrust such assumptions and at the same time
agree that structure in realistic fiction, of the most highly developed sort,
appears simpler than in metaphysical romance, that the construction
usually strikes us as cleaner and, indeed, somehow more natural.

It is well to remember, however, that the nineteenth-century realists,
unlike the romantic poets, had much more than just an eighteenth-century
attic to clean out. Homeric epic begins, of course, *in medias res*, and the
extreme complications of romance go back at least to the Milesian tales,
which are characterized by all the structural conventions the realists sought
to eliminate: multiple-voiced narration, digressions, episodes, double and
triple plotting, and the mixture of genres. Apuleius is even more difficult
in this respect than the Greeks, and the narrative-within-narrative-within-

1. *The Gates of Horn: A Study of Five French Realists* (New York, 1963),
p. 19.

narrative structures of Persian and Indian fiction are so elaborate that it is virtually impossible, at least for noninitiates, to find meaningful patterns in them. The problem, moreover, is almost as great when we turn to medieval cyclic romance, of which Eugene Vinaver has written:

> Since it is always possible, and even necessary, for several themes to be pursued simultaneously, they have to alternate like threads in a woven fabric; one theme interrupting another and again another, and yet all remaining constantly present in the author's and the reader's mind. The adventures which constitute the great cycles of romance thus become a part of a carefully thought-out design of fantastic dimensions.[2]

Nor do Jean de Meung, Boïardo, Ariosto, or Sidney make things significantly simpler for their readers. The conventions, if that is all they were, had become so deeply imbedded that by the nineteenth century they seemed in some quarters to indicate not only the time-honored, but perhaps even the natural way of telling a story. Some realists liked, indeed, to see themselves as fighting a Romantic revolution in fiction, but no Bishop Hurd among them could point to a "Fairie Spenser," just a couple centuries back, who represented a lost tradition of wholesome simplicity.

On the contrary, Bishop Hurd, as Robert Kiely has recently pointed out, "defends the technical diversity and thematic excesses of medieval literature as aesthetic virtues and dismisses the notion that they represent a breach of decorum."[3] Roger Sale, a more recent admirer of Spenser than Hurd, also justifies complex narration, and in terms which are most relevant to the argument we shall be presenting. Without reference to the theory of Schiller's discussed in the second chapter of our study, Sale defines "dramatic" and "undramatic" precisely as we have been defining them. Spenser is undramatic, he writes, in the sense that "there is no consistency to the narrative, no coherent fictional world, and little in the way of causal connections between episodes."[4] "The author of a dramatic work," Sale continues, "is skeptical and uses his story to discover his sense of life. The author of an undramatic work is certain and does not need his story to discover a sense of life he already commands. . . . Most undramatic authors are in some sense visionary; they know their world and move freely within its boundaries."[5]

Nineteenth-century realism, since it is based on a positivistic, nonvisionary, unmetaphysical worldview, tended to see the complexities of the earlier literature, not only as meaningless, but as adverse to its own at-

2. *The Rise of Romance* (Oxford, 1971), p. 76.
3. *The Romantic Novel in England* (Cambridge, Mass., 1972), p. 28.
4. *An Introduction to the Faerie Queene* (Seattle, 1967), p. 28.
5. *Ibid.*, p. 26.

tempts at discovering psychological truths. Realists jettisoned certain conventions, therefore, and some novelists liked to believe that they were creating without the encumbrance of a tradition of any kind. The best of the realists, however, knew that they were writing with a strong classical orientation and that such a commitment carried along with it plenty of conventions, including the convention of apparent simplicity. So although it is true that their purpose was to free literature from a set of rules which had become useless and detrimental to them, their accomplishment was to enslave it in a different, although almost equally traditional manner.

The revolt was not even a new one, but had begun in Western literature soon after Aristotle's *Poetics* were recovered. In this respect, the differences between the epics of Tasso and Ariosto can be instructive. Narrative complications are still present in the *Gerusalemme*. When we compare it with *Orlando Furioso*, however, which was written before there was much influence from the newly discovered Aristotelian principles, the mixture of voices and genres in Tasso seems strictly controlled and to be exercised with strong restraint.[6]

The two parts of *Don Quixote* also illustrate the point, for Cervantes was caught precisely in the middle of the first critical controversy between dramatic and undramatic form. He airs the subject, characteristically, with a thoroughly undramatic digression in which the Canon begins by severely criticizing the Aristotelian disunity of the chivalric romances and of the Milesian tales from which he believes they derived. " 'Never,' concluded the Canon, 'have I seen any book of chivalry that held the body of a story completely with all its members so that the middle was consistent with the beginning and the end with the beginning and the middle. Rather they are made up of so many disparate members that it would seem the author's intention was to create a chimera or monster rather than a well-proportioned figure.' " (Henry James seems to be talking here, or perhaps he had been reading here, for even the ungainly monster—James calls him loose and baggy—is employed by both critics as a metaphor describing digressive narrative.) But then, in a surprising turnabout, the Canon rhapsodically defends the complex or "loose method" because of the great freedom it gives the artist to present idealized characters and to display all the branches of his accumulated knowledge:

6. In his "Introduction" to *Jerusalem Delivered* (trans.) Edward Fairfax (New York, 1963), John Charles Nelson accounts for this change by noting "the large body of poetic theory based on the rediscovery," and he cites especially the example of Bernardo, "who had attempted to 'elevate' the chivalric *Amadigi* to the rank of a heroic poem according to Aristotelian precepts by basing a unitary action upon a single 'perfect' hero" (p. xxvi).

He might take as his theme . . . all these attributes that go to make an illustrious man perfect, as shown sometimes in a single individual and other times as shared among many. All of which being done in an easy-flowing style, with a skilled inventiveness that draws insofar as possible upon the truth of things, the result would surely be a web woven of beautiful and variegated threads, one which when completed would exhibit such a perfected beauty of form as to attain the most worth-while goal of all writing, which as I have said is at once to instruct and entertain. These books, indeed, by their very nature, provided the author with an unlimited field in which to try his hand at the epic, lyric, tragic, and comic genres and depict in turn all the moods that are represented by these most sweet and pleasing branches of poetry and oratory; for the epic may be written in prose as well as in verse.[7]

Part I of *Don Quixote* is itself the sort of heterogeneous work in the loose form which the Canon has been describing. Nor did it escape the censure of contemporary, rules-minded critics.

In response to such criticism, Part II is a much more orderly and more obviously unified production. There were times, however, when Cervantes could not resist a petulant though humorous digression of protest at the enforced restraint.

They say that in the original version of the history it is stated that the interpreter did not translate the present chapter as Cid Hamete had written it, owing to a kind of grudge that the Moor had against himself for having undertaken a story so dry and limited in scope as is this one of Don Quixote. For it seemed to him he was always having to speak of the knight and Sancho, without being able to indulge in digressions of a more serious and entertaining nature. He remarked that to go on like this, pen in hand, with his mind fixed upon a single subject and having to speak through the mouths of a few persons only was for him an intolerable and unprofitable drudgery.

By way of relieving the monotony, in the first part of the work he had employed the artifice of introducing a few *novelas* . . . that, so to speak, had nothing to do with the narrative proper. . . . [But] in this second part it was not his intention to insert any more tales of that kind, whether separate or interwoven with the narrative as a whole, but rather only a few episodes that resembled them, arising naturally out of the course of events, and even with these he meant to be sparing, employing as few words as possible in the telling. He goes on to say that, while thus confining himself closely within the narrow limits of the plot, he wishes it understood that he has sufficient ability and intelligence to take the entire universe for his theme if he so desired and he asks that his labors be not looked down

7. *The Ingenious Gentleman Don Quixote de La Mancha*, Part I, Chap. 47.

upon, but that he be given credit not for what he writes, but for what he had refrained from writing. (Chap. 44)

We should not be misled by the tongue-in-cheek style of this passage, for the seriousness of Cervantes' commitment to the loose or nondramatic form is amply attested by the narrative complexities of *Persiles y Sigismunda* (1617).

By the end of the seventeenth century, although works in the loose form continued to be written, the question seemed to have been settled as a matter of critical theory. And in the absence of an unrecovered treatise on the epic, even some writers of fiction chose to govern their narratives by rules which they understood were intended to apply to dramatic composition. Aristotle's rules were, after all, the clearest and most authoritative set of rules available. Thus, in the preface to *Incognita*, Congreve explains how he has modelled his novel (he says it is not a romance) on dramatic lines. Richardson, in contrast to Smollett, who saw the novel as "a large diffuse picture," and Fielding, for whom fiction was "a comic epic poem in prose," regarded his *Clarissa* as a "Dramatic Narrative."[8] Thus Belford writes to Lovelace, "What a fine subject for Tragedy would the injuries of this Lady, and her behaviour under them, both with regard to her implacable friends, and to her persecutor, make!" He goes on to praise the dramatics of Clarissa's story over those in Rowe's *The Fair Penitent*.[9] And according to the definition from Schiller which we have been using, Richardson was, in fact, writing the most dramatic work of long fiction to date, although certainly not the least convention-bound.

An epistolary novel may seem the ultimate form of multiple narration, and especially one like *Clarissa*, which employs so many "interpolated" poems, meditations, exempla, and brief background and parallel-ground stories; Richardson is nevertheless right in saying that he wrote "without the aid of digressions and episodes foreign to the principal end and design."[10] The nonnarrative material, which always flows easily from the actions the letter writers describe, is usually short and remarkably infrequent by eighteenth-century and earlier standards. Many readers-in-a-hurry have complained about the slow pace of *Clarissa*, but the action is never entirely halted by retarding digressions. On the contrary, Richardson concentrates minutely on his central action, and the dramatic unity is astounding for so long a work. Compare it, for instance, with an epistolary novel like *Humphry Clinker*, with its several lines of interest, its subplots, and

8. *Clarissa; or, The History of a Young Lady* (Oxford, 1930), VIII, 309.
9. *Ibid.*, VII, let. 44.
10. *Ibid.*, VIII, 325.

its thematic rather than dramatic concerns. Richardson's vehicle moves at only steam-roller speed, and many passengers have therefore found it possible to hop off without serious injury or regret. The dramatic novel had far to go after *Clarissa*. But the point is that the story never slows its moderate pace, and it never stops until the very end. And this is the essence of the dramatic as Schiller was to define it.

Independently of narrative theory, there may also be a traditional British propensity towards the undigressive simplicity of cause-and-effect structures. I am generalizing grandly here, and am speaking only in the most relative terms, for complicated structures remain very much the norm until quite recently; but there seems usually to be some tendency in the direction of sustained cause-and-effect narration when we compare certain important British works with the Continental masterpieces which influenced them. If we continue to use the term "dramatic" to indicate the kind of vehicular, nonretarding structuring described by Schiller and Goethe as appropriate to drama,[11] then it appears that *Roderick Random*, in spite of its episodes, is considerably more dramatic than *Gil Blas*, where the main action is interrupted time and again so that interpolated narratives can keep us abreast simultaneously of several subplots. Similarly Milton is *relatively* more dramatic than Tasso, and Spenser than Ariosto. Malory, it appears from several modern critical studies, worked quite consciously at reducing the digressions and dream visions which complicated his French sources, "unraveling," as Lumiansky writes, "the interwoven threads of the *Mort Artu* in order to present . . . episodes as complete units."[12] Another critic argues that "Malory's themes depend upon a sense of historical time. It is essential that events in the development of Arthurian society be seen in a sequence in which their cause and effect can be made apparent."[13] *Le Morte Darthur*, therefore, which for a nineteenth-century realist like Mark Twain stood as the essence of nondramatic narrative,[14] is in fact strongly dramatic when compared to its sources and analogues. And pre-Chaucerian English love lyrics, as contrasted with French, have been called "remarkable" for the "way in which a

11. See Chap. II, pp. 57–59.

12. "The Tale of Lancelot and Guenevere," *Malory's Originality: A Critical Study of Le Morte Darthur* (ed.) R. M. Lumiansky (Baltimore, 1964), p. 2.

13. Elizabeth T. Pochoda, *Arthurian Propaganda: Le Morte Darthur as an Historical Ideal of Life* (Chapel Hill, N.C., 1971), p. 65. Similarly, Thomas C. Rumble writes that in attempting "to portray the real tragedy of Arthur's realm," Malory strove "to make clearer than ever the causes of that tragedy." "The Tale of Tristram: Development and Analogy," in *Malory's Originality*, p. 145.

14. *A Connecticut Yankee in King Arthur's Court* (New York, 1923), Chap. XV.

dramatic situation and a complex state or feeling are evoked in a few lines."[15] Thus it appears that, with and without Aristotle, the British appetite for a story that moves along has always been keen.

Walter Scott exemplifies better than anyone else the instinctive nature of this British drive for the dramatic, because unlike other writers who contributed to the realistic revolution, he began, in spite of his interest in the ballads, with no theory favoring dramatic narration. On the contrary, it appears that he wanted to write nondramatically, and, as indicated by the beginning of *Old Mortality*, by the various narrative shifts in *Redgauntlet*, and by the general excellence of his interpolated tales, he could have been one of the most imaginative practitioners of metaphysical fiction. But what Karl Kroeber says of Scott's narrative poetry, "that he was incapable of using effectively any technique which complicated the direct expression of his story,"[16] applies also to his novels, which no matter how they are begun, always settle down at last into the, for him, more comfortable dramatic mode. Almost unbelievably, Edie Ochiltree of *The Antiquary* is never permitted to narrate any of the old legends he is supposed always to be telling.

In the introduction to *The Bride of Lammermoor*, where Dick Tinto criticizes the author for writing too much in the dramatic and not enough in the descriptive mode, Scott is using the term "dramatic" to mean simply the practice of telling a story through "scenes of mere conversation" rather than through described action. But Scott's interesting attempt during the early pages of the narrative proper to see his characters as though they were figures from paintings is nondramatic in a more profound sense, and the picture gallery scene in which Edgar is recognized as the double of his ancestor Malise of Ravenswood looks backward to *Orlando Furioso* and *The Faerie Queene* as it looks forward to *Pierre* and *The Marble Faun*. Nevertheless, what Scott admits concerning his penchant for conversational scenes is true also of his instinct for cause-and-effect narrative. "My favourite propensity," as he writes in the same introduction, "has at times overcome me." And *The Bride of Lammermoor* lapses into one of the great works of nineteenth-century dramatic fiction, for all its Bryonism, an indispensible work in the direction of the realistic novel.

At length, in *The Fair Maid of Perth*, which is, next to *Quentin Durward*, the most dramatic of the Waverley Novels, cause-and-effect narration is

---

15. Peter Dronke, *Medieval Latin and the Rise of the European Love Lyric* (Oxford, 1968), I, 114. In *The Ballad of Tradition* (New York, 1957), Gordon Hall Gerould writes that the ballad tradition, which had a particularly strong influence on British narrative art, stressed telling a story "by letting the action unfold itself in event and speech . . . objectively with little comment or intrusion of personal bias."

16. *Romantic Narrative Art* (Madison, 1960), p. 179.

justified in terms which, if he had not made up his mind to be obtuse on the subject of Scott, should have satisfied even E. M. Forster:

> The incidents of a narrative of this kind must be adapted to each other, as the wards of a key must tally accurately with those of the lock to which it belongs. The reader, however gentle, will not hold himself satisfied with the mere fact that such and such an occurrence took place, which is, generally speaking, all that in ordinary life he can know of what is passing around him; but he is desirous, while reading for amusement, of knowing the interior movements occasioning the course of events.[17]

In other words, according to Forster's own definitions, Scott is saying that fiction requires plot—psychological causality—rather than mere story.

When we turn to the French realists, we note the strong influences both of Scott's British instincts and of general dramatic theory. Stendhal and Flaubert expressed, and probably they genuinely felt, an artistic distaste for Scott; both were followers, nevertheless, who structured their works on the common and essentially dramatic theme of disillusionment. As Harry Levin writes, "Scott . . . had paved the way for the sociological novel. Stendhal's contribution [was] to take the present for his period, to write a historical novel of his own time."[18] And French realism is almost insistently dramatic. Stendhal, who regarded "the novel as the comedy of the nineteenth century," wrote fiction accordingly. "Transform your comedies into novels and print them," he advised in *Racine et Shakespeare*.[19] As for tragedy, Flaubert's *Madame Bovary*, although a novel, is perhaps the finest example of the century.[20] Balzac, of course, called his novels *comedies* when he referred to them in the aggregate. An individual work like *Le Père Goriot* might be described as a "drama . . . that is all true" or "an obscure but appalling Parisian tragedy."[21] And he interrupted the narration of *Eugénie Grandet* to forewarn, "In three days a terrible drama would begin, a bourgeois tragedy, without poison, dagger or bloodshed, but, for the

17. *The Fair Maid of Perth* (Boston, 1900), II, 109.
18. *The Gates of Horn*, p. 121.
19. Quoted in *The Gates of Horn*, p. 108.
20. Harry Levin writes of Flaubert: "He told Louise Colet that the method of *Madame Bovary* would be biographical rather than dramatic, yet biography seems to branch out into drama at all the stages of Emma's career. . . . [Moreover] the three-part structure allows the novelist, with a classicism seldom encountered in novels, to give his conception a beginning, a middle, and an end: to study first the conditions of Emma's marriage, then her Platonic romance and her carnal affair, and finally the train of consequences that leads to her death. Different leading men play opposite her, so to speak, in these three successive parts: Charles in the first, Rodolphe in the second, Leon in the third." (*Ibid.*, pp. 259–260).
21. *Le Père Goriot* (trans.) Jane M. Sedgwick (New York, 1956), pp. 2 and 105.

actors in it, it would be crueler than all the tragedies enacted in the famous family of the *Atridae*."[22]

Moreover, in the case of Balzac, there was no squeamishness about the acceptance of the sometimes clumsy Scott as an influence. "Indeed," György Lukács writes, "one may say that the specific form of the Balzac novel emerged in the course of his coming to grips, ideologically and artistically, with Scott. . . . With Balzac the historical novel, which in Scott grew out of the English social novel, returns to the presentation of contemporary society."[23] In *Le Père Goriot*, Balzac calls *The Heart of Midlothian* a masterpiece, and he classes Scott with the dramatist Molière. His own intention, he writes, is different from theirs only in that he hopes to be as fine and dramatic as they were, using real rather than ideal characters.[24]

Anthony Trollope represents a combination of most of the elements we have been discussing as relevant to dramatic structure. Trollope had the highest admiration for Richardson and Scott, a strong interest in classical literature, a compelling, scholarly concern with the history of the drama, and the powerful English instinct for straightforward, no-nonsense storytelling. Thus he wrote in *An Autobiography*:

> There should be no episodes in a novel. Every sentence, every word, through all those pages, should tend to the telling of the story. Such episodes distract the attention of the reader, and always do so disagreeably. Who has not felt this to be the case even with *The Curious Impertinent* and with the *History of the Man of the Hill*. And if it be so with Cervantes and Fielding, who can hope to succeed? Though the novel you write be long, let it be all one.[25]

Realism had still some distance to go before it could attain the kind of Aristotelian unity Trollope is calling for here, but it is significant that when the genre did come of age, its masters, James and Joyce, still spoke

---

22. *Eugénie Grandet* (trans.) Lowell Bair (New York, 1959), p. 123. In *The Dramatic Construction of Balzac's Novels* (Eugene, 1940), Ray P. Bowen demonstrates not only that the *Comédies humaines* are peopled with dramatic characters and built on classic lines, but that they contain "very important features of acts and scenes, settings, and dialogue" (p. 12). Balzac, according to Bowen, adheres closely to the unities of place and plot (p. 73), and "in his three great works, *Le Père Goriot, La Recherche de l'absolu* and *Eugénie Grandet*, Balzac describes at the outset those settings in which most of the action will take place, puts his characters in them, turns on the electric switch, as it were, and the characters thereafter perform in accord with the descriptions he has lent them" (p. 99).

23. *The Historical Novel* (trans.) Hannah and Stanley Michell (London, 1962), pp. 81–85. Levin writes that "it was Walter Scott . . . who merited . . . [Balzac's] profoundest acknowledgement for having elevated the novel to the philosophical value of history" (*The Gates of Horn*, p. 117).

24. P. 149.

25. II, 56.

in metaphors of the theater and stressed the necessity of making their works more dramatic.

What I am arguing, once more, is that the movement of realism was not a simple matter of emancipating fiction from the old narrative conventions and achieving a free, much less a new form. To a large extent, the realists sought to liberate fiction from its old romance and epic allegiances, only to enlist it under a banner of almost equal antiquity, that of the drama defined along classical lines. So little did the realists emancipate fiction from artistic restraints that by 1846 Archibald Alison could fault Bulwer, as opposed to Scott and Cooper, for his failure to adhere to the dramatic *rules* of unities.[26] Before the end of the century Trollope could regret that Dickens created "in defiance of rules,"[27] and Charles Dudley Warner could pronounce a book like *Uncle Tom's Cabin* "defective according to the rules of the modern French romance."[28]

These criticisms indicate precisely the orientation which Schiller and Goethe had considered inappropriate for fiction. Moreover, it was the direction in which, as Bulwer correctly anticipated, Walter Scott's influence was leading the novel and from which Bulwer tried to rescue it. We have seen that Bulwer always responded to the sort of rules-governed criticism cited above by pointing out the radical distinction between drama and narrative, as, for instance, in the following passage from *Caxtoniana*:

> I often see in our Reviews a charge against some novel that this or that is "a defect of art," which is, when examined, really a beauty in art—or a positive necessity which that department of art could not avoid—simply because the Reviewer has been applying to the novel rules drawn from the drama, and not only inapplicable, but adverse, to the principles which regulate the freedom of the novel.[29]

Bulwer saw the realists and the accompanying criticism as intrusions of French taste, similar to the foreign influences which governed English literary thought during the Restoration and had made Shakespeare almost unavailable to his countrymen. He was very much an internationalist, but he regarded the French spirit as primarily rational rather than imaginative, and unfitting therefore as a guide to narrative fiction. He struggled to restore sanity, at least in England, not only through his critical statements, but also in his fiction, which, after *Eugene Aram*, was programatically nondramatic, and, in the opposite direction, by his plays, which he

---

26. "The Romantic Drama," *Blackwood's*, LX (Aug. 1846), 171.

27. *An Autobiography*, II, 71.

28. "The Story of Uncle Tom's Cabin," in *Uncle Tom's Cabin* (Boston, 1896), I, xlvii.

29. "On Certain Principles of Art in Works of the Imagination," *Caxtoniana* (Edinburgh and London, 1863), II, 163–164.

tried to make so dramatic as to out-Aristotle Aristotle. *Richelieu* exists in two versions: one with digressions for those who wish to read it as fiction, and a much sparer and more dramatically unified acting version. According to the manuscript preface he wrote for his version of *Oedipus*, even Sophocles was not dramatic enough to suit him—"speeches [in the Greek] not conducive to the catastrophe, nor descriptive [?] of the narration have been rejected."[30] His whole career may thus be judged as an attempt to preserve and purify the traditions in which he worked.

Where Bulwer may have erred, it seems to me, was in failing to recognize what the success of Scott might have taught him, that the French narrative rules struck a sympathetic chord in Englishmen, who, as I have suggested, had been tending towards cause-and-effect narration from long before the rediscovery of the *Poetics* and the formulation of Lockean psychology. Realism was so easily naturalized in England because it was truly at home there, and from the English point of view, it was Bulwer who was trying to import foreign, specifically German, standards.

Wordsworth had similarly misjudged the taste of his countrymen when he attempted the German mode in *The Excursion*, with its multiple narrators and its many digressive discussions on matters social, political, philosophical, and religious. Karl Kroeber writes, "In *The Excursion* Wordsworth tries to pass beyond the relatively rational and objective unity of *The Prelude*'s story. . . . It strives towards a supra-realistic art." But, as Kroeber continues, it was the "precisely contrary" development of Byron and Scott which "contributed to the shaping of the nineteenth-century novel," and Wordsworth, I think, did not become an important influence on English fiction until after the much delayed publication of *The Prelude* with its greater dramatic unity. *The Excursion*, again according to Kroeber, "led towards a more consciously anti-prosaic style of visionary poetry."[31]

Yet it was the Wordsworth of *The Excursion*, whom, as we have noted, Bulwer recommended as a Teutonically inspired antidote to Lockean psychology. He also recommended the Germans themselves for this purpose, and he never tried to disguise the fact that many of his own ideas had been derived from Schiller and Hegel. His aesthetics have also a source in Richter's distinction between the closely plotted dramatic novel and the "EPIC or romantic novel," a sort of "Poetic encyclopedia" without beginning or end.[32] And there is an ultimate source in *Wilhelm Meister* it-

---

30. In the Lytton collection at Hertford, Herts. Printed with the kind permission of the Hertfordshire County Record Office and the owner of the collection, Lady Hermione Cobbold.

31. *Romantic Narrative Art*, p. 112.

32. See René Wellek, *A History of Modern Criticism 1750–1950* (New Haven, 1955), II, 104.

self, where Goethe had argued that "in the novel, it is chiefly *sentiments and events* that are exhibited. . . . The novel must go slowly forward, and the sentiments of the hero, or some means or another, must restrain the tendency of the whole to unfold itself and conclude."[33]

In Germany, these theories led to a whole literature of encyclopedic and, according to English taste, utterly formless novels, not only by Goethe and Richter, but also by Novalis, Tieck, Brentano, Eichendorff and Friedrich Schlegel. M. H. Abrams has demonstrated throughout his recent book, *Natural Supernaturalism*, that it would be understatement to say that such works were merely influenced by metaphysics. Rather, like *The Recluse* and *Sartor Resartus*, they represent significant and original contributions to idealistic philosophy. Such British Germanophiles as Carlyle and Bulwer were quick to perceive this fact and to proclaim that German fiction was much deeper, much more necessary to the psychic well-being than were the novels of Scott and the realists. But the more insular critics regarded even Goethe and Richter with a barely respectful distaste. According to De Quincey, *Wilhelm Meister* "has not gained, and will not gain, any attention in this country; and this is not only because it is thoroughly deficient in all points of attraction to readers formed upon our English literature, but because in some capital circumstances it is absolutely repulsive. . . . As a novelist, Goethe and his reputation are problems to Englishmen."[34] English criticism either ignored or positively hooted at the structural extravagances of the lesser known and less prestigious German Romantics.

The metaphysical novelists, in the face of these visceral and theoretical reactions to the Germans, and despite the frequent application of the same strictures to their own works, were nevertheless serious practitioners of the loose method. Melville is the most conspicuous example in this respect, and certainly the reviewers gave him sufficient correction, which he consistently refused to take. *Billy Budd*, whatever else it may or may not be, can hardly be regarded as a testament of Melville's acceptance of critical advice, not when we consider the various genres represented in the endings. And his earlier works—not only *Mardi* and *Moby-Dick*—are defiantly loose in their construction. He stands out, however, largely because he refused, as the other metaphysical novelists did not, to disguise his bewildering mixture of narrative voices, modes, and genres with smooth transitions.

The others in his school, however, were equally committed to the loose method, although perhaps not so obviously. Bulwer developed such skill

33. Carlyle's translation, Bk. V, Chap. VII.
34. "Goethe," *Encyclopaedia Britannica*, 7th ed.

in combining the various elements or conventions into apparently sequential structures that he enjoyed a reputation, challenged only infrequently,
as the master architect of Victorian fiction. The reviewer for *The Examiner*
(October 26, 1834) stated that *The Last Days of Pompeii*, "in its construction as a work of art, in its general keeping, *its trouble and its repose,*
. . . is the most masterly production that we have read for years. We question, indeed, whether in this respect it has ever been equalled. Rembrandt
never flung light and shade into one great effect with a pencil more true
and fatal."[35] This praise is taken from an extremely friendly review, but
harsher critics, like W. C. Roscoe, were willing to grant Bulwer at least
this one excellence:

> As a constructive artist Bulwer is indisputably great; and his works stand
> in this respect above those of every contemporary, we may almost say every
> rival [of any age]. . . . In truthfulness, in wisdom, in humour, in good taste,
> in all that marks higher poetic power, and in some respects a higher nature,
> Fielding stands immeasurably above Bulwer; but in skill of construction,
> in command of intricate combinations of facts, Bulwer may certainly claim
> to rival, if not to excel him who is justly esteemed to stand first in the
> ranks of the writers of prose fiction. There is something marvellous in the
> grasp he has of the whole design, and with the skill and ease with which he
> evolves all intricacies of plot, with which, without straining his characters or
> his incidents, he marshals all his materials and concentrates his various
> forces on one result.[36]

And even Trollope, who finds very little else to praise in Bulwer, notes the
success of his plots. "The reader never feels with him, as he does with Wilkie
Collins, that it is all plot, or, as with George Eliot, that there is no plot.
The story comes naturally without calling for too much attention, and it is
thus proof of the completeness of the man's intellect."[37]

This reputation of Bulwer's, which in the quotations just presented
spans almost fifty years, is remarkable in view of the fact that few of his
works contain anything at all like dramatic unity. As we have said, Bulwer
always insisted, and his fiction was itself an important part of the argument,
that "a novel is not a drama."[38] Almost all his romances contain more than
one plot, and participate in more than one genre. *The Caxtons*, perhaps his

35. P. 676.
36. "Sir E. B. Lytton, Novelist, Philosopher, and Poet," *The National Review*,
VIII (Apr. 1859), 308.
37. *An Autobiography*, II, 74.
38. *My Novel*, Pt. V, Chap. I. Richard Stang writes that "for Bulwer unity of
action in the Aristotelian sense is unnecessary; all that is necessary is unity of
theme." *The Theory of the Novel in England, 1850–1870* (New York, 1959),
p. 124.

most realistic work, is narrated by almost as many voices and through almost as many modes (first person, third person, in letters, and through playlets) as *Moby-Dick*. Like Goethe, in *Wilhelm Meister*, and like Melville, in *Mardi, Pierre* and *The Confidence-Man*, Bulwer frequently interrupts his narratives to provide discussions of literary technique. *The Pilgrims of the Rhine* and *My Novel* make systematic use of this thoroughly undramatic device. And Bulwer's rule for episodes and digressions, which abound in all of his works, is simply that they may not be "episodal to the main design."[39] French taste, he held to be superficial. "Do not govern a Goethe, or even a Richter, by a Boileau."[40]

Wuthering Heights, which struck so many of its early readers as an artless tale, includes dream visions, diary entries, letters, and is narrated by seven different voices. The Gondal narrative, which mixed poetry with prose, was obviously even more seriously complicated or loose. Hawthorne's interpolated tales, in *The House of the Seven Gables, The Blithedale Romance*, and *The Marble Faun*, have not usually told seriously against him in the criticisms of Aristotelian-minded readers because he manages always to relate them causally to the plots, but they must be regarded, nevertheless, as instances of complex and undramatic structure, as must his matter-of-fact introductions and strange, mystical endings, which we shall discuss in a later section of this chapter.

Dickens experimented with the "loose method" from the very beginning of his literary career. The gradually darkening vision of *Sketches by Boz* is achieved not only by shifts in genre from the frivolous accounts of "Our Parish" through the "Scenes" and "Characters" to the "Tales," but also by changes in subgenres within each of the last three sections, so that the movement is always from the superficial or trivial to the near tragic. "Scenes" concludes with a dramatic description of a condemned man's last night in Newgate; "Characters" ends with a picture of young girls and boys being initiated into vice and hardened into crime; and "Tales" arrives at last at the frenzied melodrama of "The Drunkard's Death."

Throughout the rest of his career Dickens tried with varying degrees of success to get back to this thoroughly loose form, unified only by theme, with which he had tentatively experimented in *Sketches*. *Master Humphrey's Clock* was apparently intended to provide him a format for just such a structure, but the public demand for a consecutive narrative caused him quickly to abandon the project. Later on, in the periodicals he "conducted," other opportunities were afforded, especially in the annual Christmas numbers, each of which consisted of a set of narratives, placed within a single frame and supposedly related to a single theme. But in the 1850s and

39. "A Word to the Reader," *Ernest Maltravers* (London, 1837).
40. *The Pilgrims of the Rhine* (London, 1834), Chap. XVIII.

1860s, when these Christmas numbers were published, Dickens was too busy with other projects to do all the work himself and was forced, or preferred, to farm out most of the stories to other writers. Thus, though he issued specific instructions to his collaborators, he found it impossible successfully to dictate a theme and sometimes even a genre to a heterogeneous collection of independent authors. "As yet," he wrote to Forster on November 25, 1859, "not a story has come to me in the least belonging to the idea (the simplest in the world; which I described in the most elaborate manner); and every one of them turns, by a strange fatality, on a criminal trial."[41] If, as he desired, he could have harnessed the various talents of such writers as Wilkie Collins and Mrs. Gaskell to his own visions, he would perhaps have achieved the ultimate success in the mixed mode, but he had finally to give up the idea in disappointment, and only a few of the frames by his own hand are of any lasting literary value. Perhaps Dickens' only real success in the thoroughly mixed mode came with his public readings, where he juxtaposed various passages from his published works with new pieces written for the occasions and achieved the form which seems to have given him the most personal satisfaction.

But while Dickens was bound throughout most of his life to more conventional structures, there are very few of his works which do not contain a meaningful juxtaposition of genres. Each of the books involves, of course, a combination of elements from comedy, satire, and melodrama. Beyond this, the so-called "interpolated tales" in *Pickwick Papers*, which now appear to have been written seriatim[42] and to have been a part of an overall plan, have been interpreted as providing "a meaningful variation in point of view from the main plot.... They explore the themes of the novel from an internal, psychological rather than an external, social point of view."[43] Such first person or interpolated narratives serve a similar purpose in *Nicholas Nickleby*, *David Copperfield*, *Bleak House*, and, most obviously, in *Little Dorrit*, where Dickens felt a need to justify Miss Wade's narrative with precedents from Fielding and Smollett.[44]

Dickens also makes frequent use of other genres as parts of his consecutively plotted longer works. There is a humorous poem in *Pickwick Papers*, a fairy tale in *Little Dorrit*, there are theatrical productions in *Nicholas Nickleby*, *The Old Curiosity Shop*, and *Great Expectations*,[45] and dreams

41. Quoted in *The Life of Charles Dickens* (London, 1966), II, 474.
42. See Robert Patten, "The Art of *Pickwick's* Interpolated Tales," *ELH*, XXXIV (1967), 349–367.
43. William F. Axton, *Circle of Fire: Dickens' Vision and Style and the Popular Victorian Theater* (Lexington, Ky., 1966), p. 78.
44. Letter to Forster, *Letters of Dickens*, II, 776.
45. For Dickens' use of the theater in his novels, see Charles Wolfe, "Charles Dickens and the *Theatrum Mundi*," (diss. University of Kansas, 1970) and

in *Oliver Twist, Martin Chuzzlewit, Bleak House,* and *The Mystery of Edwin Drood.* One notes also the historical present tense "Retrospects" of *David Copperfield,* which periodically interrupt the action and, according to Sylvère Monod, "slow down the rhythm of the story thanks to their contemplative character."[46] And in *Bleak House,* of course, Dickens alternated on something like a regular basis between first-person and third-person narration.

It used to be very much the fashion to assume that many of these modal inconsistencies were the result merely of the author's unbridled imagination and his desperate need to fill up monthly numbers. An insistence on generic consistency was, indeed, a staple of nineteenth-century criticism. Thus Walter Bagehot wrote in 1858:

> In cases in which Mr. Dickens has attempted to make a long complicated story, or to develop into scenes or incidents a plan in any degree elaborate, the result has been a complete failure. A certain consistency of genius seems necessary for the construction of a consecutive plot. An irregular mind naturally shows itself in incoherency of incident and aberration of character.[47]

Dickens, therefore, was well aware of this demand for dramatic coherency, which his works were judged to leave unsatisfied, and he tried, when he could, to be like Bulwer in covering over the breaks between genres with smooth transitions. In *David Copperfield* and afterwards, the "interpolated" tales are much more strongly connected to the plot line than in his earlier novels, and he said that his idea concerning Miss Wade's narrative in *Little Dorrit* was to make "the introduced story so fit the surrounding" material as to render it "impossible of separation from the main story." He wanted "to make the blood of the book circulate through both."[48] Moreover, Dickens criticized the severe and mechanical way in which his friend Wilkie Collins narrated his novels, with all the seams showing. No doubt, he would also have been critical of Melville's defiant method.

Nevertheless, to construct their books all in one genre and in a thoroughly dramatic manner would have defeated the main purposes for which Dickens and the others wrote their metaphysical novels. To begin negatively, there was no epistemological reason which legislated, as was the case with the realists, against the use of the loose form. The metaphysical novelists were not skeptical. They did not use the story to discover a sense of life, but rather to express, as Spenser had done, a visionary understanding of life.

Joseph Butwin, "The Paradox of the Clown in Dickens," *Dickens Studies Annual, Volume 5* (ed.) Robert B. Partlow, Jr. (Carbondale, Ill., 1976), pp. 115–132.

46. *Dickens as Novelist* (Norman, Okla., 1967), p. 304.

47. "Charles Dickens," *The National Review,* VII (1858), 476–77.

48. Letter to Forster. *Letters of Dickens,* II, 776.

Like Cervantes in Part I of *Don Quixote*, the loose method gave them an opportunity to try their hands "at the epic, lyric, tragic, and comic genres"[49] so that they could put forward the knowledge they already possessed. Thus the conventions which the realists had to abandon were not detrimental to the aims of metaphysical fiction. On the other hand, the new dramatic conventions which the realists had to impose for the sake of their own epistemology constituted a useless and constraining strait-jacket for the metaphysicals.

But this argument, which does not distinguish between the needs of the metaphysical novel and other visionary literature, is not sufficient justification for the against-the-grain structural excesses we have described. It remains for us to demonstrate that the old narrative conventions were not only harmless to the methods of our writers but positively useful and meaningful to their aims. For this purpose we shall have to look more closely at the structures of some metaphysical novels and at the two-part vision which the "loose method" facilitated in them.

II: THE TWO-PART VISION

Stephen Blackpool of *Hard Times* arrives by slow degrees at the state of defeat symbolized by his fall into an abandoned mine, the Old Hell Shaft. His life is crushed by a series of social and psychological circumstances which the end-of-the-century naturalists might have exaggerated, but could hardly have improved upon. Thus Barbara Hardy writes, "the virtue of *Hard Times* lies in a new kind of truthfulness about social conditioning."[50] Stephen redeems himself and the others, however, by a process which seems to belong in an entirely different genre of literature, by contemplating a mystic star. This history indicates a double vision on Dickens' part which, according to several critics, is seriously at odds with itself.

We have heard another important modern critic express the commonly held conviction that "faith in experience is one of the conditions of good fiction," but the critic's more specific and perhaps more significant reservation about *Bleak House* is not that the turning away from experience and toward Esther Summerson offends against his own world view, but that it "seems to contradict" everything else in the book's created world.[51] Similarly, Professor Hardy objects to the heroines of "encapsulated" virtue[52] who survive unsmirched in the midst of Dickens' magnificently rendered world of experiential wear and tear. One can doubt if Professor Hardy would even have interested herself in Dickens if his works did not contain

49. Chap. 47.
50. *The Moral Art of Charles Dickens* (London, 1970), p. 14.
51. George Levine, *The Boundaries of Fiction* (Princeton, 1968), pp. 71–72.
52. *Moral Art of Charles Dickens*, p. 5.

this "new kind of truthfulness about social conditioning," but, she does not object to the mystic heroine per se, whom, as we have seen, she can enjoy in the purer context offered by the story of Cinderella. Rather it is the mixture which seems to cause the difficulty.

Coming at the same problem but from the opposite direction, Graham Smith believes that the trouble with Little Nell is that Dickens was unable to stick to the kind of romance-allegory toward which he was striving in *The Old Curiosity Shop* and which Hawthorne later achieved with *The Scarlet Letter*:

> In such a work, questions of credibility and reality are subordinated to those of imaginative truth. Although their specific characteristics make them very different, Nell would possess more credibility if she were regarded as the same literary type as Hawthorne's Pearl. Her inferiority to Hawthorne's creation is due to the fact that Dickens is unable to discipline his exuberant genius into the pallid brilliance of allegory. In *The Scarlet Letter*, Pearl is not juxtaposed with characters and situations of a more fundamentally realistic kind than she is herself. But Dickens cannot resist indulging in this formal weakness, and, as a result, Nell is thrust into circumstances that make her appear ridiculous. The same fate would have overtaken Hester Prynne herself if she had been forced to exist within the covers of the same book as Dick Swiveller.[53]

Here again, the critical bias is not in favor of one sort of character or story over another; rather it is a demand for generic consistency, which amounts really to a demand for consistency of vision.

The two-part vision, which is reflected in the structure of Dickens' romances and, indeed, of most metaphysical novels, provides an obvious problem for critics. The number two, which is the symbol for disunity in classical numerology, is a difficult concept to harmonize. A single action presents no obvious structural or philosophical problem. Three parts not only make for convenient beginninngs, middles, and endings; they also leave room for thematic resolutions, *deus ex machina* interventions, or Hegelian syntheses. A double structure, by contrast, is susceptible to falling into halves—critics often call such action broken-backed—and the themes emanating from the two parts often seem contradictory. These difficulties are especially acute in the metaphysical novel where the parts call glaring attention to themselves because they are rendered in different genres and because the two visions they illustrate seem to offer a juxtaposition of opposites—skeptical pessimism and mystical affirmation. And when these two visions are perceived in Dickens, Bulwer, Hawthorne's *The House of the Seven Gables*, and sometimes even in *Wuthering Heights*, then the

53. *Dickens, Money, and Society* (Berkeley and Los Angeles, 1968), p. 29.

fashionable critical phrase to describe the juxtaposition is "a failure of nerve."

Melville critics have been far more charitable. Thus, Richard Chase, noting in Melville's works this same combination of contradictory elements —tragedy and comedy, realism and romance—concludes that the author's intention was a sort of heroic irresolution. According to such a reading, Melville did not want us to choose between the dramatically unsatisfying affirmations of Babbalanja or Ishmael and the heroic but self-destructive defiances of Taji or Ahab; rather he pitilessly exposed for us both horns of the dilemma which were goring his own soul. The classic extrinsic support of this view is Hawthorne's analysis of Melville's character, based upon their meeting near Liverpool in 1856:

> Melville, as he always does, began to reason of Providence and futurity, and everything that lies beyond human ken, and informed me that he had "pretty much made up his mind to be annihilated"; but still he does not seem to rest in that anticipation; and, I think, will never rest until he gets hold of a definite belief. It is strange how he persists—and has persisted ever since I knew him, and probably long before, in wandering to-and-fro over these deserts, as dismal and monotonous as the sand hills [on?] which we were sitting. He can neither believe, nor be comfortable in his unbelief: and he is too honest and courageous not to try to do one or the other. If he were a religious man, he would be one of the most truly religious and reverential; he has a very high and noble nature, and better worth immortality than most of us.[54]

Moreover, the obvious admiration expressed in this passage suggests that Hawthorne may also have been describing his own case—it was, in fact, a typical nineteenth-century condition of mind—and if so, then Hawthorne can be seen as here suggesting a tempting interpretation of the tragicomic nature of many of his own best works.

We should, I believe, resist this easy explanation for both authors. Chase and others have usually defined Melville's courage in terms of the refusal to express a positive or negative belief which, because of his honest confusion, he could not fully endorse. But Hawthorne said something different from this: "He can neither believe, nor be comfortable in his unbelief; and he is too honest and courageous not to try to do one or the other." Thus for Hawthorne, at least, it was dishonest and cowardly to remain willingly between doubt and conviction, and by extension, I would argue, dishonest and cowardly to write books merely descriptive of that condition. The brave man tries to fight his way through to a definite position, either to comfortable faith or, if necessary, to honest despair. Thus, while a sense of tormented doubt may have existed in Hawthorne and Mel-

54. *English Notebooks*, Nov. 20, 1856, pp. 432–433.

ville, and while such a conflict is highly flattering to our own twentieth-century feeling for relativistic chaos, it is unlikely that open-ended ambiguity could have been the intended structure of their romances.

"Allegory," Angus Fletcher asserts, "does not accept doubt; its enigmas show instead an obsessive battling with doubt. It does not accept the world of experience and the senses; it thrives on their overthrow, replacing them with ideas."[55] Romance and tragicomedy are kindred genres to allegory in that all three are, according to one's point of view, either defenses against, or attacks upon, skeptical pessimism. Frye has written that "something nihilistic and untamable" lies very close beneath the surface of romance,[56] and, indeed, the Milesian tales, which were favorite sources for Robert Greene and for the writers of Jacobean tragicomedies, show regularly how a world of realistic violence—of rapes and murders—can be both fully acknowledged and yet successfully overcome by mystic commitment.

It is never a question in these genres of stoically paying your money and either weakly taking your choice or bravely retaining your heightened sense of confusion. Even in Plato, as Fletcher has stated, the ironic stance, from which Socrates argues that all his wisdom consists in a recognition of his ignorance, does not cancel out the mythic affirmations. Rather the irony prepares us for the vision, making the vision both necessary and useful:

> The mythic core of certain Platonic dialogues; e.g., the *Symposium* and the *Phaedrus*, can thus be understood, I believe, as affecting us in two ways: like poetry it does indeed transport us to an ideal world and thereby denies the truth of our sense experiences, but it also renews faith in the ideal grounds of belief, action, and thought and then lets us return more confidently to mundane problems.[57]

And heroic irresolution was certainly not the intention of the English metaphysical novelists who employed a two-part vision and structure. In *Wuthering Heights*, for instance (even though Richard Chase pops up here again to be unconvinced by its positive aspect[58] and would like, perhaps therefore, to welcome it into the American tradition[59]), the author does not want us to be in doubt between the ways of its two heroines. Clearly, the second Catherine succeeds where her mother has failed, and she has

55. *Allegory: The Theory of a Symbolic Mode* (Ithaca, N.Y., 1964), pp. 322–23.
56. *Anatomy of Criticism* (Princeton, 1957), p. 305.
57. *Allegory*, p. 233.
58. "The Brontës: A Centennial Observance," *Kenyon Review*, IX (1947), 487–506.
59. See *The American Novel and Its Tradition* (Garden City, N.Y., 1957), p. 4.

done so in the time-honored fashion of the fairy tale—by being less calculating, less timorous, more generous, more open-hearted than her predecessor. Chase complains that Brontë has cheated to effect this optimistic conclusion, that she has switched genres on us, from Gothic romance to domestic idyl, but just such a change is the essential and aesthetically valid procedure of Emily Brontë and the four romancers with whom we are principally dealing.

The metaphysical novelists agreed strongly on one point: that the realistic or skeptical or materialistic world view could lead only to spiritual defeat. When we were discussing their passive heroes, we noted how Bulwer's Kenelm Chillingly blamed his education in "the Realistic school" for robbing him of his motive power, for crippling his greatness of soul and the potential greatness of all his countrymen. The case against realism is made most strongly in this very late work, but the indictment has been present in Bulwer from the very beginning. We have already heard him speak in 1833 of the enslavement of the English mind to the Lockean system, and in *Ernest Maltravers* he wrote that "the philosophy limited to the reason" is impoverishing "both to the artist and to the man of action" (Bk. IV, Chap. V).

But realism is not only the gray spirit which starves the heroism of Bulwer's sympathetically conceived characters, it also feeds the evil of his antagonists, releasing them from moral restraints. The villain of *Ernest Maltravers* is Lumley Ferrers, an arch-realist, a successful and cynical man of the world, who boasts he has nothing of the poet about him. Jean Nicot, the villain of *Zanoni*, is a realistic artist, a painter "not of gods and saints, but mortals" (Bk. II, Chap. VII). In *The Caxtons* Francis Vivian is wicked in his youth because he lacks imagination, "that sweet purifier of moral intellect":

> For though we are taught in our youth to be on our guard against imagination, I hold it . . . to be the divinest kind of reason we possess, and the one that leads us the least astray. In youth, indeed, it occasions errors, but they are not of a sordid or debasing nature. . . . and . . . even the erratic flashes of an imagination really healthful and vigorous deepen our knowledge and brighten our lights. . . . Of such flashes my friend was as innocent as the sternest matter-of-fact person could desire. Fancies he had in profusion, and very bad ones, but of imagination not a *scintilla*. His mind was one of those that live in a prison of logic and cannot, or will not, see beyond the bars: such a nature is at once positive and sceptical. (Bk. VIII, Chap. III)

Of course, there was a strong tradition from Gothic romance and from Jacobean tragedy which virtually legislated that the villain be a man of powerful intellect, often a Machiavellian realist. The title character of Charles Brockden Brown's *Ormond* is a monster of reason, who argues flawlessly, as he prepares to rape the heroine, that it is irrational for her to prefer death to dishonor. From this tradition of villainy Hawthorne drew frequently, especially for his ambiguous Faustian characters—Rappaccini, Aylmer, Ethan Brand, Chillingworth. But there is a less unmitigated form of villainy in Hawthorne's works. His worst scoundrel, Judge Pyncheon, like Faulkner's Jason Compson, is not a brooding genius. He is a matter-of-fact citizen who prides himself on his immunity from the airy nonsense which emanates from the worlds of sentiment and imagination. Like the devils of Bulwer, Hawthorne's Archimago is a full-fledged and glad believer in experiential reality. Thus, for Hawthorne, the only power to be derived from the realistic world view is the power to do evil.

Dickens does not go quite so far in his indictment of the spirit of realism. In his vision, a belief in experience does not necessarily make a man a villain; Dickens' devils—Quilp, Harthouse, Blandois—are closer to the conventional Enemy of Man and can be justified only in the way Melville explains Claggart of *Billy Budd*, as instances of "Natural Depravity." On the other hand, "What is known as *knowledge of the world*," writes Melville, is not very helpful when we try to understand these "exceptional characters,"[60] and Dickens seems to say that such a knowledge, or the exclusive reliance on it, is not very helpful either as a defense against the demonic world.

In *Hard Times*, Gradgrind's utilitarian school produces monsters like his star pupil and his son, but Gradgrind himself is not diabolical. On the contrary, he means very well by his children and for humanity. Nevertheless, his "hard Fact" approach to life affords the real devil his opening, so to speak, and it leaves Louisa defenseless in the face of his temptations.

In the plan for the tenth number of *Hard Times*, Dickens calls James Harthouse a "genteel demon." In the text he describes him as a Byronic Lucifer.

> When the Devil goeth about like a roaring lion, he goeth about in a shape by which few but savages and hunters are attracted. But, when he is trimmed, smoothed, and varnished, according to the mode; when he is aweary of vice, and aweary of virtue, used up as to brimstone, and used up as to bliss; then, whether he take to the serving out of red tape, or to the kindling of red fire, he is the very devil. (Bk. II, Chap. VIII)

Harthouse is the spirit of lassitude and, like Goethe's Mephistopheles, the spirit of cynical skepticism. He does not believe in anything, either in imagination *or* experience, but he has enlisted himself under the banner of the utilitarians on the practical advice of his senior devil of a brother. "Jem," the brother had said, "there's a good opening among the hard Fact

60. *Billy Budd Sailor (An Inside Narrative)* (Chicago, 1963), p. 75.

fellows, and they want men. I wonder you don't go in for statistics" (Bk. II, Chap. II). And Harthouse does so, without convictions, but quite successfully. "The not being troubled with earnestness was a grand point in his favour, enabling him to take to the hard Fact fellows with as good a grace as if he had been born one of the tribe, and to throw all other tribes over-board, as conscious hypocrites" (Bk. II, Chap. VII). Of course, the realistic Gradgrinders, the true believers in experience, are very much troubled with earnestness, but it was Dickens' purpose, as expressed in the plan for Weekly No. 12, "To shew Louisa, how alike in their creeds, her Father and Harthouse are?—How the two heartless things come to the same in the end? Yes—do it almost imperceptibly." And when Louisa, tempted to the edge of the abyss, having "almost repulsed and crushed . . . [her] better angel into a demon" (Bk. II, Chap. XII), appeals to Gradgrind for principles which might save her from the devil's lure— "Now, father, you have brought me to this. Save me by some other means" (Bk. II, Chap. XII)—he has, of course, no help to offer her. His philosophy, his faith in experience, is declared bankrupt.

It is at this point in a work like *Hard Times* that the author seems also to lose his faith in experience. The genre changes abruptly and so, apparently, does the vision. But the plan of a metaphysical novel, we must remember, has been thoroughly preconceived, and thus, the authors never entertained such a faith. Novalis, one of their strongest influences, had instructed that materialism is an exercise in superficiality: "The more limited a system is" he wrote, "the more it will please the worldly wise. Thus the system of the materialists, the doctrine of Helvétius and of Locke as well, has had the greatest success among that class."[61] Hawthorne's admiration for Samuel Johnson was substantial, but he recognized that his own "native propensities were towards Fairy Land." Johnson, he believed, "meddled only with the surface of life, and never cared to penetrate further than to ploughshare depth; his very sense and sagacity were but a one-eyed clear-sightedness."[62] We have already seen how Bulwer sought to free his culture from its slavery to Lockean materialism, and, as Cazamian wrote long ago, "Dickens' whole work is a huge attempt to destroy the psychological effects on the public of an apathy based on reason."[63]

The distinction between the English novel of development and the German and German-influenced *Bildungsroman,* which grew from it, must

61. From *Blütenstaub* in *Hymns to the Night and Other Selected Writings* (trans.) Charles E. Passage (New York, 1960), p. 69.

62. *Our Old Home* (Columbus, 1970), p. 122.

63. *Le Roman Social en Angleterre*, abstracted and translated by Stephen Wall in his book *Charles Dickens: A Critical Anthology* (Harmondsworth, 1970), p. 243.

again be stressed. Experience works to mature the hero of the former because he is an egoistical, untamed, or naïve child who must pass through some sort of Meredithian ordeal to learn firmness, unselfishness, and self-restraint. Conversion is too mystical a word to describe the process. The hero is matured by his hard collisions with the world. Disillusionment is the principal theme of realism, and when the work of realism is also a novel of development, the disillusion is a healthful, medicinal draught. But such a formula would be meaningless for the hero of romance whom we have been describing. He has already had his encounter with the world, has already suffered the consequent disillusionment, and it has not redeemed him. Exactly the contrary is true. Teufelsdröckh simply doesn't need more bad luck. Holgrave will not benefit from still more knocking about. Clennam will not come to his senses in prison as Peregrine Pickle or even Mr. Pickwick did, nor, most emphatically, will Bartleby the Scrivener. With the characters of the metaphysical novelists we are in much deeper spiritual water than Lockean psychology ever charted or was intended to navigate.[64] What these romancers thought their century needed was not a continued faith in experience, but, desperately, a belief in something else.

There was nothing positive which the metaphysical novelists could do with their perceptions of the world of experience. Dickens said Puckishly in *American Notes*, "If I were a Bostonian, I think I would be a Transcendentalist" (Chap. III), and his religious reaction to Niagara Falls, described later in the same book, suggests that he might not have made such a bad one. Nevertheless, although he recognized Carlyle as the master of this school and as his own master,[65] this was one direction in which he could not follow. Neither could Hawthorne or Melville, despite their strong Boston connections, find their way to the infinite through the finite, for they saw the transcendental state of mind as the impetus towards Faustian quests, which led, as surely as flat materialism, to destruction and death. Ahab with his chivalric lance and Ishmael with his scientific notebook, like Cooper's Natty Bumppo and Dr. Bat, are both interpreters of the natural world; but in Melville they are both certain to fail. Even Bulwer, for all his admiration of Goethe, Novalis, and Wordsworth, could not follow the natural to the supernatural. "Is not the history of superstition," he asks, "a chronicle of the follies of man in attempting to get answers from external nature?"[66]

---

64. Roy R. Male has pointed out that the association of Lockean psychology and the soul-destroying power of modern industry is made explicit in Melville's "The Tartarus of Maids." *Hawthorne's Tragic Vision* (Austin, Tex., 1957), p. 32.

65. See Letters to Carlyle, 13 July 1854 and 13 April 1863. *Letters of Dickens*, II, 567, and III, 348, and see Michael Goldberg, *Carlyle and Dickens* (Athens, Ga., 1972).

66. *Kenelm Chillingly*, III, XII, p. 187.

Thus, another means towards structural unity, the Neoplatonic way of the one and the many, was closed to the metaphysical novelists.

In these attitudes, of course, our writers were not unlike the tragic realists, who, from Stendhal to Hardy, also believed that man, whether his world was viewed skeptically or transcendentally, was certain of destruction. The two schools differed, however, both in their final positions and in their intentions. As Fletcher writes, "The mimetic poet using metaphor is only trying to understand nature; his art attempts to bring about catharsis of spent emotion. By means of his 'message,' on the other hand, the allegorical poet is . . . trying to control his audience."[67]

And so it comes back to the a priori vision of metaphysical fiction and the author's attempt to use it as a means of redeeming his world. If he could be content to leave his readers, perhaps even to confirm them, in their tragic condition, then they, already lost, would follow him contentedly in the description of the inevitable downhill progress of his characters, nod a grimly sophisticated head, and admire both his success of nerve and the unity of his structure. But the metaphysical novelist did not conceive his function in these terms.

Dickens and the others might at least have avoided censure if, since they anyway doubted the experiential world, they had not insisted on portraying it so palpably as to establish the structural and thematic dichotomies in their works. In the genre to which they were committed, however, and in the times during which they wrote, such an evasion would have constituted the real failure of nerve. The simplest criterion which distinguished comedy from romance in the Renaissance was that in the former the problem is either less serious or less seriously treated, and we know at all times that the obstacle to happiness will ultimately be overcome. As we have heard Frye observe concerning Shakespeare's late romances, "they do not avoid tragedies but contain them."[68] In this regard, James Kincaid has written, "the optimism of *Our Mutual Friend* is real, but it is based on very pessimistic premises. As the mock resurrection of Riderhood suggests, no light desires are satisfied in this world, and the comic satisfaction can come only to the truly initiated."[69]

Robert Louis Stevenson felt that he was entitled to his optimism because it did not develop from a life of physical comfort but of continual pain, and nineteenth-century critics were frequently of the opinion that Browning's hopeful poetry was especially worth listening to because the dark psychology of some of the monologues showed that he was not speaking out of a blissful ignorance of evil. But these attitudes do not state the case

67. *Allegory*, p. 192.
68. *Anatomy of Criticism*, p. 184.
69. *Dickens and the Rhetoric of Laughter* (Oxford, 1971), p. 248.

fully. It was not simply a matter of earning one's stripes. There was also a conviction that a visionary could not achieve true optimism, as distinguished from merely expressing an optimistic position, unless he had undergone a dark night of the soul.

The principal decades during which the metaphysical novel flourished, though they were hospitable to satire, romance, and, if not tragedy, at least a tragic view, were too uncertain to permit the unquestioned optimism of comedy. Before Darwin and Marx appeared to promise briefly a new species and a new social order, one had to live in hell, as Carlyle said Dante had done, before he was either qualified or had the capacity to speak about heaven.

> Commedias that come out *divine* are not accomplished otherwise. Thought, true labour of any kind, highest virtue itself, is it not the daughter of Pain? Born as out of the black whirlwind; true effort, in fact, as of a captive struggling to free himself.[70]

Schelling expresses the same idea:

> this two-dimensional fission between mind and outer nature, and between the mind and its own natural impulses, although it is in itself an evil, is the very act which releases the energy that sets in motion the speculative philosophy whose basic aim . . . is to cancel all cognitive and moral separation and opposition in a restored and enduring unity.[71]

Thus the metaphysical novelists had to give themselves up entirely to the hated "new kind of truthfulness about social conditioning," the expression of which Barbara Hardy regards as Dickens' chief virtue. They had to present the experiential world view as compellingly as possible before they could even generate the energy to contradict it with the opposite epistemic method.

Out of Carlyle's black whirlwind, the hell of sensual apathy and materialistic lassitude, the second vision was released. If it does not move us, as the evidence from some of our leading critics would seem to indicate, the reason may be that we have found a way to live untragically in the first vision. Or it may be that the second or mystic vision was never good enough to begin with, which may be saying the same thing again, for if the mystic vision had been sufficient, would it not have prevented our sad accommodation to the skeptical world view? But the worth of the metaphysical solution in the metaphysical novel must be argued by the writers themselves. The literary historian can only try to report their beliefs and

70. Carlyle, *Of Heroes and Hero Worship and the Heroic in History* (London, 1897), Lecture III.

71. Paraphrased by M. H. Abrams in *Natural Supernaturalism: Tradition and Revolution in Romantic Literature* (London, 1971), p. 182.

to show how some winds of the intellectual climate of the times seemed to favor them, to give the writers some confidence that their metaphysics might provide an adequate response to the growing positivism of their century.

The metaphysical novelists, through the agencies of Carlyle and Bulwer, were immediate heirs of both German and English Romanticism. They built on a tradition, therefore, which, as M. H. Abrams has demonstrated, held imagination and intuition higher than any other faculty of the mind, a tradition established by the greatest philosophers of the age and by its acknowledged literary masters.

> At no other place and time have literature and technical philosophy been so closely interinvolved as in Germany in the period beginning with Kant. The major German poets and novelists (as well as Coleridge and later Carlyle, in England) avidly assimilated the writings of the philosophers; many of them wrote philosophical essays; and all incorporated current philosophical concepts into the subject matter of their principal works of the imagination. And on their part philosophers remained closely in touch with literature; Schelling and Hegel themselves wrote poetry, and both these thinkers gave literature and the arts a prominent—Schelling, in his central period, the cardinal—place in their metaphysical systems.[72]

And again:

> Philosophers such as Fichte, Schelling, and Hegel, imaginative writers from Blake and Wordsworth to Shelley and the young Carlyle in England, and Hölderlin and Novalis in Germany, as well as others who, like Schiller and Coleridge, were equally metaphysicians and bards, conceived themselves as elected spokesmen for the Western tradition at a time of profound cultural crisis. They represented themselves in the traditional persona of the philosopher-seer or the poet-prophet . . . and they set out, in various yet recognizably parallel ways, to reconstitute the grounds of hope and to announce the certainty, or at least the possibility, of a rebirth in which a renewed mankind will inhabit a renovated earth where he will find himself thoroughly at home.[73]

This was the background for the role of the metaphysical novelists of the mid-nineteenth century and the apparently legitimate philosophical warrant for their faith in the power of the imagination to overcome "hard Facts."

They lived, moreover, at a time when, as a result of this tradition, the fairy tale or *Märchen* had become a serious and sophisticated genre of fiction and when visionary poetry, especially by Wordsworth and Tennyson, was held in the highest repute. "Romanticism," according to Montague Sum-

72. *Ibid.*, pp. 192–93.
73. *Ibid.*, p. 12.

mers, "is literary mysticism,"[74] and by the middle of the century, even the most occult aspects of the metaphysical position seemed to fall within the legitimate province of the writer. Thus John Senior has written:

> The world view of the romantic movement is occultism. At least insofar as romantic poets expressed philosophical and cosmological ideas, these ideas were occult. Consider just the greatest names out of thousands—Shelley, Blake, Hugo, Nerval, Gautier, Goethe, Novalis. [On the next page he adds Balzac and Bulwer.] . . . If all these great figures had merely dabbled, if it were only a matter of table turnings and the like, we should dismiss it as a diversion of genius; but occult ideas are involved in their greatest works.[75]

Around the middle of the century, spiritualism, especially mesmerism, enjoyed vogues which in some circles amounted almost to respectability. Harriet Martineau, of course, was a tireless champion, and Dr. Elliotson, the distinguished mesmerist physician, was fashionable among the writers.[76] Even Prince Albert is supposed to have said at a palace party that some medical men "were conducting themselves improperly in refusing to investigate the facts of mesmerism."[77]

Chauncy Hare Townshend, who was a friend of both Bulwer and Dickens, is especially important to our study because in his view mesmerism was not only a useful but also an optimistic science. From the beginning, animal magnetism had been predicated on a disquieting belief in double identity. Mesmer's graduation thesis at the University of Vienna was on Paracelsus, and all mesmeric thought developed from the notion of dual planetary attractions operating on the human psyche. The early magnetizers observed that their subjects, while in the trance state, displayed second and quite distinct personalities, and while some debate existed as to whether the alternate identity was an unconscious, previously submerged part of the subject's psyche or simply the projection of the mesmerist's own mind, there was general agreement that the second state was more brilliant, more interesting than the first. However, there was also pretty general agreement among the early believers in the unconscious mind that the second state was more evil than the first. Mesmerism was discredited by several reports of the French Academy of Medicine because, among other things, it was believed to be more sexual than spiritual, and the science rather quickly achieved the Gothic and anachronistic distinction of being forbidden by the Holy Roman Inquisition. But even the disciples of Mesmer, who believed it was beneficial for the hysterical patient to air his sup-

74. *The Gothic Quest* (London, 1939), p. 18.
75. *The Way Down and Out: The Occult in Symbolic Literature* (Ithaca, 1959), p. 50.
76. Dickens, Bulwer, and Thackeray were his patients.
77. R. K. Webb, *Harriet Martineau* (New York, 1960), p. 231.

pressed identity, and the artists, who held that the unconscious was the source of all their inspirations, feared they were meddling with a dark and dangerous, perhaps with a forbidden part of the soul. G. H. Schubert called his important study *Die Nachtseite der Naturwissenschaft* and, as M. H. Abrams has pointed out, "there is in Richter's concept of the unconscious. . . [a] sinister component."[78] The *Doppelgänger*, a coinage of Richter's, is usually a satanic figure as he appears in Romantic fiction—in Hoffmann and Hogg, for instance. And even the French psychologists of the end of the nineteenth century—Charcot, Janet, Binet—who took up the concept and prepared the way for Freud, believed that the glittering alter ego was, at least, socially less acceptable than the respectable waking self. Stevenson's *Strange Case of Dr. Jekyll and Mr. Hyde*, Wilde's *The Picture of Dorian Gray* and Conrad's "The Secret Sharer" all reflect this psychomorality.

On the other hand, Townshend, in his *Facts in Mesmerism or Animal Magnetism* (1839), argued that subjects in the trance state are not only intellectually but *morally* superior to their waking selves, "lifted nearer to the fountain of all truth."[79] He finds them more honest, more sincere, more pious, more refined, more benevolent, and not at all sexual. "It is true that mesmeric patients act from impulse," he writes, "but then their impulses are good."[80] Townshend was a clergyman. In 1851, William Gregory, Professor of Chemistry at the University of Edinburgh, wrote that "the sleeper, in the magnetic state, has a consciousness quite separate and distinct from his ordinary consciousness. He is, in fact, if not a different individual, yet the same individual in a different and distinct phase of his being; and that phase, a higher one."[81] In America, Emerson, who

78. *The Mirror and the Lamp* (New York, 1953), p. 211.
79. (Boston, 1841), p. 160.
80. *Ibid.*, p. 194.
81. *Letters to a Candid Inquirer on Animal Magnetism* (London, 1851), p. 84. Of course, not everyone shared this trust. Browning was highly suspicious, and Hawthorne had serious reservations. In *The Sentimental Novel in America* (Durham, N.C., 1940), Brown notes that some of the many writers who employed animal magnetism in their works did so to warn their readers against it: "Mesmeric influence . . . was as commonly exerted by the villains as by the heroes and heroines." Timothy Shay Arthur [the author of *Ten Nights in a Barroom*], who assigned mesmerism to "a disorderly, and, therefore, evil origin," noted ominously [in *Agnes; or, The Possessed* (Philadelphia, 1848)] that "A woman may be made to believe that any person is her . . . husband, and she will act accordingly; and afterwards she will have no recollection of it, excepting as the operator pleases." (p. 188)
But Brown also recognizes mesmerism as one of the principal ingredients in the American "Pot of National Uplift," heated with what one novelist was pleased to call "moral electricity" (p. 181).

was not an enthusiast, accounted for the spectacular success of mesmerism by pointing out:

> It was human, it was genial, it affirmed unity and connection between remote points, and as such was an excellent criticism on the narrow and dead classifications of what passed for science; and the joy with which it was greeted was an instinct of the people which no true philosopher would fail to profit by. . . . The popularity of Combe's Constitution of Man; the humanity which was the aim of all the multitudinous works of Dickens, the tendency even of Punch's caricature, was all on the side of the people. There was a breath of new air, much vague expectation, a consciousness of power not yet finding its determinate aim.[82]

The metaphysical novelists were among those "true philosophers" who did not "fail to profit by" the general "instinct." They were all visionaries to greater or lesser degrees and were genuinely involved with such matters as mesmerism and spiritualism. The ghosts in *Wuthering Heights* are not Radcliffean claptrap; they are as real and as immediate as the living characters. The principal dramatic problem in *Jane Eyre* is solved by mental telepathy. Melville's Cosmopolitan in *The Confidence-Man* is both a mesmerist and a magician.[83] Hawthorne, despite his fears and reservations, had a compelling personal interest in mesmerism,[84] which figures strongly in two of his major works, *The House of the Seven Gables* and *The Blithedale Romance.* Dickens was himself an enthusiastic, adept mesmerist, one of the strongest supporters of Dr. Elliotson, who was his medical authority on the matter of Krook's death by spontaneous combustion. In a letter to a protégé, the tubercular John Owers, Dickens advised, "If my own life . . . were in peril, I would trust it to him implicitly."[85] Recommending the spiritualist Chauncy Hare Townshend, for whom he later acted as literary executor, he wrote Lady Blessington, "I am a believer in earnest."[86]

82. *Complete Works of Ralph Waldo Emerson* (Boston, 1903–04), X, 337–39. Quoted in Taylor Stoehr, "Hawthorne and Mesmerism," *Huntington Library Quarterly*, XXXIII (1969), 35.

83. Melville's serious preoccupation with occult religious phenomena has been powerfully argued by H. Bruce Franklin in *The Wake of the Gods: Melville's Mythology* (Stanford, 1963).

84. In "Hawthorne and Mesmerism" Taylor Stoehr writes that "The magical power of imagination was Hawthorne's chief theme in his writings, and the usefulness of the new pseudoscience lay in its adaptability to this theme. His art could be taken as a variety of mesmerism, a spell he wove over his readers, which might change their lives, and for which he might be responsible" (p. 58).

85. Aug. 24, 1841. *The Pilgrim Letters of Charles Dickens*, II, 369.

86. June 2, 1841. *Ibid.*, II, 292. The earnestness of his belief and its very great relevance to his fiction has just recently been demonstrated by Fred Kaplan in *Dickens and Mesmerism* (Princeton, 1976).

Another even older friend of Townshend's and an equally willing supporter of Elliotson's was Bulwer-Lytton, whose interests and beliefs encompassed the full range of spiritualism.[87] In *A Strange Story* (1862), Bulwer testifies explicitly to his conviction that the visionary condition is more real than the experiential world, but this had really been his position throughout most of his long career. Thus he wrote in 1849:

> I am a believer in the duality of the mind—all of us have two minds, one of which we take into the world, carry into clubs, walk the streets with, and use every day. Then there is another mind in which we pack up such sentiments as the world has not spoiled, our potential emotions, our conceptions of what is pure or heroic—a mind that vanishes when we walk into Bond Street, and are mere men among men! [88]

A variant of the same thought occurs in Bulwer's *Alice; or, The Mysteries* (1838), where Evelyn "most sensibly felt how little our real life is chronicled by external events,—how much we live a second and a higher life in our meditations and dreams. . . . Of the two ideal worlds that stretch beyond the inch of time on which we stand, Imagination is perhaps holier than Memory" (Bk. I, Chap. II). And in *What Will He Do With It?* (1858) Bulwer wrote that "we learn to read the human heart . . . through sympathy," not through experience; "if the Poet be born, not made, is it not because he is born to sympathise with what he has not experienced? (Pt. XII, Chap. II). In Bulwer's very first novel, the supposedly autobiographical *Falkland* (1827), the hero compares himself to Shakespeare's Prospero, whose magic is, of course, specifically equated to the poet's creative faculty. Later, in one of his *Caxtoniana* essays, Bulwer was to call

---

87. In *Bulwer Lytton as Occultist* (London, 1927), C. Nelson Stewart writes that "if one were asked to name the book which more than any other provided a matrix for the building-up of a modern theosophical philosophy in the English language, *Zanoni* seems the inevitable choice" (p. 1). Stewart argues throughout his book that Bulwer was an initiate of a secret Rosicrucian society and that occult studies were the center of his life. Robert Lee Wolff has recently made the same case much more substantially in *Strange Stories: Explorations in Victorian Fiction— The Occult and The Neurotic* (Boston, 1973), which contains an exhaustive account of Bulwer's occultism: "Bulwer's active studies in the occult began in the early 1830s and became increasingly important to him as the years went by. Astrology, alchemy, mesmerism, clairvoyance, hypnotism, spiritualism, and magic: he investigated them all at first hand, and wrote about them all." (pp. 148–49)

Wolff demonstrates Bulwer's associations with many of the important hypnotists, mesmerists, and occultists of his time—Braid, Elliotson, Townsend, Home, Eliphas Lévi (Alphonse-Louis Constant)—and he shows how a developing knowledge of spiritualism is demonstrated in Bulwer's fiction from *Godolphin* (1833) to *The Coming Race* (1871).

88. Letter to Lord Walpole, quoted in The Earl of Lytton, *The Life of Edward Bulwer, First Lord Lytton* (London, 1913), II, 128.

this power of the poet's "the normal clairvoyance of the imagination,"[89] but he had been arguing from as early as *Godolphin* (1833) that occultism is simply the power of the trained imagination. "This world," says a character from *Godolphin*, "is given up to two tribes of things that live and have a soul,—the one bodily and palpable as we are; the other invisible to our dull sight—though I have seen them—Dread Solemn Shadows, even in their mirth; the night is their season as the day is ours; they march in the moon beams; and are borne upon the wings of the winds. And with them, and by their thoughts, I raise myself from what I am and have been."[90]

A similar optimistic and higher belief in the visionary world is central to all the metaphysical novelists. Sometimes, as in Hawthorne's "A Select Party," this faith is expressed as forthrightly as in Bulwer—"The dominions which the spirit conquers for itself among unrealities become a thousand times more real than the earth whereon they stamp their feet saying, 'This is solid and substantial; this may be called a fact' "[91]—but always the mystical position is at least implicit in the themes and illustrated in the structures of Hawthorne's works.[92] From as early as his college days, Hawthorne liked to think of himself as Oberon, the master magician who, in Shakespeare's play, stands for the author, motivating his characters, interpreting their actions, and introducing his audience to the mystical ramifications of farcical human behavior. The showman of "The Seven Vagabonds," an "old magician," entertaining "his guests with a mask of shadows,"[93] is, like Bulwer's Falkland, also compared to Prospero, who magically structures the action of *The Tempest* so that he may redeem its fallen world. Fancy fulfills a similar function in the allegorical story, "Fancy's Showbox," when he undertakes to convert the aged Mr. Smith by projecting representations of the latter's contemplated, although never performed crimes; and the painter of "The Prophetic Pictures" prevents a murder which his portraits had foreseen and very nearly caused, interposing "himself between the wretched beings, with the same sense of

---

89. *Caxtoniana*, I, 39–54.

90. Chap. LXI. Elsewhere in *Godolphin* he had called, as we have seen, for "a philosophical romance . . . a metaphysical *Gil Blas*." In *Ernest Maltravers* he tried to write a *Wilhelm Meister* of the practical life. "Preface to the Edition of 1840," *Ernest Maltravers* (London, 1873), pp. 7–8.

91. *The Complete Works of Nathaniel Hawthorne*, II, 71.

92. In " 'Young Goodman Brown' and Hawthorne's Theory of Mimesis," *NCF*, XXIII (1969), Taylor Stoehr writes that Hawthorne's tales "tell us that things need not be what they seem, that there is always another, better world possible to faith," and that "the means to this faith is itself through fiction and related activities of the imagination, dreams and visions" (p. 408).

93. *Complete Works of Hawthorne*, I, 394.

power to regulate their destiny as to alter a scene upon the canvas. He stood like a magician, controlling the phantoms which he had evoked."

Perhaps the finest example of the Prospero figure in nineteenth-century fiction occurs in *The Marble Faun*, where Miriam is less a character caught up in the action of the story than she is a high priestess of the carnival and the mystical controlling force in the lives of all her friends. It is not too much to say that Miriam structures all the action of the romance. First she recognizes Donatello's mythic significance and plays nymph opposite his faun during the chapter called "The Sylvan Dance." This part of the story is Donatello's, as Miriam dramatically announces at its conclusion: " 'Hush; leave me!' . . .'Your hour is past; his [the Model's] hour has come!' " (Chap. X). And as though with a touch of the wand, she changes the very genre of the book from innocent pastoral to Gothic romance. In the second section, the Model's hour, Miriam authorizes the murder of her double, ergo of herself, and thereby transforms the naïve faun into the guilt-laden, Byronic Count of Monte Beni, who broods in his dark tower. There she mourns with him, a secret guest in his Gothic tomb, patiently preparing him and the story for still another transformation. " 'High noon!' " said the sculptor. " 'It is Miriam's hour!' " (Chap. XXXIV).

In this last section, starting with her mystic marriage in the square of Perugia, Miriam turns pure magician. She has one more role to assume in relation to Donatello, who has been a demigod, an aristocrat, and is now ready at last to become a man. She now plays *contadina* as the two go about the countryside as peasants. But Miriam operates during this section in relation to all the characters as a sort of fairy queen in medieval romance. She has some mysterious connection with Hilda's abduction to the land of ideal forms, where the pale, stern virgin will somehow be changed into a warm household Madonna, fit for a good man's love. And she arranges for the softened Hilda's reappearance at the carnival to coincide exactly with Donatello's arrest, her own sacrifice. In the meantime, between moments of meaningful life with the faun she has converted into a man, she performs a feat which, in terms of Hawthorne's previous writing, seems even more miraculous, she transforms an artist into a lover. Part of Miriam's motivation for delaying the release of Hilda lies, no doubt, in her desire to have a few more happy moments with her own lover, but from the way she teases Kenyon, it appears that she uses the delay also to worry this cautious aesthete into anxious concern for Hilda, and therefore into warm life. And certainly in her "sacred hour" (Chap. XLIX) as Queen of the Carnival, Miriam is authoress of all the symbolic assaults made on Kenyon—the sunflowers and nettles which the giantess offers him, the plaster-gun shot taken at his heart, the cauliflower the young man throws at him, and the rosebud, which the transformed Hilda tosses. Miriam's final acts in the story are to bestow an authorial blessing on the two lovers she has magically created and to send them a mystic ornament as a wedding gift.

The Prospero or Oberon figure is also central to Dickens. In *Our Mutual Friend* Noddy Boffin carries a magical staff or wand which seems to whisper to him, and he constructs an elaborate "Pious Fraud" to redeem the heroine. Old Martin Chuzzlewit was modeled on another of Shakespeare's ambiguous, grace-dealing characters, the Duke from *Measure for Measure.* Indeed such quasi-mystical figures, taken both from Shakespeare and the fairy-tale tradition, occur almost everywhere in Dickens' works. Riah, the old Jew of *Our Mutual Friend* is a fairy "godmother" to Jenny Wren and Lizzie Hexam, as, more ambiguously, are Magwitch and Miss Havisham to Pip in *Great Expectations.* One of the "interpolated" tales of *Pickwick Papers* recounts how a drunken sexton was converted by a benevolent goblin, and this is, of course, the serious pattern of both *A Christmas Carol* and *The Chimes.*

The benevolent goblin, who represents the imagination, stands also for the author, Charles Dickens, all of whose novels are magical attempts to save the drunken sextons of his society.[94] And when we consider that Hawthorne's Prospero characters are all artists of some sort, it is perhaps not too much to suggest that the authors of the metaphysical novel saw themselves, as their masters in the previous generation had urged, in the role of mystical priest to a faithless generation. Like the writers of allegory and myth whom Angus Fletcher describes, each conceived his function as that of "the magician . . . trying to control nature" rather than merely to understand it, and seeking to sway his audience to redemption "by magic devices."[95]

Many critics have acknowledged at least aspects of this commitment on the part of the metaphysical novelists and have regretted it as a poor thing to set beside the sensible experiential world, which was bound to overwhelm it. Thus, Howells, who had some admiration for Dickens' "ethical intention," remarks:

94. In *Imagination Indulged! The Irrational in the Nineteenth-Century Novel* (Montreal and London, 1972), Elliott Gose interprets the seemingly omnipotent Inspector Bucket of *Bleak House* as illustrating the motif we have just been describing, and he argues "that there are vital connections between Inspector Bucket as detective-magician and Dickens as writer-magician" (p. 94). Gose sees Bulwer as another of these writer-magicians.

95. *Allegory: The Theory of a Symbolic Mode* (Ithaca, N.Y., 1964), pp. 191–92.

People always knew that character is not changed by a dream in a series of tableaux; that a ghost cannot do much towards reforming an inordinately selfish person; that a life cannot be turned white, like a head of hair, in a single night, by the most allegorical apparition; that want and sin and shame cannot be cured by kettles singing on the hob; and gradually they ceased to make believe that there was virtue in these devices and appliances.[96]

The metaphysical novelists were not insensible to this tendency of mind, and surely they must have known that by juxtaposing their magic with a powerfully rendered version of the material world, they ran the risk of making the reader's return to skepticism even less gradual than it might otherwise be. Since they were trying to redeem the world from a seemingly triumphant materialism, they must have possessed a fair estimate of the power they were opposing. But neither did they suppose that their own visions, derived from the greatest sages and writers of the century in which they were born and greeted in the years of their maturity by what Emerson called "an instinct of the people," were flashes of mere stage magic. The romantic metaphysicals had given them a philosophy, and modern occultism, washed clean of its old diabolical associations, seemed certainly to offer them a possible means of escape from the stultifying faith in experience. There were serious structural liabilities to be overcome, but the new mysticism seemed to give them precisely what they and a great many of their contemporaries had been calling for, a key to the prison of a phenomenal world which appeared to separate them from the exercise of their greater human potentials.

III: THE TWO-PART VISION: PARALLEL STRUCTURE

As realism developed in the nineteenth century, more and more of the old narrative conventions of the loose method became unpopular with the critics. Multiple narration, digressions, episodes, the mixture of genres were inimical both to the epistemic method of the realists and to the dramatic unity they were trying to achieve. These devices were, therefore, rather quickly swept away. Double or parallel plotting, on the other hand, was a convention which the realists took much longer to discard. Eventually, even this structural relic was purged from the novel, as it had been from the drama, but in the middle of the nineteenth century it still had such unromantic professors as Thackeray and Trollope.

The metaphysical novelists continued to use parallel plots because the convention was important to them in a number of ways. William Empson's chapter "Double Plots" in *Some Versions of Pastoral* bristles with valuable

96. "Criticism and Fiction" in *Criticism and Fiction and Other Essays*, p. 83.

suggestions. At one point, sounding like Schiller on epic versus dramatic form, Empson writes:

> The device sets your judgment free because you need not identify yourself firmly with any one of the characters (the drama of personality is liable to boil down to this); a situation is repeated for quite different characters, and this puts the main emphasis in the situation not the characters. Thus the effect of having two old men with ungrateful children, of different sorts, is to make us generalise the theme of Lear and feel that whole classes of children have become ungrateful, all nature is breaking up in the storm. The situation is made something valuable in itself, perhaps for reasons hardly realised; it can work on you like myth.[97]

Parallel plotting, therefore, emphasizes theme over character, and a recognition of this tendency was one of the things which made the technique useful to the philosophical romancers and which ultimately turned the realists, for whom theme had to develop from a firm identification with character, toward unity of action, the single plot.

A double-stranded story also facilitated the double vision of the metaphysical novel, an obvious point. In the preface to the second edition of *The Disowned* (London, 1829), Bulwer wrote that he had decided to give his book two separate plots because he wanted "to make two marked divisions: human nature, as we see it in ordinary life, and human nature in its rarer attributes." Similarly, his *Rienzi* balances a pastoral love idyl against an epic tale of dynastic ambition, thus giving us the two world views which characterize so many works in his school and of his tradition. As Empson writes:

> The interaction of . . . two plots gives a particularly clear setting for, or machine for imposing, the social and metaphysical ideas on which pastoral depends. What is displayed on the tragi-comic stage is a sort of marriage of myths of heroic and pastoral, a thing felt as fundamental to both and fundamental to the health of society.[98]

On the other hand, the two plots of *Vanity Fair* do not present opposed visions of reality. Both heroines accept the materialism of the society Thackeray has posited; they differ only in that the sympathetic Amelia becomes a willing victim to these values, while knavish Becky tries to use them to aid her ambition. The one girl sacrifices herself to George Osborne, a tawdry imitation of tawdry George IV, to whom the other aspires. Thackeray laments this vision, but unlike the metaphysical novelists, he has nothing to set against it, and he can use his parallel plots,

97. (Norfolk, Va., n.d.), p. 54.
98. *Ibid.*, pp. 30–31.

which differ neither in meaning nor in genre, only to give his sad truth a double emphasis.

Thackeray unifies his two-plot novel, not only by this singleness of vision, but also, as all realists achieve unity, by providing strong causal connections between the plots. Just as he makes the ending of each heroine's story an inevitable effect of its beginning, so he relates the separate strands with constant dramatic interactions. Becky courts Amelia's brother and seduces her husband. At the climax she provides the information which sets Amelia free to marry Dobbin. So *Vanity Fair* is really only one story, after all. Trollope is also a master of this technique of unifying his works by actions between the plots. *Can You Forgive Her?* and *The Way We Live Now* are especially remarkable in this respect. Although the Mary Garth plot of *Middlemarch* stands rather by itself, the other three plots are connected by interactions, and several other of George Eliot's novels are reduced to single actions by the central device of confronting the heroine —Maggie, Eppie, Esther, even Gwendolen—with moral and dramatic choices, represented by the heroes of the separate lines of narrative development.

Metaphysical novels, in which the two plots embody contradictory visions and are rendered in different subgenres, and where the author is not a believer in a materialistic cause-and-effect universe, lack all the obvious means towards unity. However, parallel plotting is not a liability to be overcome in the metaphysical novel; it is, indeed, the primary source of power, a "power of suggestion," which Empson says "is the strength of the double plot. Once you take the two parts to correspond, any character may take on *mana* because he seems to cause what he corresponds to or be Logos of what he symbolises."[99] And as Angus Fletcher writes concerning "magical causation" in allegory, "When plots and subplots are combined in certain ways, the effect of interplay between them is a causal one. . . . The agents of allegory can [thus] help, hurt, change, and otherwise affect each other 'as if by magic.' "[100] This is certainly what happens in Hawthorne's *The Marble Faun*, where the pairs of characters in the two plots— Miriam and Donatello, Hilda and Kenyon—never interact meaningfully with one another except on the spiritual level. Ahab and Ishmael, Scrooge and Tiny Tim, never even speak together, and yet there is a spiritual relationship between them which might not have been possible if they had existed together in a simple, unified, cause-and-effect plot.

Such mystical relationships across the plots cannot occur in works of pure realism. No one ever supposes that Amelia's goodness will save

99. *Ibid.*, p. 34.
100. *Allegory*, p. 182.

Becky. Even in somewhat realistic works which permit spiritual influence, like *Middlemarch*, the magic seems to stop at the borders of each individual story. Thus, Dorothea can save Ladislaw, who belongs to her own story, but, though she tries to rescue Lydgate, and though he recognizes that her heart is as large as the Virgin Mary's, her power does not reach so far. Gwendolen Harleth is at least improved, if not redeemed, by an influence from the parallel plot, but then *Daniel Deronda* is very nearly a metaphysical novel and has consequently suffered attacks from the same schools of critics who have criticized the apparent disunity in Dickens and Melville.

In the metaphysical novel the influences move easily across the plots, whether the double structure is sequential or parallel. We have already noted that the characters from the second plot of *Wuthering Heights* liberate their elders in the first.[101] In *A Tale of Two Cities*, after the genre has shifted to allegorical melodrama, a character from the English *mal du siècle* plot is able literally to save his opposite, a character from the French plot of inherited guilt. And when *The House of the Seven Gables* has made its change from gentle realism to Gothic fantasy, Hawthorne suggests that, if he had lived, even Jaffrey Pyncheon might have been redeemed by the wonders of the night he has passed with his ghostly ancestors (Chap. 18). Indeed, just such an unlikely conversion, accomplished through a similar juxtaposition of genres, was exactly the pattern of *A Christmas Carol* and *The Chimes*.

The most obvious two-genre, two-plot romance of the period is *Bleak House*, where Dickens, using no reconciling frame device, continually alternates an anonymous, present-tense, seemingly omniscient narrative with the highly subjective reminiscences of Esther Summerson. The juxtaposition of these two plots has been a favorite topic of critical discussion, but the elements have seldon been reconciled. One reader sees the impersonal plot as written in open competition with Thackeray, and the Esther plot in rivalry with Charlotte Brontë.[102] Others, viewing the narratives as illustrating some of the categories of Northrop Frye, maintain that "*Bleak House* has the dialectical structure of romance," which opposes winter and spring worlds,[103] or that the conflicting world views of the two narrators

---

101. At the end of his chapter on "Double Plot" Empson tosses us the following scrap: "And *Wuthering Heights* is a good case of double plot in the novel, both for covert deification and telling the same story twice with the two possible endings." *Some Versions of Pastoral* (London, 1935), p. 86.

102. Lionel Stevenson, "Dickens' Dark Novels," *Sewanee Review*, LI (1943), 404–405.

103. Joseph I. Fradin, "Will and Society in *Bleak House*," *PMLA*, LXXXI (1966), 108.

are embodied in genres which Frye places on either side of the "novel"—"anatomy" and "romance."[104]

These archetypal readings are attractive to me, and I follow them except to their conclusions, which are that since Esther does not succeed in reconstituting the entire diseased society but only in brightening "the corner where she is," *Bleak House* must be regarded finally as "a parody of romance,"[105] or that the book must be understood rather in the way in which Richard Chase understands *Moby-Dick*, as the work of an author content to illustrate "opposing world views" and to show how "these views can color the world."[106] Before arguing with these conclusions, however, I should like to review in some greater detail the two worlds and world views described by the separate narrators of *Bleak House*.

The anonymous voice speaks, indeed, from a winter world of sterility and confusion. It is a world in which literally nothing ("nothink") of any consequence is known because, as it seems, the old forms of authority—the aristocracy, the church, the legal structure—have worn out and become meaninglessly inoperative. *Bleak House*, according to this voice, is a book of orphans for whom no one will take responsibility because no one can understand either his own relationship to society or his consequent duty to humanity. Lady Dedlock and Mrs. Rouncewell do not know of the continued existence of their children. The Lord Chancellor, the legal and/or symbolic guardian of all the orphans, is officially ignorant of Gridley and literally unaware of Jo, the most obvious of all the orphans. If the parents would speak, would only acknowledge the children who are dying around them every day, then, the anonymous voice insists, society could have a general pattern and a man might be able to exist in it. But how is it possible for anyone to act responsibly when he is so radically ignorant, when like Krook, the parody of the Lord Chancellor, everyone is too unschooled to read life correctly and too suspicious even to accept instruction?

Bleak House is thus a work about social conditions, but it is more profoundly a study of the condition of man, for such ignorance as we have just described, though it is most acutely apparent in a period of political laissez-faire, is really man's lot everywhere and at all times. Consequently any society is a labyrinth which each man enters without the aid of an Ariadne's thread, and where he is more than likely to encounter the monsters of starvation, disease, perhaps even murder, certainly of death. It is a terrifyingly dangerous world we live in, and most of the people here are trying desperately to find a way to survive.

104. Doris Stringham Delespinasse, "The Significance of Dual Point of View in *Bleak House*," *NCF*, XXIII (1968), 254.
105. "Will and Society in *Bleak House*," p. 108.
106. "The Significance of Dual Point of View in *Bleak House*," p. 264.

The example of helpless Jo seems to demonstrate that perfect ignorance is the poorest defense in such a chaos. Knowledge, said the founder of British empiricism, is power, and the materialistic inhabitants of the winter world seek through knowledge the power to keep themselves from falling into pits, the power to build a Chesney Wold somewhere in the dark labyrinth or at least some modest fortification from which other wanderers cannot order them to "move on" and risk further exposure to the terrible menaces. Consequently, men seek knowledge for self-protection, and thus *Bleak House* is also a book of detectives—Mrs. Snagsby, Guppy, Bucket, Tulkinghorn—who believe that if they can only put enough facts together, they will amass a plan for the entire labyrinth, a plan which will allow them to exist in safety.[107]

The theory under which these characters operate may seem logical enough because it is the plan by which most of us have chosen to live. But as the case of Tulkinghorn shows, the theory fails because of the impossibility of its minor premise: even Tulkinghorn, who knows more "important" secrets than anyone else, cannot know everything. He fears George, who is harmless, and his stupid misunderstanding of Hortense, who refuses the English cash nexus, costs him his life. Partial knowledge, even almost complete knowledge, will not do in such a situation. It simply makes a man more fully aware of the potential dangers around every next corner, so that Tulkinghorn lives his life in constant terror, compulsively discovering and eating up secrets in the desperate and false belief that they may save him. It is a vague hope, at best, and Tulkinghorn has no clear idea of what good the individual secrets will do him or how he can use them. His fury at Lady Dedlock is not in Sir Leicester's behalf but in his own, since she threatens to deprive his collection of one of its best secrets by making it public.

Other characters try to gain knowledge by turning to the old and worn-out authorities. Mrs. Snagsby, in addition to her free-lance detective work, tries to derive certainty from religion. But even Jo can see that Mr. Chadband is only "a-speakin' to hisself" (Chap. 47). Volumnia and Mrs. Rouncewell listen attentively to Sir Leicester, who likewise has no wisdom to impart. Most significantly, the Chancery suitors turn to the Lord Chancellor. Poor Richard Carstone, as George Eliot would undoubtedly have called

107. In *Charles Dickens: The World of His Novels* (Cambridge, Mass., 1958), J. Hillis Miller writes: "everywhere in *Bleak House* we see characters who are engaged in an attempt to vanquish the chaos of a merely phenomenal world. These characters, in one way or another, try to discover in the world an intelligible order, an authentic relationship between events. And this will happen, they know, only if they can find the world patterns of events which are meaningful to them." (p. 167)

him, is the closest approach to a transcendental hero in the works of Dickens. With something like the determination of Melville's Ahab, who has resolved to have satisfaction from Moby Dick and to force his enemy to give up the ultimate secret, Richard, after a youth of wavering indecision, bends all his energies to make the Protean Lord Chancellor deliver a verdict. Of course, neither the jurist nor the whale are saying anything, supposing either has anything to say, but these failures do not in the least lessen the tragic heroism of the intrepid pursuers.

This then is the winter world of the anonymous narrator—another "damp, drizzly November" of the soul, a place of chaos, peopled by desperate men and women, trying ambitiously to discover some master plan which can never be vouchsafed them. It is characterized by deceit and violence, and symbolically, by the prevailing east wind, which brings confusing fog, contagion, and deadly cold to England, as it brought locusts in Exodus and divine retribution in *The House of Seven Gables.*

Bulwer's *My Novel, by Pisistratus Caxton; or, Varieties in English Life,* which appeared in *Blackwood's* during the two years before Dickens wrote *Bleak House,* and at the time when the two writers had their closest professional relationship,[108] is also a first-person to third-person encyclopedic novel. Bulwer so disliked the statement—knowledge is power—that he refused to believe Bacon had authored it, and *My Novel* is calculated to disprove the aphorism. Thus Randal Leslie "the still spirit of Intellectual Evil" (Book IX, Chap. X) believes, like Tulkinghorn and the other detectives of *Bleak House,* "there is no knowledge which has power more useful than that of the secrets of men" (Book VII, Chap. XXI). Leslie maintains this conviction, which leads him to villainy, although he is admonished by Parson Dale, Bulwer's moral spokesman, that "Intellectual Power refined to its utmost, and wholly void of beneficence, resembles only one being. . . . the Devil; and even he, sir, did not succeed" (Bk. VIII, Chap. VIII).

In *My Novel* the devil is frustrated by a redeeming heroine, who, as we have already seen, always represents the nonintellectual force in Bulwer's works. Violante, "the woman who exalts" (Final Chapter), breaks the spell with which the world of positivistic questors like Randal Leslie had robbed the passive hero of his motive power to do good for others. Thus the naïve overcomes the sophisticated and renders the good powerful.

In *Bleak House,* where this same allegory is much more powerfully mythicized, Esther Summerson, poor, weak, modest, not very clever, has her own plot and is set, rather unequally it would seem, against the winter

---

108. Dickens had just named a child after Bulwer, and he was directing a production of Bulwer's *Not So Bad As We Seem* to benefit the new Guild for Literature and Art, of which the two writers were cofounders.

world of intellectual, Faustian questors. She comes up to London from Windsor and Reading, out of the west, in the very teeth of the evil wind; and then, in spite of the cold, she makes her gradual way northward, like the summer sun after which she is named, to St. Albans, to Lincolnshire, and eventually all the way to Yorkshire. I do not agree with those critics who suggest that she represents merely a posited alternative or with those who believe that she fails. Esther's is a constantly triumphant progression. Accepting the theory that complete knowledge is beyond the possibility of her weak comprehension—indeed it is of everyone's—and that to quest for it is both wasteful and evil, Esther instinctively concentrates, as Carlyle had urged, on the work closest at hand. Instead of charting the terraquatious globe, she illuminates a small corner of it. By the end of the book she has kindled four hearth fires which were cold before her influence began—the fires at Caddy Turveydrop's, at Charley's, and at the old and new Bleak Houses. And while she has not yet redeemed the entire world, such an expectation belongs to the world of the self-defeating Faust figures, her discredited alternatives.

Nevertheless, the dissatisfaction of the critics is understandable. Judged as a real person, Esther's accomplishments are remarkable—she saves John Jarndyce, Ada, Caddy, Charley, and Allan Woodcourt, and she brings final comfort to Richard and Jo—but clearly Dickens wants us to see her as something more than a real person. As William Empson says of Donne's double-plotted *First Anniversary,* "The only way to make the poem sensible is to accept Elizabeth Drury as the Logos,"[109] and, since this is equally true of *Bleak House,* Esther's accomplishments as a religious figure, the new hope of the world, may seem to fall somewhat short. Even if we grant, as indeed we must, that the terms of the salvation she offers require that the orphans fall into her direct influence and that the whole society cannot be redeemed until her hearth fires spread gradually throughout all of England, there remain certain questions concerning her power. She seems to leave some important problems of the winter plot unsolved. Why, for instance, can't she preserve Jenny's child or Gridley, and why can't she save Jo alive, or at least Richard, with whom she has so many opportunities?

I think the answer to these questions may be that Esther has not come into her full powers at the times when her failures occur. She is by no means the static character she has so often been taken for, although her development, like the development of romance characters in general, does not come about through the easy to follow novelistic cause-and-effect processes we are used to tracing. She changes nevertheless from a power-

109. *Some Versions of Pastoral,* p. 84.

less, guilt-ridden little girl, convinced of her own unworthiness,[110] to a well-adjusted and loving mother, still humble, but confident in her benevolence. Her name is Esther, and her fate, like that of the Biblical heroine, is to rise from a despised birth to become the beautiful and redeeming queen of her oppressed, leaderless people. Moreover, her development is made possible by a process which would be unusual in a realistic novel, by the spiritual interactions between the two plots, interactions which are especially meaningful in light of the care Dickens has taken to separate the plots generically.

Esther is central to her own plot. Her mother, Honoria, the imprisoned snow queen, is the heroine of the winter narrative. The spiritual interaction between these plots and genres begins when Esther accepts the guilt and suffering which has been shunned by her mother and the impersonal world she rules. As Carlyle had shown in *Past and Present*[111] and as Dickens ratified both in *Bleak House* and *Dombey and Son*, contagious disease is the last resort of outcasts to demonstrate their human relationship to an indifferent society. The sickness, therefore, transmitted through Jo and Charley, was intended for Lady Dedlock, who had permitted it to spread; but Esther receives it gladly, especially when she speculates that her disfigurement will lessen her resemblance to her mother and thereby hide her mother's sin. Her disease also awakens her mother's conscience and begins the melting process which will eventually change Esther, who is the only certain bastard of *Bleak House*, into the only actually acknowledged child of all the orphans in the book, and therefore render her the queen, capable of leading and redeeming the *Bleak House* world.

Esther's illness drives Honoria "nearly frantic" (Chap. 36), and brings about a partial redemption, as indicated by her tearful though secret recognition of Esther and by the full awakening of her sense of guilt. The immediate result of this breakthrough is to renew in Esther all the old feelings which have been hindering her full development. Typically, Esther begins by taking the guilt upon herself:

> I hope it may not appear very unnatural or bad in me, that I then became heavily sorrowful to think I had ever been reared. That I felt as if I knew it would have been better and happier for many people, if indeed I had never breathed. That I had a terror of myself, as the danger and the possible disgrace of my own mother, and of a proud family name. That I was so confused and shaken, as to be possessed by a belief that it was right, and

110. Esther, at this stage of her development, is best described by William Axton, "The Trouble with Esther," *Modern Language Quarterly*, XXVI (1965), 545–557.

111. *Past and Present*, Bk. III, Chap. II.

had been intended, that I should die in my birth; and that it was wrong, and not intended, that I should be then alive.

These are the real feelings that I had. I fell asleep, worn out; and when I awoke, I cried afresh to think that I was back in the world, with my load of trouble for others. I was more than ever frightened of myself, thinking anew of her, against whom I was a witness; of the owner of Chesney Wold; of the new and terrible meaning of the old words, now moaning in my ear like a surge upon the shore, "Your mother, Esther, was your disgrace, and you are hers. The time will come—and soon enough— when you will understand this better, and will feel it too, as no one save a woman can." With them, those words returned, "Pray daily that the sins of others be not visited upon your head." I could not disentangle all that was about me; and I felt as if the blame and the shame were all in me, and the visitation had come down. (Chap. 36)

As the passage indicates, guilt is not a new feeling for Esther. Her sense of extreme unworthiness has been a dominant feature of her character since her early education, preventing her full participation in life and curtailing her in her efforts to help others. But now her guilt is fully focused for the first time. It has been removed from the unconscious to the conscious mind, and Esther is able to face it at last. Thus after this initial submission, and after she has been reassured by letters from her loved ones at Bleak House, Esther is able to assert her innocence, and in terms which indicate her symbolic function in the story: "I knew I was as innocent of my birth as a *queen* of hers; and that before my Heavenly Father I should not be punished for birth, nor a *queen* rewarded for it." [112]

This is the beginning of Esther's queenly power, which had long lain dormant.[113] But her strength has far to grow before it will be fully effective as a redemptive force. To be guiltless as a queen is not enough, although Esther is at least capable now of giving absolution to Jo, *Bleak House*'s symbolic orphan. She is also able to inspire Allan Woodcourt, who first shrinks back from Jo "with a sudden horror" (Chap. 46), so that Allan can bring atonement to Esther's spiritual and disease-related brother by leading him in a thematically significant "Our Father." Nevertheless, in this intermediate state, she is powerless to slow Richard's destructive career, and she is incapable of admitting, even to herself, that she loves Woodcourt. Instead she promises herself to Jarndyce, a suitably loving husband, such as her mother had chosen, but an older man who, again like Sir Leicester, will not ultimately fulfill her by making her a mother. At this

112. Chap. 36. My italics.

113. According to Elliott Gose's reading, John Jarndyce is a white magician who has been trying to awaken this queenly identity in Esther. *Imagination Indulged!*, pp. 76–85.

point Esther appears, although innocent of her mother's sin of pride, to be following in her footsteps.

As previously noted, Dickens read *The Scarlet Letter* just a few months before he began writing *Bleak House*.[114] He was not favorably impressed, but the thematic similarities between the two works are great enough to suggest at least that we have to do in both cases with an important romance motif. Honoria's secret recognition of Esther is, if not influenced by, then certainly analogous to the nighttime scene in Hawthorne when Dimmesdale stands secretly upon the scaffold with Hester and Pearl. Neither act is a sufficient recognition, and Esther, like Pearl, must remain spellbound until she is acknowledged fully. Esther is free to redeem the winter world fully only after it, as represented by its queen, Lady Dedlock, is ready to make the proper gesture towards her.

Honoria's true identity consists in her motherhood. Everything else about her is a disguise, an evasion of her real self and of the legitimate responsibility which, like all the other parents of her winter world, she has failed or refused to recognize. Her life as Lady Dedlock "(who is childless)" (Chap. 2), represents her most elaborate evasion, but she also masquerades, to Jo's confusion, as her own servant. Jo subsequently mixes her up with Esther, and Miss Flite mistakes her significantly for the Lord Chancellor's termagant wife, who is allegedly responsible for the jurist's failure to make definitive judgments. Only in her last action does Honoria become symbolically herself, when, driven by terror and her conscience, she hastens away from her life as Lady Dedlock and puts on the rags of Jenny, who has been defined throughout the book with strict reference to her motherhood. Jenny is the mother of the dead child, as Honoria, before she began her masquerades, believed herself to be.

Hillis Miller writes that "in assuming at last the self she has so long been fleeing, Lady Dedlock achieves the only kind of freedom possible in Dickens' world, the freedom to be one's destined self."[115] But she also achieves something across the plots and genres in relation to Esther, her daughter and queenly successor. Honoria's death, in a book of symbolic deaths and diseases—spontaneous combustion, gout, smallpox, etc.—is, almost literally, a melting of the weeping snow queen, and it is probably at the moment of her physical reunion with the decomposed body of

114. Letter to Forster, [July 1851]. *Letters of Dickens*, II, 335. The letters which have been published so far do not prove that Dickens read *The House of the Seven Gables*, but Hawthorne's romance was popular in England at the time Dickens' own "House" novel was being written, and the scene in which the narrator gloats over the murdered body of Tulkinghorn suggests that Dickens may have read the chapter describing Judge Pyncheon's death.

115. *Dickens: World of His Novels*, p. 205.

Esther's father in the foul, running graveyard that Inspector Bucket ultimately acknowledges Esther. There is almost a coronation speech: "When a young lady is as mild as she's game, and as game as she's mild, that's all I ask, and more than I expect. She then becomes a *Queen*, and that's about what you are yourself."[116] And Trooper George, using characteristically humbler language, salutes her as "a pattern young lady" (Chap. 63).

Now Esther, like Hawthorne's Pearl after her father's public and daylight recognition of her, has come fully into her own.[117] Now, at last, she can admit to herself that she loves Woodcourt and she can take advantage of her guardian's generosity by becoming Woodcourt's "household goddess" and the mother of his children. More important, as queen *and* mother, she has replaced all the false parents and those who acted falsely *in loco parentis*. She can begin now to save the English orphans. Hers is, as Skimpole describes it, a "little orderly system," which, for Conversation Kenge, would never do in a great country; but it is nevertheless the only hope for England, and as Dickens optimistically concludes, her hearth fire is spreading.

Like Carlyle, whom he followed as much as he could,[118] Dickens had no universal Morrison's Pill to cure the ills of society. He had only Esther's little system. And he was as willing as Carlyle to "let Bobus and Company sneer, 'That is your Reform!'"

> Yes, Bobus, that is our reform, and except in that, and what follows out of that, we have no hope at all. Reform, like Charity, O Bobus, must begin at home. Once well at home, how will it radiate outwards, irrepressible, into all that we touch and handle, speak and work, kindling ever new light, by incalculable contagion, spreading in geometric ratio, far and wide,— doing good only, wheresoever it spreads, and not evil. . . . Light once kindled spreads till all is luminous.[119]

Of course, Carlylean rhetoric will hardly convince those readers who, though willing to concede that Esther provides perhaps the best hope, are unable to convince themselves that the hope is very good or that Dickens could really have believed in it. As Professor Hardy complains, "We are left with the constructiveness of the good housekeeper and the good doctor, rewarded with each other, cosily settled in their rustic 'Bleak House,' whose 'doll's rooms' strike some readers as an impropriety after Tom All Alone's. . . . We are asked to move from the powerful indictment to this weak doll's

116. Chap. 59. My italics.
117. Both Pearl and Esther, after they have achieved proper status, marry into aristocracies like fairy-tale princesses.
118. See letters to Carlyle July 13, 1854 and April 13, 1863. *Letters of Dickens*, II, 567, and III, 348.
119. *Past and Present*, Bk. I, Chap. IV.

house conclusion."[120] Once again, I find it easy to sympathize with this disappointment, especially since I recognize, in the reference to Ibsen, the tone of Women's Liberation. The book seemed to promise a more striking finale—either a spectacular redemption, such as Sydney Carton was later to provide, or at least a thundering despair; certainly not a YES, in zephyr. But, from the metaphysical novelist's point of view, our very disappointment is a symptom of the disease which he has undertaken to cure in us, and, which is more important, it is a necessary part of his treatment that our false expectations for heroic conclusions, either positive or negative, not only be permitted, but even encouraged.

We are now at the very heart of the so-called Dickens problem and of the identical problem modern critics have with Hawthorne and Melville. The realists have convinced us that writers of fiction owe us a certain honesty, that novelists should never appear intentionally to have misled us. Most graphic and narrative art, of course, is illusion, but the novel, at least from the time of Defoe, has laid special claim not only to a higher, but to a literal truthfulness. It is on this basis that James is so severe with Trollope. The requirement of suspense does permit the holding back of certain information, but some realists were uncomfortable even with this license, and they either did without suspense or eliminated the omniscient author so that they might establish a technical alibi for the evasion. Thus we do not know the essential fact that Chad Newsome and Madame de Vionnet are lovers until quite late in *The Ambassadors* because Strether, rather than James, is the post of observation.

How far from this scrupulosity we seem to be in a work like *Our Mutual Friend*, where, as Graham Smith writes:

> Boffin belongs to the tradition of Dickens' genially eccentric old bene-factors, and yet we feel convinced that Dickens is prepared to sacrifice him in the interests of artistic truth. His failure to do so is damaging . . . to the entire novel, but it makes nonsense of the earlier stages in which we watched Boffin's breakdown. . . . Such manipulation of people, in life or in art, is at once arrogant and frivolous. It cannot be denied that the weakness of the Boffin strand seriously undermines the novel's artistic unity. We sense in it a failure of nerve.[121]

Of course, no one believes that Dickens first intended the "breakdown" to be legitimate and then changed his mind for the sake of a happy ending. Smith calls "Boffin's moral degeneration . . . a well-intentioned sham,"[122] and his serious admiration for *Great Expectations* indicates that he does

---

120. *Dickens: The Later Novels* (London, 1968), p. 21.
121. *Dickens, Money, and Society*, pp. 182–83.
122. *Ibid.*, p. 182.

not always object to being tricked by a novel, so long as all the narrative controls are right, and when the surprise does not contradict his own world view. In the end it doesn't really matter to the reader (of course it matters terribly to the deluded Pip) whether the fortune comes from Magwitch or Miss Havisham; Pip's expectations were evil in either case, and both benefactors are ultimately exposed as corrupt. But in *Our Mutual Friend* Dickens first convinces us that he shares our skeptical faith in the irresistible force of money to destroy even the best of men. Boffin's degeneration into mean miserliness seems to be a magnificent demonstration of the power of social conditioning. Then Dickens blandly informs us that it was all a trick, perpetrated to teach Bella Wilfer, whose self-confidence had been destroyed by just such a faith as ours, that this force can indeed be resisted by the greater power of love. Smith calls the deception "one of the biggest disappointments in literature."[123]

We have previously suggested a relationship between *Our Mutual Friend* and some of Shakespeare's dark comedies, where such "well-intentioned shams" are common (cf. *Measure for Measure, All's Well that Ends Well, Much Ado about Nothing, The Winter's Tale, The Tempest*, the much lighter *Love's Labour's Lost, A Midsummer Night's Dream, The Taming of the Shrew*, and the much darker, although still not quite tragic, *Romeo and Juliet*).[124] Usually Shakespeare makes his audience a party to the deceptions, but in *King Lear*, which was based on a tragicomedy and later played as one for over a hundred years, the structure, according, at least, to virtually all nineteenth-century interpreters, was designed first to convince the audience that life may indeed be as foul and meaningless as they suspected, before bringing back Edgar and Cordelia to assert the contrary.[125] So considered, *Lear*, the classic of parallel plotting, whose strong influence on Dickens and Melville has frequently been acknowledged, is a gigantic trick played on the audience, a manipulation of people, both in life and in art. Perhaps it was a failure of nerve to answer "As flies to wanton boys" with "Ripeness is all," and, if the play had been a Dickens novel, with greater opportunities for scenic deception,

---

123. *Ibid.*

124. Interestingly, this motif of benevolent deceptions, which is used so frequently in Shakespeare, is not a common feature of Renaissance drama, and there are no sources for most of the Shakespearean subplots in which it figures.

125. This interpretation has been hotly contested in our century, especially by William Elton (*King Lear and the Gods*, San Marino, Calif., 1966), but it still represents, I believe, the view of many Shakespeare critics. Perhaps the most comprehensive reading occurs in Herbert R. Coursen's *Christian Ritual and the World of Shakespeare's Tragedies* (Lewisburg, Pa., 1976). Coursen maintains that the optimistic penultimate is a legitimate statement, but also a missed opportunity. "*King Lear*," he writes, "is a comedy swallowed up in tragedy" (p. 237).

the "leap" from the "cliff" might have seemed to some nihilistic disciples of "the new philosophy" even a bigger disappointment in literature than Noddy Boffin's incorruptibility does to a century of behaviorists. But Shakespeare's manipulation of his audience and of Gloucester is certainly neither frivolous nor arrogant. As Edgar says, "Why I do trifle thus with his despair, / Is done to cure it." In *The Winter's Tale*, where, as in *Our Mutual Friend*, the audience is deceived along with the character, Leontes decrees, "If this be magic, let it be an art / Lawful as eating."

Surely no work of the nineteenth century encourages the expectation for a negatively heroic ending more strongly than *Moby-Dick*, but while the climax of the Ahab plot satisfies our longing magnificently, Ishmael's story concludes with a gentle, and, some readers have felt, an unearned acquiescence. Ishmael does not precisely leap from Ahab's boat as cowardly Pip jumps from Stubb's or as sensible Mohi and Yoomy dive from Taji's. Ahab does not permit defection—"the first thing that but offers to jump from this boat I stand in, that thing I harpoon" (Chap. 135). Rather Ishmael is, as he says, "flung out," and he "helplessly" drops astern. On the other hand, Ishmael does not cling to the gunwale to prevent the accident, as Ahab does, nor does he act with sufficient dispatch to get back into the boat, like the two sailors who went overboard with him. And in the epilogue Ishmael hangs tenaciously and gratefully to the coffin-lifebuoy, whispering his quiet yes in response to Ahab's NO, in thunder.

This ending has occasioned only somewhat less general disappointment than the ending of *Bleak House*, and the double-centered structures which dictated the conclusions of both works have presented a most perplexing problem to critics of fiction. Some readers have refused the challenge by simply wishing one of the two centers away, along with the Zionist plot of *Daniel Deronda*[126] and the Harmon-Wilfer plot of *Our Mutual Friend*.[127] And we have heard arguments that such works merely present alternative irreconcilable visions, expressing a dramatic confusion on the parts of the authors, arguments which I have rejected because I cannot see the authors in question as intentional advocates of uncertainty. Rather, I have maintained that although Melville and Dickens recognized the compelling power of the negative vision, they rendered it, as they and their contemporaries believed Shakespeare did in *King Lear*, so that it might be ultimately rejected.

In *Little Dorrit*, one set of characters, led by Gowan, Miss Wade, Blandois, and Mrs. Clennam, see the world as a prison, and such a perception

126. See F. R. Leavis, *The Great Tradition: George Eliot, Henry James, Joseph Conrad* (London, 1948), pp. 80–85.

127. See Taylor Stoehr, *Dickens: The Dreamer's Stance* (Ithaca, 1965), pp. 206–208.

seems at times to be indeed the vision of the book. If we accept it, as Clennam temporarily accepts it, and as Dickens believed his countrymen had accepted it, then we have no choice but to regard ourselves also as prisoners, and no choice, therefore, but to *be* prisoners. On the other hand, Dickens has given us a title character who perceives the literal prison as a loving world and who is capable of turning "its iron stripes . . . into stripes of gold" (Bk. II, Chap. 30) by nourishing Clennam's and our own starved imaginations.

The world's reality, as the post-Kantian metaphysicals had argued, is entirely a matter of perception. Thus Abrams describes the basis of Romantic art and philosophy:

> Whether a man shall live his old life or a new one, in a universe of death or of life, cut off and alien or affiliated and at home, in a state of servitude or of genuine freedom—to the Romantic poet, all depends on his mind as it engages with the world in the act of perceiving. Hence the extraordinary emphasis throughout this era on the eye and the object and the relation between them. Whatever their philosophic differences about what is and what only seems to be, the major poets coincide with Blake's view that "As a man is, So he Sees," that "As the Eye—Such the Object," and that "the Eye altering alters all"; therefore, that to see the world wrongly is to see the wrong world, but to see it aright is to create a new earth and new heaven.[128]

This proposition, that reality is a question of perception, is nowhere better illustrated than by the parallel plots of *Bleak House*. Here, for instance, are two descriptions of Chesney Wold, the ancient seat of the Dedlocks, who rule the sterile, winter world. It is first presented to us by the "omniscient" narrator, the spokesman for the dark view of reality:

> While Esther sleeps, and while Esther wakes, it is still wet weather down at the place in Lincolnshire. The rain is ever falling, drip, drip, drip, by day and night, upon the broad flagged terrace-pavement, The Ghost's Walk. The weather is so very bad, down in Lincolnshire, that the liveliest imagination can scarcely apprehend its ever being fine again. Not that there is any superabundant life of imagination on the spot, for Sir Leicester is not here (and, truly, even if he were, would not do much for it in that particular), but is in Paris, with my Lady; and solitude, with dusky wings, sits brooding upon Chesney Wold. (Chap. 7)

Esther, the rival narrator, supplies the missing imagination. Here is her description of the identical scene:

> There was a favourite spot of mine in the park-woods of Chesney Wold, where a seat had been erected commanding a lovely view. The wood had been cleared and opened, to improve this point of sight; and the bright

128. *Natural Supernaturalism*, p. 375.

sunny landscape beyond was so beautiful that I rested there at least once every day. A picturesque part of the Hall, called the Ghost's Walk, was seen to advantage from this higher ground; and the startling name, and the old legend in the Dedlock family which I had heard from Mr. Boythorn, accounting for it, mingled with the view and gave it something of a mysterious interest, in addition to its real charms. There was a bank here, too, which was a famous one for violets; and as it was a daily delight of Charley's to gather wild flowers, she took as much to the spot as I did. (Chap. 36)

These are indeed, alternative views of reality, but they are not of equal, practical value, and since, according to metaphysical philosophy, we can have one or the other of them, Dickens did not expect us to find the choice difficult.

Almost every reader is startled to discover, through Esther's description, that Bleak House, the residence in St. Albans, so thoroughly belies its name:

It was one of those delightfully irregular houses where you go up and down steps out of one room into another, and where you come upon more rooms when you think you have seen all there are, and where there is a bountiful provision of little halls and passages, and where you find still older cottage-rooms in unexpected places, with lattice windows and green growth pressing through them. (Chap. 6)

Is Bleak House really so charming a place? Of course it is, although you would not think so if the other narrator had described it first. According to his view, the irregular building, with its confusing halls and passages, would have been bleak enough. But his is the despairing, unimaginative vision, characteristic of a materialistic century, from which Dickens is trying to convert us by the juxtaposition of his parallel plots.

In *Our Mutual Friend* Dickens simply made obvious the dual techniques he had been using to affect this conversion in all his mature works. There Bella Wilfer is redeemed by two agencies, one positive and the other apparently negative. Bella's belief in her own mercenary weakness, a lack of self-confidence based on a low and unimaginative view of human nature, must be overcome before she can break the spell which has kept her from declaring, even to herself, the love she feels for John Roksmith (Harmon). Dickens saves her through the influence of Lizzie Hexam, the Madonna or redeeming heroine of the parallel plot, and by Boffin's "Pious Fraud," the central action of Bella's own story. The fraud, until it is exposed as such, seems to contradict the Madonna, just as the "new kind of truthfulness about social conditioning," which Barbara Hardy admires in the earlier novels, seems to make nonsense of the heroines of "encapsulated virtue." When we recognize, however, that the new kind of truthfulness was also a pious fraud, a "glaring instance," intended for the reader's conversion, the contradiction disappears, and the two visions of the metaphysical novel work together against the materialistic world view of the nineteenth century and of our own.

IV: THE TWO-PART STRUCTURE: SEQUENTIAL FORM

Bulwer's *A Strange Story* (1861–1862) is the nineteenth-century romance which sets out most directly to contradict materialistic with occult psychology. Joseph Fradin has written that this work is concerned with the idea that "man's experience in trance may be as revealing of his essential nature and the nature of reality as the daylight world of his senses.... From trance may well up the most profound truths. Bulwer.... was seeking in the deepest levels of consciousness some secret power which might transcend the 'absorbing tyranny of everyday life,' a power which might make whole again the world disintegrating about him." [129] Bulwer embodies his idea by showing the conversion to a belief in mysticism of a no-nonsense physician whose "favorite phrase was 'common sense.' " The doctor, who begins as an avowed follower of Locke and Condillac, undergoes what Fradin properly calls "a journey of discovery, of the nature of his self and the world. Forced into a confrontation with the inexplicable powers for good and evil, Fenwick learns not only that there is a higher reality, a realm of the spirit, but also that reason and science cannot discover it." [130]

Since a work with such a theme virtually required the depiction of both the skeptical and the visionary world views, Bulwer very carefully structured his romance around this necessity. During the first part of the book, when common sense rules, and where occult matters are mentioned only to be laughed at, the action takes place in one of "the wealthiest of our great English towns" (Chap. 1), whose social world Bulwer describes with all the attention to ordinary detail of a writer of realistic satire. *A Strange Story* starts out as though it were intended to be a novel of manners. At the conclusion, however, creatures from the occult world dominate in wild visions, set in a vague, sublime Australian wilderness.

A Strange Story is an especially important work for our discussion because it also demonstrates the influence of Dickens and, as we later shall see, perhaps of Hawthorne, thus relating these writers to the tradition in which Bulwer was working. Dickens' influence is certain and direct, for

129. " 'The Absorbing Tyranny of Every-day Life': Bulwer's *A Strange Story*," *NCF*, VI (1961), 13–14.
130. *Ibid.*, p. 8.

A Strange Story was written at his special invitation, to be published in *All the Year Round*, and the always conscientious editor took an unusually strong interest in the developing manuscript. For one thing, Dickens' advice was constantly solicited by the nervous author. In the decade just passed, Bulwer had achieved the critical successes of his lifetime with his safely domestic Caxton novels, which represented a studied retreat into realism after the fiasco of *Lucretia*.[131] He was extremely uncertain about the wisdom of returning to the occultist and sensational fiction of his earlier career, and as the letters show, he sought Dickens' counsel at every turn. Moreover, Dickens responded to this need not only as a responsible editor with a financial interest in the magazine, but also as a personal friend and colleague.

We have already spoken of Dickens' largely neglected counsel that Bulwer not burden this book with excessive notes and prefatory explanations. On the other hand, it appears that Bulwer accepted most of Dickens' advice concerning other matters. For our purposes it is most significant that Dickens proposed, although he attributed the suggestion to Wills, his assistant, that *A Strange Story* be lengthened to include "some new touches of character and ordinary life."[132] In response, Bulwer, who had already submitted revised proofs, appears to have developed Mrs. Colonel Poyntz, the most important of the realistic portraits from the early chapters. And Dickens praised the addition as "a remarkable, skillfully done woman. The whole idea of the story turned in a masterly way towards the safe point of the compass."[133] Thus it appears that Bulwer, acting on Dickens' advice made the beginning of *A Strange Story* more realistic, and, interestingly, he did so at almost precisely the same time when he was persuading Dickens to change the ending of *Great Expectations* in the direction of romance.[134]

Bulwer accepted Dickens' suggestion because, unlike the admonition not to preface, it did not go against the grain of his temperament or even of his usual practice. *Pelham*, Bulwer's first fully-acknowledged romance, begins as a glittering example of the silver fork school of society fiction, but it ends as a Gothic detective story. The sequential split between realism and romance is sometimes so distinct in Bulwer's works that when *Go-*

---

131. For a fuller account of this aspect of Bulwer's career see my article, "Raphael in Oxford Street: Bulwer's Accommodation to the Realists" in *The Nineteenth-Century Writer and His Audience* (eds.) Harold Orel and George J. Worth (Lawrence, Kan., 1969), pp. 61–74.

132. Letter to Bulwer, 15 May 1861. *Letters of Dickens*, III, 220.

133. Letter to Bulwer, 12 July 1861. *Ibid.*, III, 229.

134. See my article "Bulwer-Lytton and the Changed Ending of *Great Expectations*," *Nineteenth-Century Fiction*, XXV (1970), 104–108.

dolphin was published anonymously in 1833, a friendly reviewer for *The Examiner* speculated that it was "the work of two hands of very unequal power. . . . The book is of two parts; the first, worldly, which is all clever; the second, romantic, which is somewhat flaring and extravagant. . . . As in the portraiture of the world as it is, the author resembles Bulwer, so in the portraiture of the world of romance, he strongly reminds us of Godwin, but in his questionable manner."[135] And this is very close to the effect at which Bulwer had aimed, when in one of the digressions of *Godolphin* he called for a worldly romance:

> I want someone to write a novel which shall be a metaphysical 'Gil Blas'; which shall deal more with the mind than Le Sage's book, and less with the actions; which shall make its hero the creature of the world, but a different creation, though equally true; which shall give a faithful picture in the character of one man of the aspect and effects of our social system,— making that man of a better sort of clay than the amusing lacquey was, and the product of a more artificial grade of society. The book I mean would be a sadder one than Le Sage's but equally faithful to life. And it would have more of romance. . . . romance of idea as well as incident,—natural romance. (Chap. XX)

A similar two-part, sequential structure characterizes so much of Bulwer's fiction that a reader like Kenneth Burke, who believes "a work has form in so far as one part of it leads the reader to anticipate another part, to be gratified by the sequence,"[136] should be constantly frustrated in reading it. *The Pilgrims of the Rhine* begins as a collection of tales and ends as a *Bildungsroman. Kenelm Chillingly*, one of Bulwer's very last productions, starts out in the picaresque tradition and concludes as a love story.

Dickens, therefore, was not suggesting an unusual technique when he advised Bulwer to emphasize the realism at the beginning of an occult novel. The idea was not new to Bulwer, nor was it new to Dickens, who sometimes structured his own books similarly. In both of Dickens' historical novels, for instance, he breaks the continuity of action by dividing it abruptly into distinct time blocks. "How as to a story in two periods— with a lapse of time between, like a French Drama," he wrote in his Memorandum Book (1855–1865) sometime before he began work on *A Tale of Two Cities*.[137] No one, so far as I am aware, has attempted to gloss this puzzling comment, but, while the practice has a precedent in French historical fiction, where *The Charterhouse of Parma* was heavily

135. May 10, 1833, p. 309.
136. *Counter-Statement* (Chicago, 1957), p. 124.
137. *Letters of Dickens*, III, 786.

criticized for just such a division, it was surely a violation of the principles of unity to which the French theater absolutely subscribed. On the other hand, the two-period story provided a convenient structure for Dickens' thematic purposes.

In *Barnaby Rudge* the fevered nightmare quality of the novel's second time period presents, as in a dream vision, the disunited society realistically and comically described in the first, a society in which Protestants contend with Catholics, rich with poor, servants with masters, fathers with sons, and women with men.[138] But the change in subgenre not only emphatically renders the true situation of the first thirty-two chapters; it transports the reader into a world of symbolic melodrama, where the defeated juveniles of the world of realistic comedy, Joe Willet and Edward Chester, can reappear as rescuing heroes.

And the same opportunity exists in *A Tale of Two Cities*, when the shift from historical realism to thinly disguised religious allegory permits Sydney Carton, hitherto trapped in the world of English realism, to perform his act of Christ-like renunciation. I am not suggesting that there is no religious allegory in the first part of the book and no historical realism in the last. The first section, entitled "Recalled to Life" has obvious religious overtones, but the emphasis is on the domestic scene and the down-to-earth English characters. In the last section the allegory surfaces in an apocalyptic world of irrationality and terror, and the book climaxes, of course, with a crucifixion.

In these works of Dickens, as in the metaphysical novels of Bulwer, the emphatic change in genre represented and facilitated an abrupt turn towards redeeming mysticism. Ample precedent for such a pattern existed, not in French drama, even as liberated by Victor Hugo, but in late Gothic fiction, where Godwin usually took a firm stance in reality before springing into the clouds. Poe's visionary *Narrative of Arthur Gordon Pym* also began realistically. And the first scenes of *Melmoth the Wanderer*, which may have influenced the kitchen opening of *Wuthering Heights*, are almost Edgeworthian.

Another obvious precedent for the structure we have been describing, and perhaps a strong influence on it, was the English pantomime. Note

138. In *Dickens and the Rhetoric of Laughter*, James Kincaid notes this structure and interprets it in a somewhat similar fashion: "just about one-half of the novel is spent in assuring us that we are safe and, correspondingly, that our fantasies are supportable, our fears easily dismissed, and our tyranny certainly justifiable. It is a novel based on reversal; the second half reverses the tendencies of the first half and negates its assurances. Safe daylight becomes night, the fairy tale becomes a nightmare, the comic wooden inflexibility is engulfed in fire, and the assumption of immunity is cruelly exploded. It is a novel whose very heart is rhetorical and whose themes are defined by its structure." (p. 107)

this description of the sort of popular theatrical entertainments which so fascinated the young Dickens that he edited the *Memoirs of Joseph Grimaldi*, the greatest of the nineteenth-century pantomime clowns:

> When the pantomime scenes were brought together to make a complete piece, the entertainment was arranged on a fixed plan. During four or five scenes, known as "the opening," a simple story was unfolded, involving the familiar quadrilateral of two lovers, the grim father, and the unwanted suitor. At the moment when the lovers were about to be separated, the good genius arrived, and turned them into Harlequin and Columbine, the father to Pantaloon, the suitor to Clown. . . . Then came the comic business, directed by magic and prolonged throughout a dozen scenes, in which Harlequin and Columbine were vainly pursued by the disreputable characters. . . . Just before the end the lovers would be caught by the pursuer, in what was known as "the dark scene," and the magic wand would be seized by Clown—at which point the Fairy would arrive, extract a promise from Pantaloon, a promise on behalf of the young couple, and transport everyone to the final scene, which was a very grand affair indeed.[139]

The pantomime thus began as something resembling a realistic comedy and, when its problems seemed to become unsolvable within this genre, made a sudden and radical shift to the fairy tale.

And the fairy tale itself, as we have already shown in our discussion of the disappearing characters of *Wuthering Heights*, provided an even more immediate pattern for the two-part, two-vision, sequential structure of some metaphysical novels. Here the influence is most clear on Dickens, who conceived of himself, on at least one occasion, as essentially a writer of adult variations in this genre.[140] "In a utilitarian age, of all other times,"

---

139. V. C. Clinton-Baddeley, *All Right on the Night* (London, 1954), pp. 206–207. A much expanded and more scholarly treatment of the same material appears in David Mayer III, *Harlequin in His Element: The English Pantomime, 1806–1836* (Cambridge, Mass., 1969), and, as it relates to Dickens, the subject is treated at length in Charles Wolfe's unpublished dissertation, "Dickens and the *Theatrum Mundi*" (Univ. of Kansas, 1970).

140. Forster wrote that "No one was more intensely fond than Dickens of old nursery tales, and he had a secret delight in feeling [when he wrote the Christmas Tales] that he was here only giving them a higher form." *The Life of Charles Dickens* (London, 1928), p. 317. Important and suggestive work has been done in this area of Dickens studies by a number of scholars, most valuably, perhaps, by Harry Stone in "The Novel as Fairy Tale: Dickens' Dombey and Son," *English Studies*, XLII (1964), 567–579, and Michael C. Kotzin in *Dickens and the Fairy Tale* (Bowling Green, Ohio, 1972). Kotzin writes: "Dickens . . . was a descendant of the Romantics, who prized the imagination (the Romantic term—he more often uses "fancy") as a faculty that makes men happy and truly good, but who feared it was in danger in the modern, utilitarian world. For Wordsworth it is nature that inspires and guides the imagination. . . . Dickens, drawing upon his different, later, more urban childhood and adult experiences, substituted for na-

Dickens wrote in 1853, "it is a matter of grave concern that Fairy tales should be respected. . . . a nation without fancy, without some romance, never did, never can, never will hold a great place under the sun."[141] The genre was particularly valuable to Dickens because, as Gissing notes, he could combine it with eighteenth-century realism.[142] Thus he was able to include both of the visions we have been discussing. Dickens' best modern biographer, Edgar Johnson, writes that from near the very beginning of his career, when he wrote *Pickwick Papers*, he devised "a new literary form, a kind of fairy tale that is at once humorous, heroic and realistic."[143]

There are many fairy-tale elements in Dickens' fiction, but perhaps the one most germane to our discussion of two-part sequential form is "the bad wish granted" motif from such stories as "The Golden Touch," "The Sorcerer's Apprentice," and "The Fisherman's Wife" ("The Man Without a Country," *Dear Brutus*, and "The Monkey's Paw" are more recent examples).[144] In these tales a character is punished and sometimes educated when a controlling power allows his fondest wish to come true. With Dickens, because the bad wish can usually be unwished after the education has taken place, the motif is used to tell a Faust story, but with a beneficent devil. His most obvious large-scale use of this sort of instruction by goblins occurs in *Great Expectations*, where Pip is allowed to become the gentleman he wanted so desperately to be, and in *Little Dorrit*, where "the fairy came out of the Bank and gave . . . [Dorrit] his fortune" (Bk. II, Chap. 12) so that Amy could realize her terrible ambition of seeing her father free of debtors' prison. Pip turns into a snob and a predator, like all the conventional gentlemen of *Great Expectations*, and William Dorrit becomes, of course, more deeply imprisoned than ever by the materialism of the greater world he had been "freed" to enter. The makers of these bad wishes, perceiving the results, are permitted to unwish them. They have thus gained a true vision, which allows them to go home and, in the case of Amy Dorrit, empowers her to redeem Arthur Clennam from the Marshalsea by a more legitimate, though equally mystical method. The motif occurs also, and, I believe, most elaborately, in *Our Mutual Friend*. Boffin is Prospero and the good fairy both of the pantomime and the *Märchen* as

---

ture what Wordsworth saw as less effective but still helpful, the fairy tale. In his [Dickens'] view, then, the tales, more than mere escape and more than teachers of such simple virtues as forebearance, are nurseries of fancy." (pp. 39–40)

141. "Frauds on the Fairies," *Household Words* (Oct. 1, 1853), p. 97.

142. *Charles Dickens: A Critical Study* (London, 1898), pp. 28–30.

143. *Charles Dickens: His Tragedy and Triumph*, I, 173.

144. I am indebted for this insight to Professor Max Keith Sutton, who believes the motif is central in nineteenth-century romance.

he pulls all the strings of Bella Wilfer's life and, by moving her to wish herself poor again, saves her from the debilitating world view, her destructive self-image, and frees her to become the mendicant's bride.

Hawthorne, the author of "The Birthmark" and of the best known version of "The Golden Touch."[145] makes powerful use of the bad wish formula in *The House of the Seven Gables*. After the death of the judge, Clifford is given his long dreamed-of freedom and discovers there is nothing he can do with it. Similarly, Holgrave gets his revenge and begins to feel the abyss open under his feet. Only after these disillusionments have been experienced and acknowledged, moreover, can the redeeming mystical powers of the book be released.

It was, of course, the German Romantics who had first dignified the fairy tale, making it an important part of their very serious literature, and it is therefore to Germany that we must look for the most significant models of the two-part sequential structure. *Wilhelm Meister*, which Bulwer regarded as the only really satisfactory metaphysical novel, is in two distinct parts, the first generally realistic and the second highly mystical. *Faust* and *Heinrich von Ofterdingen* are similarly constructed to achieve a related effect. There is, moreover, as we might expect, a philosophical justification for the structure in German metaphysics, where Schelling's *Transcendental Idealism* interpreted the two-part format of God's Testament(s) and Homer's epic(s) as mystical renderings of history:

> History is an epic composed in the mind of God. Its two main parts are, first, that which represents the departure of humanity from its center out to its furthest alienation [*Entfernung*] from this center, and second, that which represents the return. The first part is, as it were, the *Iliad*, the second the *Odyssey* of history. In the first part the movement was centrifugal, in the second it becomes centripetal. . . . Ideas, spirits, had to fall away from their center and introduce themselves into separateness in nature, the general sphere of the fall, in order that afterward, as separates, they might return into the Undifferentiated and, reconciled with it, remain in it without disturbing it.[146]

The realistic, first part of a metaphysical novel depicts the alienation, of which the skeptical world view was both cause and symptom, and for which the mystical conclusion was supposed to provide a radical cure. As M. H. Abrams argues, *The Prelude* and *The Rime of the Ancient Mariner*, which end with the poets' ability and compulsion to produce the poems we have

145. See *Tanglewood Tales*. Hawthorne added the beloved daughter to the story.
146. Translated by M. H. Abrams and quoted in *Natural Supernaturalism*, pp. 223–24.

just read, are therefore structurally circuitous in the fullest sense, but he also shows how this German motif became central to Blake, Shelley, Carlyle and much of what we value in early nineteenth-century literature and thought.

> The historical process was often represented . . . as a circuitous journey back home. So represented, the protagonist is the collective mind or consciousness of men, and the story is that of its painful pilgrimage through difficulties, sufferings, and recurrent disasters in quest of a goal which, unwittingly, is the place it had left behind when it first set out and which, when reachieved, turns out to be better than it had been at the beginning.[147]

We have previously heard Sylvère Monod's argument that *David Copperfield* might have been called " 'The Growth of the Novelist's Mind' in emulation of Wordsworth's subtitle for *The Prelude*" (see p. 72 above). And it is true that both Pip and Esther Summerson are also writers who must undergo painful pilgrimages before they can find home and render the discovered vision which their narratives have embodied. Similarly, Bulwer's Pisistratus must undergo a circuitous journey, to Australia and back, before he can be the first-person narrator of *The Caxtons*, which turns out to be a prelude, a Wordsworthian "ante-chapel" to Bulwer's "gothic church," the succeeding Caxton novels, of which Pisistratus is the fictional author. An earlier and much more highly mystical romance of Bulwer's, *Zanoni* (1842), belongs also in this metaphysical tradition of the circuitous journey, for the apparent author of the book turns out to be one of its central characters, the artist Glyndon, who may represent the young Bulwer and who can become a writer only after Zanoni's magic has redeemed him.[148] Thus the circuitous journey of Romantic literature is also a sequential pattern for the metaphysical novelists.

Moby-Dick is very much in the same tradition. The breezy young man of the realistic first chapters, who asks us to call him Ishmael, is, as I suggested earlier, more analogous to Jonah, God's reluctant prophet. All the backing and stalling of the beginning may therefore be interpreted as an effort to put off the vision—it takes the *Pequod* much longer than any other of Melville's ships to get underway—and the shift in emphasis to Ahab's

147. *Ibid.*, p. 191.
148. This position is powerfully argued by Robert Lee Wolff in *Strange Stories*, pp. 230–32. Wolff maintains that Glyndon was intended as a self-portrait of Bulwer himself and that "*Zanoni* is the spiritual autobiography of his youth." The interpretation that Glyndon is the author appears also, I understand, in Pietro Bornia's *Il Guardiano della goglia* (Naples, n.d.). I have not had an opportunity to look at Bornia's book, but his argument is summarized in Allan Christensen's *Edward Bulwer-Lytton: The Fiction of New Regions* (Athens, Ga., 1976), pp. 242–43.

story can be read as an outright evasion. Or rather, the change of protagonists is an attempted evasion, for the narrator is not permitted, after all, to avoid his mission. Like the Biblical Jonah, who gets to Nineveh in spite of himself and, as Melville points out, by the fastest possible route,[149] Ishmael is trapped, by observing the suicidal quest of the *Pequod*, into the realization that he should be writing a book instead of living one. Thus Murray Krieger says:

> Let us take seriously the fiction that Ishmael is the author of the tale. On the very first page of his writing and at the outset of the events he is relating . . . he described the "damp, drizzly November" in his soul which had forced him to take the sea as therapy. The journey of the *Pequod* cured him indeed, and it was that cure that saved him for the *Rachel*, that symbol of a chastened but still warmly responsive humanity. But the journey of the *Pequod* is also the writing of the book. So is it too much to say that Ishmael is saved also by this creating of Ahab and Ahab's [tragic] vision by seeing him through and purging the Ahab within himself through Ahab's necessary death?[150]

From the first, Ishmael's Jonah's-mission has been to expose the false quests of his century, suicidal endeavors based either on a positivistic or a transcendental faith in the material universe. There are a number of familiar nineteenth-century quests in *Moby-Dick*, each of which has the whale as its object. Earlier we spoke of Ishmael's own scientific attempt to master his subject. Ahab's purpose is, of course, the most heroic and archetypical. He is Faust and St. George, Perseus and Napoleon, and he is instinctively informed with the transcendentalisms of Carlyle, Emerson, and Goethe. He is also a master navigator and naturalist. Ahab mobilizes the entire world in microcosm to seek and destroy the fabulous beast. Jason, pursuing the golden fleece, and the twentieth-century astronauts, driving to their "flashier bauble yet," as Yeats brilliantly prophesied, pale in a comparison. Under the direction of this knightly hero, the cruise of the *Pequod* is a symbolic romance, the nightmare voyage of the bad ship *Nineteenth Century*, which ends in Armageddon. Ahab dies gaining neither vengeance for himself, redemption for his society, nor knowledge for the world. His transcendental quest—the great philosophical adventure of his times—ends in complete and uninterpretable catastrophe.

The narrator has attempted to avoid this vision because he fears the social consequences and because, as we learn when he comes to speak of Moby Dick in his narration of "The *Town-Ho* Story," the very thought

149. That is, around Africa in the whale's belly.
150. *The Tragic Vision: Variations on a Theme in Literary Interpretation* (New York, 1960), p. 253.

of the terrible whale makes him physically ill. To speak of him at length
" 'would be too long a story. . . . Nay, Dons, Dons—nay, nay! I cannot
rehearse that now. Let me get more into the air, Sirs' " (Chap. 54).[151] The
narrator holds back, moreover, and perhaps most significantly, because he
fully shares in the evil quest dreams of his contemporaries and is as reluctant
as they are to settle for a Queequeg, much less an Esther Summerson. As
his allegiances to Ahab and to his own scientific quest show, there is still
the Taji in him which wants to conclude, "Better to sink in boundless deeps
than float on vulgar shoals," and which prefers, as Father Mapple would
put it, to obey himself rather than God. He must be purged of this attitude
before he can be saved. *Moby-Dick* is thus Melville's first testament of acceptance and, like his last, it is made with a most grudging reluctance.
Nevertheless, the two major plots of *Moby-Dick*, the Ishmael and the Ahab
plots, are intimately related to one another in that, taken together, they
represent both the attempted evasion and the actual fulfillment of the
author's true mission, and thus everything in the book leads to the ultimate
affirmation, the completion of Ishmael's two-part, circuitous journey.

As the psychology changes in metaphysical fiction from skeptical to
visionary, the narrative technique changes with it, as we should expect,
from dramatic to undramatic, from vehicular to retarding. Nonvisionary
narratives of earlier times, when the loose form was so conventional as
to be virtually unavoidable, display an opposite movement *toward* the
dramatic. *Orlando Furioso*, for instance, one of the most generally digressive of major Renaissance epics, settles down, when it comes within sight
of the ending, into a remarkably straightforward narration. The last three
cantos, with the exception of one long complimentary introduction, are
entirely dramatic. There are no interpolated episodes and only a single
plot. An important mixed narrative of French fiction, *La Princesse de
Clèves*, follows this same pattern, which consists of retarding the action
like water behind a barrier until the pressure becomes so great that the
dam bursts. Then the author gets out of the way, so that the story can complete itself. Thus Fielding makes his farewell to the reader at the beginning
of Book XVIII of *Tom Jones*:

> If I have now and then, in the course of this work, indulged any pleasantry
> for thy entertainment, I shall here lay it down. The variety of matter,
> indeed, which I shall be obliged to cram into this book will afford no
> room for ludicrous observations which I have elsewhere made, and which

151. I am particularly indebted at this point to Mr. Eugene F. Simon of my
1968 Melville Seminar at the University of Kansas.

may sometimes, perhaps, have prevented thee from taking a nap when it was beginning to steal on you. In this last book thou will find nothing of that nature. All will be plain narrative only.

And he keeps this promise remarkably well, restraining even his penchant for amusingly distracting chapter titles to such brief headings as "Continuation of the History," "Further Continuation," and "The History draws Near to a Conclusion." Scott, with his strong instinct for the dramatic, compares the endings of novels to "the progress of a stone rolled down hill by an idle truant boy"; it becomes "most furiously rapid in its course when it is nearest to being consigned to rest for ever."[152]

On the other hand, Spenser, who was a more disciplined writer than any of those we have just mentioned, but also much more of a visionary, complicates his structures and therefore slows his narratives as he concludes them. He begins *The Faerie Queene* and most of its books both realistically and dramatically. C. S. Lewis has written that "the opening ('A gentle knight was pricking on the playne') seems to us the most ordinary thing in the world. We have seen a hundred novels begun in the same way. . . . [with] the immediate presentation of a figure already in action."[153] But Spenser's books certainly do not end in the straightforward manner; rather they dissolve, so to speak, into masques, processions, and tours through art galleries. And this is the pattern of metaphysical fiction in the nineteenth century when the loose form was no longer a conventional necessity or even, in the eyes of most critics, an acceptable method.

Hawthorne, so frequently a disciple of Spenser, follows also in this respect. *The Scarlet Letter* begins realistically, if the first "chapter" is "The Custom House," and dramatically, if we start with "The Prison Door"; it ends, after a procession, like grand opera. *The House of the Seven Gables* opens its main narrative like *Babbitt*, by detailing a day in the prosaic life of Old Maid Pyncheon. Yet the book achieves its dénouement with a parade of ghosts and a magical transformation.

Hawthorne's structures differ, however, from those of Dickens and Bulwer which we have been describing in that his works usually display a gradual ascent from the everyday and/or dramatic to the visionary and symbolic rather than an abrupt shift from the materialistic to the mystical. Perhaps, as with the business of the authorial voice (see Chapter II), he was merely trying to achieve the effects of the metaphysical novelists without suffering their penalties, but perhaps, as Taylor Stoehr suggests when he contrasts Hawthorne with Poe, he had a deeper reason:

152. *Waverley*, (Edinburgh, 1870), Chap. 70, p. 436.
153. *English Literature in the Sixteenth Century excluding Drama* (Oxford, 1954), p. 389.

Hawthorne's narrative stance is different from Poe's because Hawthorne wants to bridge the gap between imagination and reality while Poe prefers to fall in. The former's emblems are of something, have bearing on life, while the latter's are grotesque climaxes marking the boundary-line of fantasy and its sharp division from the ordinary world, which, so far as his tales are concerned, might as well not exist. . . . The contrast between dream and reality is what interests Hawthorne. . . . While Poe wants to blot out reality and allow fantasy to fill the consciousness, Hawthorne is merely interested in exploring the relations between the two.[154]

I cannot agree that Hawthorne was ever "merely interested in exploring" anything. Exploration was the province of the skeptical realists, who had to discover their truths. But it is possible that Hawthorne thought he could better redeem the world of action, which was the true endeavor of all the metaphysical novelists, by not seeming obviously or entirely to reject everyday reality.

In any event, Hawthorne usually moves between the two worlds of metaphysical fiction by means of slow transitions. When he had no other way, he used prefaces as his "footholds between fiction and reality." "The Custom House" performs just such a function, among others.[155] Hawthorne's preface strategy in this regard is formulated in the notes for *The Ancestral Footstep*:

The Romance . . . begins as an integral and essential part, with my introduction, giving a pleasant and familiar summary of my life in the Consulate at Liverpool; the strange species of Americans, with strange purposes in England, whom I used to meet there; and especially, how my countrymen used to be put out of their senses by the idea of inheritances of English property. Then I shall particularly instance one gentleman who called on me on my first coming over; a description of him shall be given, with touches that shall puzzle the reader to decide whether it is not an actual portrait. And then this Romance shall be offered, half seriously, as the account of the fortunes that he met with in his search for his hereditary home.[156]

The narrative to which this realistic introduction was gradually to lead, Hawthorne saw as not "A picture of life, but a Romance, grim, grotesque, quaint," a "wild story."[157]

When Hawthorne did not employ functional introductions, he often-

154. "'Young Goodman Brown' and Hawthorne's Theory of Mimesis," pp. 399–400.

155. See Marshall Van Deusen, "Narrative Tone in 'The Custom House' and *The Scarlet Letter*," *Nineteenth-Century Fiction*, XXI (1966), 61–71.

156. *Complete Works of Hawthorne*, XI, 519–520.

157. *Ibid.*, XI, 491.

times found other means of moving progressively from realism, through a suitable remoteness, to the fairy precinct itself. *The Blithedale Romance* begins in prosaic Boston before moving to its "theatre a little removed from the highway of ordinary travel." When Coverdale returns to Blithedale for the last chapters, the setting has become more than just suitably remote. With its masquerade, its histrionic suicide, its moonlight dredging, the story has shifted into the realm of romance proper. *The Marble Faun* moves through a similar progression. The setting of the first chapters is the Rome of the guidebooks, a city familiar enough to travellers and readers of straightforward travel literature. There is remarkably little scenic distortion in these scenes. The middle section, set in the ancient Monte Beni castle and in pastoral Italy, is less familiar and takes on shades of Gothic fiction. And the last chapters, during which Hilda has been sequestered in the world of ideal forms and the other characters have become parts of the wild carnival, take us much farther from the phenomenal world than Mrs. Radcliffe, with her ultimate commitments to eighteenth-century rationalism, would have ever consented to. The settings here are frankly of the world of vision. Hawthorne never quite falls into "the gap between imagination and reality," but neither does Stoehr's analogy of the bridge precisely describe his method. Returning to Hawthorne's own metaphor, we should say, rather, that he guides us, ever so gradually, to the edge of a precariously overhanging precipice, from which we can view the possibilities of the mystical solution and, if we can maintain our balance, come back to a transformed real world.

Bulwer, who was one of Poe's masters,[158] sometimes does fall in, but always by inadvertence. It was he, after all, who wanted to write "a *Wilhelm Meister* of the practical life" and a metaphysical *Gil Blas*. His intention was always similar to Hawthorne's, who may have been as important an influence as Dickens on the writing of *A Strange Story*. Bulwer had recently praised *The Marble Faun* in one of his *Caxtoniana* essays,[159] and it is possible that Hawthorne's Gothic interlude at the castle of the Monte Benis, where the action is suspended while the characters and the story are gradually prepared for their mystic transformations, may have impressed him, for there is a similar attempted transition in *A Strange Story*. Between the flatly materialistic beginning and the wildly occult conclusion, Bulwer interposed a set of chapters describing an England less finely observed than earlier, an England of castle graveyards, prisons, romantic lakes and seashores, and peopled by a combination of flesh-and-blood characters and

158. See Michael Allen, *Poe and the British Magazine Tradition* (New York, 1969).

159. "On Certain Principles of Art in Works of the Imagination," *Caxtoniana*, II, 151–52.

spirit manifestations. As in Hawthorne, this central section does not succeed in connecting the two extremes of the story in any causal manner—
cause and effect are never the way of metaphysical fiction—but it does
prepare us somewhat for the visions which are to come.

It would be unwise, nevertheless, to insist on this influence, for, as was
the case with Dickens, Hawthorne was Bulwer's disciple many years before *A Strange Story* was written, and earlier works indicate that Bulwer
had long understood the wisdom of easing the reader, so to speak, into the
vision. *Night and Morning* (1841) has the typical beginning and ending
of metaphysical fiction. It starts with a hundred pages of material as dramatically realistic and unsentimental as anything in the English novel since
Jane Austen. Book I contains subject matter capable of the full Victorian
treatment, but note Bulwer's restraint in the following potentially bathetic
scene and imagine how Dickens or even Thackeray might have handled it.
Mr. and Mrs. Roger Morton have come to make arrangements for taking
little Sidney away from his mother.

> "We have settled it all," said the husband, "When can we have him?"
> "Not today," said Mrs. Roger Morton, "You see, ma'am, we must get his
> bed ready, and his sheets well aired. I am very particular."
> "Certainly, certainly," [says Catherine, the child's mother]. "Will he
> sleep alone?—pardon me."
> "He shall have a room to himself," said Mr. Morton. "Eh, my dear? Next
> to Martha's. Martha is our parlour-maid,—very good natured girl, and fond
> of children."
> Mrs. Morton looked grave, thought a moment, and said, "Yes, he can
> have that room."
> "Who can have that room?" asked Sidney, innocently.
> "You, my dear," replied Mr. Morton.
> "And where will Mamma sleep? I must sleep near Mamma."
> "Mamma is going away," said Catherine, in a firm voice, in which de-
> spair would only have been felt by the acute ear of sympathy,—"going
> away for a little time; but this gentleman and lady will be very—very kind
> to you."
> "We will do our best, ma'am," said Mrs. Morton.
> And as she spoke, a sudden light broke on the boy's mind; he uttered
> a loud cry, broke from his aunt, rushed to his mother's breast, and hid his
> face there, sobbing bitterly.
> "I am afraid he has been very much spoiled," whispered Mrs. Roger
> Morton. "I don't think we need stay any longer,—it will look suspicious.
> Good morning, ma'am; we shall be ready tomorrow."
> "Good'by, Catherine," said Mr. Morton; and he added as he kissed her,
> "be of good heart; I will come up by myself and spend the evening with
> you." (Bk. I, Chap. VIII)

And that is the end of the scene. It is followed by another, in which the mother visits the sleeping child in his new home, a scene handled less sentimentally and at least as realistically as the similar episode in *Anna Karenina*. *Night and Morning* (1841) could have been the first realistic novel of the Victorian era if that had been Bulwer's intention, but, as one might expect in a work by a metaphysical novelist, its last part is a melodramatic detective story, which reaches a suspenseful climax and then dissolves into pure romance.

Night and Morning would have been included when we discussed Bulwer's two-part novels if it were not that the transitional material separating the main visions is so elaborate as to suggest a five-part pattern, corresponding to the five books into which the work is divided.[160] After the realistic beginning, Book II is a Gothic novel, in which Sidney and his brother become outcast runaways, chased all about the countryside in the pursuit tradition established by Godwin in *Caleb Williams* and which Dickens was currently employing in *The Old Curiosity Shop*. Book III provides another surprise, a return to realism in the form of a Jonsonesque comedy of sharpsters, which despite Thackeray's public contempt for Bulwer, must have been an important influence on *Barry Lyndon*.[161] The next part serves again as a transition. It is a quiet movement, pastoral and elegiac, with lakeside and graveyard settings, which prepares us for the fireworks and romance of the final book: "Had the time yet come when the old Florimel had melted into snow; when the new and true one, with its warm life, its tender beauty, its maiden wealth of love, had risen before his hopes?" (Bk. V, Chap. XXI).

This is the romance whose calculated effects Poe compared with what he imagined to be the spontaneous and natural genius of *The Old Curiosity Shop*.[162] Calculated it certainly is, and with transitions so smooth that one probably had to be something of a student of the various subgenres involved

160. At this stage of his career Bulwer was very much given to highly elaborate structures. *Zanoni*, which appeared the next year, is divided into four distinct parts, based, as Robert Lee Wolff has demonstrated at length, on the four kinds of divine madness discussed in Plato's *Phaedrus*. *Strange Stories*, pp. 161 ff.

161. It is possible to trace at least two more such influences. *The Caxtons* revived and Victorianized the genre to which *Pendennis* belongs, and when Bulwer hit on the idea of letting Pisistratus Caxton narrate *My Novel*, Thackeray followed by having Pen narrate *The Newcomes*. Bulwer has been perversely saddled with the reputation of switching from one faddish genre of fiction to the next in an effort to keep up his sales. The truth is that he inaugurated or revived most of the styles in which he wrote and abandoned them long before they ceased to be popular.

162. "The Old Curiosity Shop and Other Tales," *Graham's Lady's and Gentleman's Magazine* (May 1841), pp. 248–251.

to recognize the changes; but *Night and Morning* is hardly a unified work in the sense in which narrative unity had usually been defined or even in the sense in which Poe was himself to define it. It is not organized around a single action or to produce a single effect; its unity derives only from the relevance and applicability of each of its parts and genres to a central idea or theme, and the particular sequence of its sections can be justified, not by a causal relationship, but by their rhetorical success in leading us gradually to the ultimate vision.

We can see a similar gradual technique again in Bulwer's "The Haunted and the Haunters" (1859), which, though intended as a sort of trial balloon and "preliminary outline" for *A Strange Story*, was written before *The Marble Faun* and, to protect the author's anonymity, without any help from Dickens. Once again, the beginning is realistic. The principal setting is a haunted house, which sounds remote enough until we mark the extraordinary care Bulwer has taken to make the place seem ordinary. His is no weather-beaten old mansion, set precariously on a windy Cornish headland; rather "It is situated on the north side of Oxford Street, in a dull but respectable thoroughfare." The characters, moreover, are also everyday types —a landlord, who was a former civil servant, an unimaginative English valet, and the narrator, himself, who reads Macaulay for his "strong daylight sense." Even the hero's dog is no mastiff, but an "exceedingly sharp, bold, and vigilant bull-terrier."

Insofar as the characters are concerned, Bulwer is beginning his ghost story with a technique which is as old at least as *Hamlet*, where the apparition appears first to the most prosaic of the characters, the hardy soldiers and the skeptical, matter-of-fact Horatio. When such people become convinced they have seen a ghost, the audience may also acknowledge it without undue shame. In this respect, where Bulwer differs from Shakespeare and from the writers of most nineteenth-century ghost stories is in his progressive ascent from the level of reality. Conventionally, the trick was to get the notion of ghosts accepted fairly early in the narrative and then to write a "realistic" story with ghosts as a given. The more realistic the characters who perceived the ghosts, the easier it was to identify with them, as in Mrs. Radcliffe's romances, and the more exquisite, therefore, would be the thrills. But in "The Haunted and the Haunters" the matter-of-fact characters drop off gradually, and in the last section even the narrator gives up the center of our attention in favor of an evil magician who has discovered the secret of eternal life.[163] Nor does Bulwer provide the conven-

163. This character and the entire last section in which he appears will be unfamiliar to most readers of "The Haunted and the Haunters" since Bulwer omitted the ending in editions appearing after the publication of *A Strange Story*. It has been the practice of almost all editors, including the editor of the recent

tional easy descent back down to everyday reality at the very conclusion.

Insofar as locale is concerned, Bulwer's story is out of line with the ghost and Gothic traditions. *Hamlet* begins with its eeriest setting and, as we have suggested earlier, the remote worlds employed by Mrs. Radcliffe and Mary Shelley were a strong aid in attaining a suspension of disbelief. Bulwer, on the other hand, begins in the ordinary world, on Oxford Street, and he progresses through an electronically transmitted spook show to trance-vision scenes of polar icefields. Instead of moving from the phenomenally remote to the psychologically immediate, Bulwer progresses from the everyday to the occult, and the narrative technique, which begins by involving us dramatically in the emotions of a ghost hunter keeping watch in a deserted house, concludes rhetorically with a flat-out vision, which concerns the ghost solely.

Some of Melville's best works display a similar shift from the dramatic to the undramatic mode of narration. Moreover, his most ambitious romances, *Mardi, Moby-Dick,* and *Pierre,* try to make use of the gradual technique, leading from the everyday world to the ultimate vision. Thus the first chapters in these works are not, as it has been fashionable to call them, false starts in realism. Like Bulwer's reviewer, who thought that *Godolphin* was written by "two hands of very unequal power," one of the first English critics of *Moby-Dick* was imperceptive when he concluded that "Mr. Melville must have changed his mind."[164] The early chapters of Melville's great works provide what one critic has called "a crescendo of oddness,"[165] which "should prepare us for the allegory to come, leading us step by step away from the factual world."[166] This was, indeed, the plan for *Mardi* as Melville himself outlined it to Murray on March 25, 1848, when he wrote that the book "opens like a true narrative—like *Omoo,* for example, on ship board—and the romance and poetry of the thing thence grow continu[al]ly, till it becomes a story wild enough I assure you and with a meaning too."[167] But the allegorical portion of *Mardi,* toward which

---

paperback, *Minor Classics of Nineteenth-Century Fiction* (Boston, 1967), to print the B-text, often without Bulwer's headnote, which explains that a portion of the story as first published in *Blackwood's* "is now suppressed because encroaching too much on the main plot of the 'Strange Story.'" As usually published, "The Haunted and the Haunters" ends with one of the dullest thuds in literature—"Subsequently he let it [the house] to advantage, and his tenant has made no complaint"—but at this point in the A-text, the really wild part of the story is just about to begin.

164. *The Athenaeum* (Oct. 25, 1851). Reprinted in *The Melville Log,* I, 430.

165. Stuart Levine, "Melville's 'Voyage Thither'," *The Midwest Quarterly,* III (1962), 342.

166. *Ibid.,* 352.

167. *The Letters of Herman Melville,* p. 71.

we have been led by the crescendo of oddness, is itself only transitional, as are the nondramatic, digressive, "middle" sections of *Moby-Dick*, *Pierre*, and *Clarel*.

The thematic relevance of such digressions has been argued by a number of critics and scholars, most significantly perhaps by Howard P. Vincent, who called the large section of *Moby-Dick* in which they occur "the cetological center." Vincent maintained that this material is "neither digressive nor diversive; it is not an intrusion. . . . From the whaling center, Melville works out to the symbolical and metaphysical circumference."[168] The connection between these seemingly digressive facts of whaling and the great actions of the characters is to be found in what Melville called the "linked analogies" between nature and the soul of man. "Not the smallest atom stirs or lives in matter, but has its cunning duplicate in mind" (Chap. 70). Vincent's word "center" is a particularly apt choice, for metaphysical novels, unlike plays or dramatic novels, do not have Aristotelian middles. To repeat, the action simply does not progress according to the rules of naturalistic cause-and-effect. Yet open any Dickens novel at the central or keystone chapter—quite literally, at the center of the book—and you are pretty certain to find the theme.[169]

The particular theme with which we have been dealing in Melville, the Percival theme or, its negative variation, the Faust theme, has almost always presented writers with a special structural weakness around the middle. The story begins spectacularly with a vow or a bargain, and it ends with a stirring supernatural confrontation. But what is to come in-between? Kittredge has shown how the *Gawain and the Green Knight* poet or his source handled this problem by an inspired act of filling in the hole in the bargain structure with a hitherto unrelated temptation story. This was also the way with Spenser in Book I of *The Faerie Queene* and, to the great dissatisfaction of Samuel Johnson, with Milton in *Samson Agonistes*. The middle sections of Marlowe's *Doctor Faustus* are so nonprogressive and have seemed therefore to represent so unfortunate a falling-off in tone and quality from the most generally satisfying beginning and ending in dramatic literature that critics have been tempted to suggest they were written by some lesser artist. Goethe, in his treatment of the same material, was apparently aware of the problem. He tried to solve it by putting a strong emphasis on the center, which he rendered thematic and encyclopedic rather than dramatic.

The cetological material forms, similarly, the thematic encyclopedia of

168. *The Trying-Out of Moby-Dick* (Boston, 1949), p. 125.
169. See William Axton, "The Keystone Structure of Dickens' Serial Novels," *Univ. of Toronto Quarterly*, XXXVII (1967), 31–50.

Moby-Dick. This digressive center represents a quest in its own right, and one of equal relevance to the aspirations of the nineteenth century as the endeavors of Ahab and the others. Ishmael counterpoints Ahab's transcendental journey with his own Voyage of the *Beagle*. In Bulwer's *A Strange Story* the commonsense hero, especially when he is most troubled by the black magic going on around him, works tirelessly on a purely materialistic treatise describing the phenomenal world. Here is another romantic dream of the Renaissance and modern times: that by a painstaking study and analysis of each separate part of nature, man will come ultimately to an understanding of the forces which baffle him. Goethe and Faust, of course, were also scientists. In *Moby-Dick* both quests must fail, however, because they are both blasphemous and because they are equally impossible. "How, now . . . Dar'st thou measure this our god!" the enraged priests shout at the irreverent scientist as he takes the altitude of the final rib of the whale skeleton which serves as a South Seas cathedral (Chap. 102). But the attempt is already concluded long before this time, for when he came to analyze the tail of his monster, Ishmael had given up his quest in utter despair:

> Dissect him how I may, then, I but go skin deep; I know him not, and never will. But if I know not even the tail of this whale, how understand his head? much more, how comprehend his face, when face he has none? Thou shalt see my back parts, my tail, he seems to say, but my face shall not be seen. But I cannot completely make out his back parts; and hint what he will about his face, I say again he has no face. (Chap. 86)

Thus ends the attempt in Melville to pursue ultimate knowledge in the encyclopedic way, and Ishmael's abandonment of this quest may well account, in a spiritual way, for his salvation.

But the transitional digressions in all of Melville's quest romances operate primarily as rhetorical links to the ultimately mystical conclusions: Taji's descent into Hautia's visionary cavern; Pierre's dream vision of Enceladus and the Spenserian illumination in the picture gallery; Ahab's rejected symphony and Ishmael's ultimate acceptance of Queequeg's mystical self-sacrifice. Angus Fletcher calls such visionary explosions attempts by Melville to pierce through all the confusion as to what is "mythical" and what is "allegorical" in the apocalyptic and prophetic traditions:

> The semantic character of these traditions would seem to be allegorical, while the metaphysical character would seem to be mythical. In much the same way a dream is metaphysically a myth, but semantically, when we interpret it, we take it to be allegory. By stressing the metaphysical nature of certain intense moments of allegorical literature [he refers specifically

to "The Symphony" in *Moby-Dick*], we do in fact also stress absolute value, since these are the very moments that would seem to be of higher importance to humanity.[170]

The metaphysical novel, therefore, uses both its realistic beginning and, sometimes, its allegorical center as means of arriving at the redeeming vision, which transcends and finally reconceives them both.

Fletcher has also explained in the foregoing passage, although it was not his specific intention, why, whether achieved gradually or abruptly, there can be no third part in the metaphysical novel, why we cannot be instructed beyond confusion as to which version of reality the author really wants us to accept. Such a final section, he suggests, would interpret the metaphysical dream or visionary moment, thereby reducing it again to mere allegory. Bulwer ended most editions of *Zanoni* with Harriet Martineau's algebraic interpretation of the story's allegorical significance. But, recognizing the weakness of such a conclusion, he introduced the key with a lengthy note, insisting that "*Zanoni* is not, as some have supposed, an allegory." As to Miss Martineau's analysis, he "leaves it to the reader to agree with, or dissent from the explanation":

> "A hundred men," says the old Platonist, "may read the book by the help of the same lamp, yet all may differ on the text; the lamp only lights the characters—the mind must divine the meaning. The object of a parable is not that of a Problem; it does not seek to convince, but to suggest. It takes the thought below the surface of the understanding to the deeper intelligence which the world rarely tasks. It is not sunlight on the water, it is a hymn chanted to the Nymph who harkens and awakes below.

Dickens, the editor, forbade the publication of a similar key at the conclusion of Bulwer's *A Strange Story*, and his own fiction, like that of Emily Brontë and Melville, ends without any cheapening, interpretive final section, either critical or dramatic. Hawthorne's Hester and Hilda specifically reject allegorical interpretations of the visionary experiences in which they have participated. *Billy Budd* concludes with a misleading newspaper account and an apparently irrelevant song, and "Benito Cereno" ends with a thoroughly undramatic transcript, which caused the imperceptive editor's reader to exclaim, "Oh! dear, why can't Americans write good stories. They tell good lies enough and plenty of 'em."[171] Melville seems resolved, here and elsewhere, wantonly to throw the vision away, but perhaps it is to discourage allegorical interpretation, even by the reader.

Usually, though, the metaphysical novelists, even Bulwer on most oc-

170. *Allegory*, p. 358.
171. Letter of G. W. Curtis to J. H. Dix, Aug. 19, 1855. Printed in *The Melville Log*, II, 504.

casions, contented themselves by presenting their preferred and uninter-preted world view last in the sequence. It is, after all, their final word, and we should try, perhaps, to take this fact as aesthetically sufficient.

If these explanations cast light on the purposes of the metaphysical novel, they may also suggest philosophic and artistic reasons for some of the other sudden changes in genre which occur elsewhere in nineteenth-century fiction, and which have generally been regarded as puzzling, if not dis-appointing. What bothers most readers of *The Mill on the Floss*, for in-stance, cannot surely be the flood, which has been laboriously prepared for, hinted at from the very earliest chapters; rather the shock comes from the abrupt shift at the conclusion, where a cerebral novel of character suddenly becomes a fast-paced adventure story, involving the romance elements of mystic conversion and even double identity. And what offends in the change of genre is the implied change in world view. Similar sudden turns into the realm of adventure and action characterize—some say mar—the conclusions of such seemingly different novels as *The Master of Ballantrae* and *Tess of the D'Urbervilles*.

In our own century, nonsequential narratives by Conrad, Faulkner, Nabokov, and, of course, Joyce have almost become the norm of our best fiction. It is not too much to say in conclusion, therefore, that the embattled and defensive Bulwer-Lytton was worth listening to when he insisted that realism, which seemed to have swept everything before it, was, after all, only another literary fashion or style. And if so, it is perhaps legitimate to suggest that competing fashions, like that of the metaphysical novel as practiced by Melville, Dickens, Hawthorne and others, warrant our con-tinued and serious attention.

Index

Design: Dave Pauly
Composition: Heritage Printers, Inc.
Printing: Heritage Printers, Inc.
Binding: The Delmar Company
Text: Linotype Garamond No. 3
Display: ATF Garamond
Paper: P&S Book, basis 50